When Parents Fail

WHEN PARENTS FAIL

The Law's Response to Family Breakdown

SANFORD N. KATZ, 1933-

Beacon Press   Boston

Copyright © 1971 by Sanford N. Katz
Library of Congress catalog card number: 77–156450
International Standard Book Number: 0–8070–4484–9
Beacon Press books are published under the auspices
of the Unitarian Universalist Association
Published simultaneously in Canada by Saunders of Toronto, Ltd.
All rights reserved
Printed in the United States of America

For Joan, Daniel, and Andrew

Contents

Preface

This book is an outgrowth of work I began at the Yale Law School where I was intellectually enriched by my association with Professor Joseph Goldstein, Dr. Jay Katz, and Dr. Anna Freud. I am grateful for the interest and encouragement they have continued to show in my work.

I wish to express my thanks to the Field Foundation for the generous financial support given to my study and to Rep. Robert F. Drinan, S.J., who as Dean of the Boston College Law School was instrumental in bringing my interests to the attention of the Field Foundation. Congressman Drinan also deserves my special thanks for the encouragement and assistance he has given me through the years.

Walter O. Weyrauch read earlier drafts of the manuscript and his comments have been of great value to me. I am grateful to my colleague William A. Schroeder who, in the final stages of the manuscript, gave me wise counsel and perceptive editorial guidance.

Miss Jane Stein, Alan Silberberg, and George Kappus assisted me in preparing the manuscript for publication and I appreciate the devotion they showed to their painstaking tasks.

I wish to thank Dean Richard G. Huber who, while Acting Dean of the Boston College Law School, facilitated my research by his cooperation in many administrative matters. I am grateful to my colleagues at Boston College Law School, to Mrs. Louis Bonelli, formerly the Administrative Assistant of the Law School, and to the staff of the Boston College Law Library for their kindnesses and courtesies during the writing of this book.

Special thanks must also go to Miss Ursula M. Gallagher for bringing to my attention useful material on adoption, to Attorney Leonard Tarr for sharing material on the *Liuni* case with me, to Attorney Robert W. Fields for providing me with the briefs in the *Alexander* case, and to the Massachusetts Society for the Prevention of Cruelty to Children for providing me with the material on the Mitchell Family, the Smith Family, and the Dorwin Family (all pseudonyms).

I should like to thank the editors of the *Michigan Law Review* for allowing me to make use of material published in my article, "Foster Parents Versus Agencies: A Case Study in the Judicial Application of the 'Best Interests of the Child' Doctrine" that appeared in 65 Mich. L. Rev. 145 (1966) and the editors of the *Georgetown Law Journal* for their permission to revise my article "Judicial and Statutory Trends in the Law of Adoption," 51 Geo. L.J. 64 (1962).

My wife, Joan R. Katz, is responsible in large measure for my familiarity with and appreciation for social work theory and practice. I am grateful to her for sharing with me her insights into and her excitement and disappointments over the state of social work, and especially child welfare, today. This book is affectionately dedicated to her in her triple role as wife, mother, and social worker, and to my two sons.

S.N.K.

Waban, Massachusetts
September 1970

Introduction

This is a book about the process of state intervention into the parent-child relationship. It discusses the circumstances, purposes, and means by which the state seeks to nourish or reorganize that relationship[1] and thereby promote the best interests of the child involved. Those interests are defined in terms of "a constellation of social values, the sharing of which is desirable for a child's adjustment in society and essential to a well-functioning family."[2]

One of the indices of the progress of a society toward the promotion of human dignity is its care and treatment of all children in all social strata. In the twentieth century, there has been a concerted effort in this country to promote the general welfare of children. Beginning with the early part of this century, which saw successful attempts to prevent the industrial exploitation of infants, state legislation has demonstrated a growing concern for the physical, moral, and intellectual development and well-being of children. Although efforts to promote these goals have often left much to be desired, the fact of concern is reflected in such measures as the requirement of compulsory education, the establishment of juvenile courts, battered child legislation, and the gradual decline in the stigma of birth out of wedlock.

In endeavoring to protect children, the state has become increasingly more involved in the parent-child relationship. Both governmental and private agencies have been empowered by state legislatures to perform duties and make decisions that were historically reserved to the parent.

In child welfare, social service agencies theoretically have the

expert knowledge and training essential to the making of enlightened decisions about children in need of care, as well as
the institutional resources, in terms of trained personnel, to implement those decisions. Consequently, the courts—historically
the institution empowered to secure the child's best interests—
have relied on the efforts of child welfare agencies and have
come to use them for the intermediate, and sometimes permanent, placement of a child whose custody must be resolved as
a result of state intervention into the family. Child welfare
agencies generally have the authority to choose the custodian
for a child and may at times be authorized to supervise the
placement of the child.

Governmental intrusion, while ostensibly directed toward
promoting the child's best interests, and thus beneficent in purpose, nevertheless often conflicts with the desires of some of
the individuals involved. The legal questions that these conflicts engender can, of course, only be resolved when there are
standards to guide the decisionmakers. What these standards
should be is an issue that permeates the entire field of child
custody.

The most fundamental question in child custody is to determine what type of situations justify public intrusion into the
normally private parent-child relationship. This determination
necessarily requires an examination of the goals that those in
authority feel should be promoted within the family relationship. Chapter One attempts to ascertain these goals and to
determine what situations are symbolic of the failure of the
parent-child relationship to live up to community expectations
and indicative of the frustration of the values society wants
furthered through the relationship.

Chapters Two and Three delve into the question of how
evidence of the family's failure to promote socially desirable
goals might be discovered. Such a failure is generally a result
of neglect, and these chapters analyze the standards and processes which can lead the courts to a finding of neglect.

When a child has been found to be neglected, and as a consequence state intervention is sought, a further question arises
as to what steps should be taken to remedy the situation, what

considerations should govern these steps, and what legislative standards should be set to guide decisionmakers in implementing these remedies. Chapter Four discusses the temporary remedy of foster care and the policy considerations underlying this response, as well as the consequences of this response, particularly for the child. Chapter Five deals with the permanent remedy of adoption, concentrating on the termination of the rights of the natural parents and the standards of selection which govern the establishment of a suitable adoptive parent-child relationship. The book concludes by outlining the possible directions that courts may take in seeking to further the best interests of the child when its custody is at issue.

NOTES

1. The analysis and terminology in this book are derived in part from those developed in J. Goldstein & J. Katz, The Family and the Law 1–5 (1965).

2. S. Katz, Book Review, 64 Mich. L. Rev. 756, 763 (1966) The "constellation of social values" incorporated in the "best interests of the child" doctrine may be described in this way: "We say that we expect children to be physically and emotionally secure; to become responsible citizens in their community and to become economically independent; to acquire an education and develop skills; to respect people of different races, religions, and national, social and economic backgrounds; to become socially responsible and honorable, and to have a sense of family loyalty." *Id.*

When Parents Fail

1

Community expectations of parenthood

Dominant cultural preferences in the United States may cause Americans to assume that a child is best reared in a family, especially the family setting in which it was born.[1] Our society prefers a family unit that is characterized by formal establishment, common residence, and economic independence. This group typically includes a married man and woman and their biological offspring. Social scientists use the term "nuclear family" to describe this group, contrasting it with the "extended family," which typically consists of a married man and woman, their offspring, and other relatives such as grandparents, aunts, and uncles.

The phrase "dominant cultural preferences" describes only a part of contemporary family life and excludes two other kinds of families found in the United States: those informally established and those which the law considers "illegitimate." Both are, to some extent, socially tolerated; neither is preferred. An informally established family gains legal recognition in some jurisdictions, since the husband and wife, while not conforming to the state's ceremonial requirements of marriage, have fulfilled other standards. The terms "common law marriage" and "informal marriage" describe the establishment of these families.[2] The "illegitimate family" is typically illustrated by the mother and her child born out of wedlock, living together, to the exclusion of the biological father.[3]

As history's most enduring institution, the family, regardless of its form or the legal label attached to it—legitimate, illegitimate, or informal—performs several functions that are both basic to individual members and necessary for the continuation

of our culture. Biologically, the family serves as that unit maintaining the reproductive function needed for the continuation
of any society, and at the same time serves to provide the basis
for "transforming a biological organism into a human being."[4]
Psychologically, the family serves to build and integrate the
basic personality structures of its members. Here parents, and
more specifically the mother, constitute the single most significant influence on the life and development of any child. As one
writer has said:

> The most important determining factor in the early phases
> of development is the child's dependence upon his parents, whom
> he needs not only for physical survival but who are also the most
> important objects in his world. The quality of his relations with
> them determine the security and satisfaction with which he involves
> himself with his external world. From the beginning of life the basic
> need of the individual, as part of a psycho-social unit, is to main-
> tain good relations with his objects—specifically people with whom
> he has close emotional ties—for only by doing so can he feel secure
> within himself and interact successfully with others.[5]

Furthermore, the family performs numerous socialization functions that allow new members of the culture to test, reject,
adopt, and adapt to the various roles required by society. It is
the family's function to inculcate children with society's values
and transmit our cultural heritage from one generation to the
next.[6] This includes the teaching of language, with all its implicit value preferences, and the developing of moral, ethical,
religious, and political attitudes.[7] Also, it is through the family
that notions of class and racial consciousness are developed.

Finally, the family is designed to perform an economic function. It is meant to be financially independent, separating its
members' economic statuses from that of the state and larger
community. The state benefits from the family's economic independence through the saving of government funds if the
family, not the government, fulfills certain human needs: housing, food, shelter, and health. Illustrations of the ways in which
the state encourages financial independence include the obliga-

tions of parental support, family inheritance laws, and tax laws which favor family relationships as contrasted with other arrangements and individuals.

In these and other ways, the law shows its preference for family living as a desirable social goal.[8] Yet it is interesting to note that the law does not give the family protection as a social institution. Judicial cases may mention *family* privacy and *family* integrity, but in reality the family as a unit is less protected than corporations. This is demonstrated when we see the judicial eagerness to accord legal protection to other arrangements and associations. Extensive litigation, for example, has resulted in setting out explicit legal rights and duties for business corporations under the Fourteenth Amendment to the United States Constitution.[9] And, in recent years, the United States Supreme Court has shown little reluctance to invoke the protection of the First Amendment's right of association to govern labor unions, religious groups, and political associations.[10] A comparable clarification in regard to the family, however, is missing. Thus, one has to go back to the individual relationships of family members to each other to determine legal protections.[11] Indeed, the family may be perceived in American law to consist of a bundle of seemingly independent legal relationships between husband and wife, parent and child, and so on.

Most of our cultural preferences for the family are nevertheless reflected in the law's pronouncements. These legal prescriptions take on importance when it is realized that law and its sanctions give weight and authority to community goals and attitudes. In the case of the parent-child relationship, community expectations of that relationship lie behind the legal definitions of parental duties.

PARENTAL RESPONSIBILITIES

It is important to state at the outset that we shall be discussing the duties of parents to their biological children, even though (as we shall see later) there are similarities in responsibilities that flow from parents to their children regardless of the relationship—biological, foster, or adoptive—involved.[12] It should also be said that as we examine the duties of parents to their children, we must keep the government's involvement in mind. Legal duties cannot be discussed without relating them to the sanctions that attach to nonfulfillment.

While traditionally the government seemingly has held superior control over children, it has stood in the shadow of the parent-child relationship. The judicial doctrine referred to as the "parental right to custody" holds that any biological parent is entitled to the custody of his child unless the parent is affirmatively shown to be unfit.[13] Many courts have claimed that the right is based on principles of morality and natural affection.[14] However, the common law history of the doctrine indicates that it may have been created for economic reasons, even though the dictates of a moral code have also had a bearing. During the feudal period, custodial rights, which had commercial value, were subject to transfer and sale; a child was primarily a financial asset to his father. During this early period, therefore, a custodial right was essentially a property right.[15] In time, as concern developed for the child's welfare and (perhaps as a consequence) as the mother became legally considered a joint custodian together with the father, the emphasis shifted from the property theory of custody toward the personal status theory;[16] that is, the natural parents, because of their relationship to the child, were presumed to be the custodians best fitted to serve the child's needs.

At the same time, the state has been a passive force, available to act as the ultimate protector of children when it deemed intervention necessary. Under the doctrine of *parens patriae*,[17] the state has invoked its power in unusual circumstances to promote certain policies for the protection of children. The history of government's role in protecting children, and concomitantly in dealing with parents in their relation to children, has been clearly one of slow expansion. Indeed, in its efforts to protect children, the state has become more directly and thus actively involved in the parent-child relationship. The old idea that a child is somehow the "private property" of its parents, with the impression of exclusivity of control—the right to enjoy an object to the exclusion of others—has thus diminished.

When one observes the expanding power of government into the family sphere, one must begin to readjust one's legal concept of family relationship, especially that of parent and child. It is not accurate to portray the parent-child relationship as one of the most jealously guarded in society—a frequently stated myth. Indeed, the greatest inroad the government has made in the family setting has been in the parent-child relationship. From a legal perspective, that relationship is probably the least secure in the family constellation. No appropriate legal remedy is presently available for the government to readjust or terminate an ongoing husband-wife relationship against the wishes of the spouses. Nor is there a remedy to readjust a sibling relationship. But the parent-child relationship is susceptible to subtle, indirect, and sometimes direct intrusions. There is a tendency to view governmental intrusions in these matters as benevolent, thus minimizing what might, in another setting or social stratum, be considered invasions into the privacy of the home.

The point is that no longer is it possible to delineate sharply the jurisdictional lines between government, parents, and children. The limits of decisionmaking power over children have become blurred. This does not mean, however, that we cannot tease out from laws regulating family relationships those responsibilities that have traditionally been relegated to the parent—in other words, the legal duties of the parent to his child.

Nowhere in American law is there a comprehensive statement that adequately describes the full range of the legal responsibilities of parents to children. These duties may be spelled out in various parts of state statutes (both civil and criminal), welfare regulations, case law, and so on. It becomes apparent from a study of these laws that they are expressions of community expectations about parenthood. And since judges and legislators are generally drawn from the middle-class environment, it should not be surprising that laws and their interpretations about parents and children reflect prevailing middle-class mores.

To present a profile of parental responsibilities, we have looked at the policies that the community wants promoted through the parent-child relationship. The pattern that emerges

from the various laws dealing with parental responsibilities implies an objective of a stable parent-child relationship. By this
we mean a relationship that is secure and autonomous—in essence, one that is basically free from governmental intrusion.

Stability and integrity: the comprehensive
value in the parent-child relationship
At birth a child is considered to be in the custody of his natural
parents. Some have looked upon the family relationship that is
established at this time as a trust which parents hold for the
benefit of their child and the state.[18] In reality, however, due to
the sheer necessities of the circumstances, parents assume control over and have immediate supervision of their infant to the
exclusion of others. Except for certain compulsory governmental health measures during the first few weeks of their
child's life, such as the silver nitrate treatment at birth and
perhaps the PKU (phenylketonuria) test later, natural parents
have the power to make routine decisions affecting their child's
life.[19]

If the "parental right to custody"—legally, a parent's control
over and supervision of his child—can be included in the bundle
of rights associated with marriage, establishing a home, and
rearing children, it can be claimed as a right that is "so rooted
in the traditions and conscience of our people as to be ranked
as fundamental" and, therefore, constitutionally protected.[20]
While neither the relationships of husband and wife, parent and
child, nor the family is explicitly mentioned in the United
States Constitution, the United States Supreme Court has employed "substantive due process" to protect the husband-wife
and parent-child relationships from unwarranted governmental
intrusion.

This notion of protecting the autonomy of the family and at
the same time legitimizing governmental intervention in the
parent-child relationship is supported by two early United
States Supreme Court cases: *Meyer v. Nebraska*[21] and *Pierce v.
Society of Sisters.*[22] In both cases the Court recognized the
limits of state intrusion into the parental right to educate children. In *Meyer,* the Court would not allow the State of Ne-

braska to prohibit parents from initiating the teaching of German in the public schools. Two years later, the Court in *Pierce* affirmed the parental right to educate children in private schools. The Court stated, "[T]he child is not the mere creature of the State; those who nurture him and direct his destiny have the right, coupled with the high duty, to recognize and prepare him for additional obligations."[23]

The principle that there is a realm of family life which the State can invade to protect children was reinforced by *Prince v. Commonwealth of Massachusetts*.[24] In that case, the United States Supreme Court held that the child labor laws of Massachusetts were reasonable restrictions on a parent's right to rear children, even if the teaching and practicing of a particular religious faith was involved.[25] The Court further held that a child's own right to observe and practice that faith is not unlimited.[26] At the same time, the Court was quick to note that the decision should not be read as a wide or vague limitation upon parental prerogatives in dealing with children. Mr. Justice Rutledge's statement in the *Prince* case illustrates the extent to which the Court believed the parent-child relationship should be secure and free from unreasonable interference from the state:

It is cardinal with us that the custody, care and nurture of the child reside first in the parents, whose primary function and freedom include preparation for obligations the state can neither supply nor hinder. . . . And it is in recognition of this that these decisions [*Pierce v. Society of Sisters* and *Meyer v. Nebraska*] have respected the private realm of family life which the state cannot enter. But the family itself is not beyond regulation in the public interest, as against a claim of religious liberty. . . . Acting to guard the general interest in youth's well-being, the state as *parens patriae* may restrict the parent's control by requiring school attendance, regulating or prohibiting the child's labor and in many other ways. . . . The catalogue need not be lengthened. It is sufficient to show . . . that the state has a wide range of power for limiting parental freedom and authority in things affecting the child's welfare; and that this includes, to some extent, matters of conscience, and religious convictions.[27]

A case that may have significance for issues in the family sphere is *Griswold v. State of Connecticut.*[28] In that case the United States Supreme Court was asked to declare unconstitutional a state statute that restricted the use of birth control devices. The Court, in holding against the State of Connecticut, declared that the statute constituted an excessive intrusion into the husband-wife relationship. Mr. Justice Douglas, writing for a divided Court, extracted from the Bill of Rights a penumbral right of marital and familial privacy. In his concurring opinion, the then Mr. Justice Goldberg utilized the Ninth Amendment to give additional support to precedent affirming the goal of integrity and security in the family. He wrote:

The entire fabric of the Constitution and the purposes that clearly underlie its specific guarantees demonstrate that the rights to marital privacy and to marry and raise a family are of similar order and magnitude as the fundamental rights specifically protected.

Although the Constitution does not speak in so many words of the right of privacy in marriage, I cannot believe that it offers these fundamental rights no protection. The fact that no particular provision of the Constitution explicitly forbids the State from disrupting the traditional relation of the family—a relation as old and as fundamental as our entire civilization—surely does not show that the Government was meant to have the power to do so. Rather, as the Ninth Amendment expressly recognizes, there are fundamental personal rights such as this one, which are protected from the abridgment by the Government though not specifically mentioned in the Constitution.[29]

The significance of Mr. Justice Goldberg's remarks about the husband-wife relationship for that of the parent-child is apparent. Indeed, the Ninth Amendment argument may become a new way of finding constitutional support for the integrity of the parent-child relationship.

That the parent-child relationship should be secure, stable, and free from unreasonable interference by the state or others is further emphasized in cases which establish the right of a parent to procedural due process and other procedural advantages when the custody of his child is being litigated. The due-process clause of the Fourteenth Amendment requires a court to notify a natural parent and to give him an opportunity to participate in a proceeding designed to determine his child's custody.[30] In addition, there is a procedural preference given natural parents in that the burden of proving a natural parent's unfitness is placed on the individual who desires to gain custody of the child over the natural parent's objections.[31]

Another, perhaps indirect, indication of a community policy favoring the integrity of the parent-child relationship is that the law discourages, and may even prohibit, the unconditional voluntary termination of the parent-child relationship. Events that might allow for a voluntary termination are the availability of a satisfactory placement for the child or a belief that denial of the termination request will be detrimental to the child's welfare.[32]

Thus, we have seen that the state places a high priority on a stable and independent parent-child relationship. To maintain this autonomy, the state, through its laws, imposes upon the parents specific minimum responsibilities and requires that they fulfill certain basic needs of their children. Without regard to priority, these are determined to be the child's need for financial security, health, education, morality, and respect for people and authority.[33] While these terms may seem clear upon first reading, they tend to cause difficulties in application and, in interpreting them, courts have often been reluctant (perhaps wisely) to set anything but vague and uncertain standards.

Financial security

One of the most basic obligations of parents toward their children is that of providing financial support. This obligation finds its basis in a general concept of moral responsibility, in natural law, in the common law, and in the statutes of the various states.[34] As a judge in an early case stated, "this [support obligation] is not only the law of the land but the plain dictate of humanity and justice."[35] Another early opinion read, "this [support] duty is recognized and discharged even by the higher orders of the animal world, and it would seem to be prescribed

as to the human father by the most elementary principles of
civilization as well as of law."[36] Despite these judicial statements, there is ample evidence to substantiate the view that the
parent's responsibility to provide support rests equally upon the
policy of preventing children from becoming economic burdens
on the state.[37]

The actual obligation demanded of parents is one that would
enable a child to be housed, fed, clothed, educated, and given
medical care in a manner that satisfies minimum community
standards. Often the cases refer to these as the "necessities" required by the child, and courts in some jurisdictions may be
quick to point out that bare subsistence is insufficient.[38] Beyond
the total consensus that these necessities are required, however,
there appears to be little agreement as to the actual level of
support demanded. Indeed—as is often true in the law surrounding the parent-child relationship—courts appear reluctant
to set anything but vague and minimum standards. Often the
only guide the court sets is that of a decent standard of living.

Also, it must be remembered that since support duties are a
public responsibility to which criminal and civil sanctions attach,[39] these duties cannot be avoided except in extraordinary
circumstances, such as destitution;[40] merely renouncing or dele-
gating the duty is without force.[41] Furthermore, when natural
parents make provision for support, those who do provide for
the child may seek restitution from the parents.[42]

Health and education

The next set of obligations owed by parents to their children is
to be found in health and education. First, parents are expected
to nurture and protect the physical and emotional well-being of
their children. Second, they are expected to provide their children with guidance and to offer them the opportunity for educational development. The position of the state, in all likelihood,
will be to intervene in the parent-child relationship only upon
a clear failure on the part of the parent to fulfill these obligations. A court, for example, will not require parents to provide
corrective surgery to treat nondangerous problems of the child,[43]
although it will require a parent to compensate a physician who

has provided professional services for a child without the knowledge of the parent.[44]

Furthermore, child neglect statutes (discussed more fully in Chapter Three) may be used as a legal basis for providing health care for the child when the parents fail to do so and that failure might lead to "immediate and present" danger to the child's health and well-being. In the usual situation, a parent refuses to consent to a surgical operation or blood transfusion deemed necessary for the child.[45] In such cases parental refusal is usually based on religious grounds, and courts are faced with the problem of overcoming objections based on both the First Amendment and an alleged parental right to rear their children as they see fit. In one well-known case, the court appointed a special guardian for the child and had the guardian order the needed operation. The court concluded that "the appointment of a special guardian was not intended to reflect adversely upon [the parents'] general standing and conduct as parents."[46] At the same time, however, the court was forced to base the appointment of the guardian upon the state's neglect statute and the general doctrine of *parens patriae*, stating that the child's right to life takes precedence over the parental rights to religious freedom and to rear children free from governmental intervention.[47]

The legal prescription of health standards are indicative of what the state will *not* tolerate: parents who severely deprive their children of physical safety, emotional security, or comfort. Violations of these standards may lead to criminal prosecution, temporary or permanent loss of custody, or state supervision of custody. Courts and legislatures have been less definite, however, as to what the requirements are for furthering a child's physical and emotional well-being *beyond* simply requiring a parent to provide his child with the bare essentials. Whether the parent must take positive steps to ensure the optimal physical and emotional health of the child—for example, by providing it with psychiatric or orthodontal care—is a question which is for the most part left unanswered.

Just as there is no clear statement of what constitutes the maximum or ideal of good health, neither is there any judicial or statutory expression of the extent to which parents must enlighten their children. The educational duty which rests on the parents begins with the birth of the child and is essentially uncontrolled during its early years. There is almost no state supervision of the duty to educate until a child reaches the age of five or six, although governmental control could be assumed prior to those ages if the child were "neglected" by not having received rudimentary education. When their children reach the age of five or six, parents are expected to enroll them in educational institutions under state regulation, to refrain from interfering with school attendance, and, in fact, to encourage their children's attendance until they reach a specific age (usually sixteen). State compulsory education acts contain criminal sanctions which apply to parents who fail to fulfill their responsibilities.

Beyond these statements, however, it is unclear whether the standard of the child's education should be set at a minimum level, at the highest potentialities of the child, or somewhere in between. Indeed, whether parents must provide their children with educational opportunities beyond statutory compulsory education is an open question, depending perhaps on the economic and social situation of the parents. Difference in expectations can be found within states. For example, courts in Ohio are split as to whether a college education is a necessity which a father must provide for his child. One Ohio court has held that a college education is not included among the "necessaries" which a parent is "legally required" to furnish a child.[48] But another court in Ohio, within a year, held that this is a relative matter and "considering the progress of society and our nation's need for citizens educated in the humanities and sciences, a college education is a necessary where the minor's ability and prospects justify it."[49]

Morality and respect
Closely associated with the parental duty to nurture health and education is the parent's responsibility to teach his child respect for authority and other persons and to provide it with a moral

environment in which it may develop sound character. This latter responsibility imposes on a parent an obligation to train his child in differentiating "right" from "wrong" and to develop his child's conscience. It also requires a parent to teach by example, that is, to conduct himself in a manner that his child may emulate. Furthermore, although this duty is rarely articulated, the parent is expected to instill in his child respect for the parent as an individual and an authority figure and, as the child matures, to implant in him respect for other persons and authorities in society. To assist in the development of respect for authority, courts give parents wide latitude in the exercise of their disciplinary powers. An underlying reason for this latitude is the belief that one way in which children learn to adjust to the mandates of society is through the proper use of discipline.

The moral conduct expected of parents is rarely defined in terms of specific religious dogma since, as individuals, parents are not required to follow the dictates of a particular religion, although the tenets of the dominant Judeo-Christian culture may influence the standards of parental conduct. The moral conduct necessary to fulfill parental responsibilities usually encompasses notions of "common decency, cleanliness of mind and body, honesty, truthfulness, and proper respect for *established* ideals and institutions" (emphasis added).[50] A parent is free to choose the method by which his child will be inculcated with a sense of morality, and he need not utilize religious training for this purpose. In fact, courts have consistently stated that parents have no duty to give their children any religious training. Parents are, therefore, as free to ignore religion in their home as they are to rear their children in a particular faith.[51] At the same time, in order to teach a child social responsibility, parents are not required to provide any special ethical training. But despite the latitude given by many courts in this area, child neglect laws of some states have been utilized in certain instances by public prosecutors, welfare officials, and others to punish parental nonconformity (that is, deviant behavior and perhaps attitudes as defined by community officials) under the theory of parental failure to instill the values of respect and morality in the child.

SUMMARY

If we take a comprehensive view of the parent-child relation-ship in the law, we see that the state expects parents to care for their children in a way that will not prompt governmental intrusion into the family universe. There are, practically speaking, basic elements of privacy and autonomy that surround the parent-child relationship. This is so even though the state has made important and what appears to be lasting inroads into functions that had been considered traditionally parental. But in most everyday activities, parents control their children's conduct and have an enormous impact on their attitudes and behavior. Allocation to parents of power and control over their children has its roots in our society's culture; it may be based on social, psychological, and even financial considerations. Quite simply, parents have traditionally reared their children in their home; society believes it is healthy, for the most part, for them to perform that function; and it is economically expedient for the state that they do so.

For the parent-child relationship to remain free from state intervention, however, parents are expected to fulfill certain obligations. They are required to provide their children with financial security, to maintain their children's health, to ensure their children's education, and to instill in their children values of morality and respect. These statements of community expectations are abstract standards and have little concrete worth outside of individual cases. These standards are applied when some event occurs in the life of either the child or parent which prompts someone to question the parental right to custody.

NOTES

1. For an examination of cultural preferences found in other countries, see N. Timasheff, *The Attempt to Abolish the Family in Russia*; M. Spiro, *Is the Family Universal?—The Israeli Case*, E. Cough, *Is the Family Universal?—The Nayar Case* in N. Bell & E. Vogel, The Family (1960). For a discussion of changing attitudes on family living in America, *see The*

Commune Comes to America, Life, July 18, 1969, at 16B. *See also* G. Gorer, The American People (1948).

2. A prevalent belief exists that only one kind of marriage is legal: marriage by license and ceremony. But other methods of marriage exist and may be legal in the United States: common law, marriage by estoppel, marriage by ratification, marriage by presumption, and so on. It is important to note that common law and other informal marriages are phenomena primarily found in marginal groups, that is, the lower classes of both the white and black populations. The prevailing statutory trend in the United States is to abolish common law marriages. For a full discussion of common law marriage and an examination of its place in contemporary America, *see* W. Weyrauch, *Informal Marriage and Common Law Marriage* in Sexual Behavior and the Law 293 (R. Slovenko ed. 1965).

3. Perhaps because of the increasing number of illegitimate births in the United States and because of traditional distaste for unequal treatment based on distinctions of birth, a gradual decline in both the social and legal discrimination against the "illegitimate family" is occurring. About one in fifteen live births in the United States is illegitimate. U. S. Department of Health, Education, and Welfare, Trends in Illegitimacy, United States—1940–1965 (1968). In some urban ghetto communities alone, more than 50 percent of live births are illegitimate. Report of the National Advisory Commission on Civil Disorders (Kerner Commission) 263 (1968). This latter percentage reflects the enormously high rate of illegitimate births among the nonwhite urban population.

The status of the "illegitimate family" under the law has historically been one of clear discrimination, as contrasted with the legitimate family. For example, early in our legal tradition the illegitimate child was considered "the child of no one," and consequently had no legal, custodial, or inheritance rights. Later its legal relationship to its biological mother was recognized in inheritance statutes, and it gained inheritance rights through her, as she did through it.

During the 1967 term, the United States Supreme Court held in *Levy v. Louisiana,* 391 U.S. 68 (1968) and *Glona v. American Guarantee & Liability Ins. Co.,* 391 U.S. 73 (1968) that the equal-protection clause of the Fourteenth Amendment protected illegitimate children from being discriminated against in wrongful death statutes. *Levy* held that an illegitimate child can recover for the wrongful death of its mother; *Glona* held that a mother could recover for the wrongful death of her illegitimate child.

Fathers of illegitimate children have traditionally been excluded from having any legal claims to their child. They share the same standing with a stranger insofar as custodial rights are concerned. Their consent is not required if their child is sought to be adopted. See *infra* Ch. 5, notes 42–

45 and accompanying text. They have no claim through intestacy laws on the estate of their illegitimate child. At the same time, the illegitimate child has been excluded through intestacy laws from sharing with legitimate siblings in the wealth of its biological father.

For a discussion of the legal problems of illegitimacy as they affect the family, *see* C. Foote, R. Levy, & F. Sander, Cases and Materials on Family Law 1–10 (1966). For a historical discussion of illegitimacy in America and the rights of illegitimate children, *see* H. Krause, Illegitimacy: Law and Social Policy (1971). *See also* H. Semmel, *Social Security Benefits for Illegitimate Children After Levy v. Louisiana*, 19 Buffalo L. Rev. 289 (1970); Note, *The Rights of Illegitimates Under Federal Statutes*, 76 Harv. L. Rev. 337 (1962).

4. W. Goode, The Family 8 (1964).

5. L. Pincus, *Relationships and the Growth of Personality* in Marriage: Studies in Emotional Conflict and Growth 17 (L. Pincus ed. 1955), cited in F. Harper & J. Skolnick, Problems of the Family 216 (Rev. ed. 1962).

6. *See* T. Lidz, The Person 46–47 (1968); S. Briar, *The Family As An Organization: An Approach to Family Diagnosis and Treatment*, 38 The Social Service Review 247 (1964).

7. *See generally* L. Berkowitz, Development of Motives and Values In the Child (1964); A. Greeley and P. Rossi, The Education of Catholic Americans (1966); M. Lewis, Language, Thought and Personality in Infancy and Childhood (1963).

8. *See, e.g.*, the statement of the policy of the Commonwealth of Massachusetts in its statute on the protection and care of children: "It is hereby declared to be the policy of this commonwealth to direct its efforts, first, to the strengthening and encouragement of family life for the protection and care of children; to assist and encourage the use by a family of all available resources to this end; and to provide substitute care of children only when the family itself or the resources available to the family are unable to provide the necessary care and protection to insure the rights of any child to sound health and normal physical, mental, spiritual and moral development." Mass. Gen. Laws Ann. ch. 119, § 1 (1969).

9. *See, e.g.*, Connecticut General Life Ins. Co. v. Johnson, 303 U.S. 77 (1938) (due process); Minneapolis & St. L. Ry. Co. v. Beckwith, 129 U.S. 26 (1889) (due process); Wheeling Steel Corp. v. Glander, 337 U.S. 562, 576–581 (1949) (Douglas, J., dissenting) (equal protection); Santa Clara County v. Southern Pacific R.R., 118 U.S. 394 (1886) (equal protection).

10. *See* Brotherhood of Railway Trainmen v. Virginia, 377 U.S. 1

(1964) (labor unions); West Virginia State Board of Education v. Barnette, 319 U.S. 624 (1943) (religious associations); N.A.A.C.P. v. Button, 371 U.S. 415 (1963) (political associations).

11. *But see* Loving v. Virginia, 388 U.S. 1 (1967) *discussed in* H. Foster, *Marriage: A "Basic Civil Right of Man,"* 37 Fordham L. Rev. 51 (1968) and W. Wadlington, *The Loving Case: Virginia's Anti-Miscegenation Statute in Historical Perspective,* 52 Va. L. Rev. 1189 (1966). *Cf.* McLaughlin v. Florida, 379 U.S. 184 (1964).

12. The legal duties to be discussed attach to the parents of legitimate children. It should be noted, however, that in the case of the "illegitimate family" (see *supra,* note 3), only the biological mother has the duties discussed here unless there has been some kind of governmental intervention, such as bastardy proceedings, to compel the father of an illegitimate child to assume certain parental duties, or unless the father has legitimatized his illegitimate child or has taken any other appropriate legal measures to assume parental responsibilities.

13. *See, e.g.,* Roche v. Roche, 25 Cal.2d 141, 152 P.2d 999 (1944); McGuire v. McGuire, 190 Kan. 524, 376 P.2d 908 (1962); Stout v. Stout, 166 Kan. 459, 201 P.2d 637 (1949); *Ex Parte* Barnes, 54 Ore. 548, 104 Pac. 296 (1909). *See also* Iowa Code § 633.559 (1963).

14. *See, e.g.,* Wilkinson v. Wilkinson, 105 Cal. App. 2d 392, 233 P.2d 639 (1951); Acomb v. Billeiter, 175 So.2d 25 (La. Ct. App. 1965); *In re* Lewis, 35 Misc. 2d 117, 230 N.Y.S.2d 481 (Surr. Ct. 1962); Anonymous v. Anonymous, 15 Misc. 2d 389, 181 N.Y.S.2d 311 (Sup. Ct. 1959); People *ex rel.* Kropp v. Shepsky, 305 N.Y. 465, 113 N.E.2d 801 (1953).

15. *See* P. Sayre, *Awarding Custody of Children,* 9 U. Chi. L. Rev. 672, 676–77 (1942); J. tenBroek, *California's Dual System of Family Law: Its Origin, Development, and Present Status, Part II,* 16 Stan. L. Rev. 900, 925 (1964).

16. For many purposes, however, the child is still treated as property; there has been a shift, but not a substitution.

17. The doctrine of *parens patriae* is said to have originated in England in the seventeenth century. It is generally explained as being derived from the Sovereign's prerogative in protecting his subjects unable to protect themselves, that is, mental incompetents and infants. Early recognition of the doctrine is found in Eyre v. Shaftesbury, 2 P. Wms. 102, 24 Eng. Rep. 659 (1722). There is some authority for basing the power of the state to invoke the doctrine only when the incompetent's property was involved. *See* Wellesley v. Beaufort, 2 Russ. 1, 38 Eng. Rep. 236 (1827).

Whatever its origin, however, *parens patriae* in its modern application gives the state jurisdiction to act when a child's interests are involved. The doctrine is discussed in Cinque v. Boyd, 99 Conn. 70, 80–81 (1923). *See also* H. Clark, Domestic Relations 572 (1968); C. Foote, R. Levy, & F. Sander, *supra* note 3 at 394 n. 13 (1966).

18. *See, e.g.*, Gardner v. Hall, 132 N.J. Eq. 64, 26 A.2d 799 (ch. 1942); Lippincott v. Lippincott, 97 N.J. Eq. 517, 128 A. 254 (Ct. Err. & App. 1925); Elliot v. Elliot, 235 N.C. 153, 69 S.E.2d 224 (1952).

19. Many states have statutory provisions regulating the silver nitrate treatment. *See, e.g.*, Conn. Gen. Stat. Rev. § 19.92 (1958); Fla. Stat. § 383.05 (1965); Ill. Rev. Stat. ch. 91 § 108 (1963). Minnesota specifically waives the test if parents object to it. Minn. Stat. § 144.12(8) (1965 Supp.). New York has enacted a statutory provision requiring the administering of the PKU test. See N.Y. Public Health Law § 2500-a (Supp. 1968).

20. Griswold v. Connecticut, 381 U.S. 479, 487 (1965) (Goldberg, J., concurring).

21. 262 U.S. 390 (1923).

22. 268 U.S. 510 (1925).

23. *Id.* at 535.

24. 321 U.S. 158 (1944).

25. *Id.* at 170 ("Parents may be free to become martyrs themselves. But it does not follow they are free, in identical circumstances, to make martyrs of their children before they have reached the age of full and legal discretion when they can make that choice for themselves.")

26. *Id.* at 171.

27. *Id.* at 166, 167.

28. 381 U.S. 479 (1965).

29. *Id.* at 495–96 (concurring opinion). *See also* Poe v. Ullman, 367 U.S. 497, 551–52 (1961) (Harlan, J., dissenting).

30. Armstrong v. Manzo, 380 U.S. 545 (1965).

31. Professor tenBroek convincingly demonstrated that the burden of

proof in favor of parental fitness applies mainly to members of the middle classes, but is substantially relaxed as to the poor. In cases involving the poor, "parental fitness" is examined rather than presumed. J. tenBroek, *California's Dual System of Family Law: Its Origin, Development, and Present Status, Part III*, 17 Stan. L. Rev. 614, 676 (1965).

The decision of the United States Supreme Court in *Armstrong v. Manzo*, 380 U.S. 545 (1965), illustrates the extent to which the Court will go to protect a natural parent's right to his child. In that case, the issue was whether an adoption decree was valid when secured by the child's natural mother and her second husband without notification to the first husband, the child's natural father. Although the natural father had subsequently obtained a hearing on his motion to vacate the decree because of the lack of notice and had presented evidence at that hearing in an attempt to establish the necessity of his consent to the adoption, the Court held that the decree was invalid. The failure of the adoption court to provide the natural father an opportunity to contest the adoption was more than a routine denial of procedural due process, because the court's action permanently deprived "a *legitimate* parent of all that parenthood implies" (emphasis supplied). The natural father's absence in the adoption proceedings gave the adoptive applicant (second husband) an undue advantage since he did not have to carry the burden of proving his own qualifications and the natural father's unfitness. In the subsequent hearing on the motion to vacate the decree, this crucial allocation of the burden of proof was reversed, for the natural father, since he was the moving party in that hearing, was required to demonstrate affirmatively his fitness to have custody of the child. The Court, realizing the decisiveness of the location of the burden of proof, was unwilling to deprive the natural father of his procedural preference in the adoption proceeding.

But see the discussion of *In re Neff* in Ch. III, *infra*, p. 77–80, which seems to indicate that once the presumption in favor of parental fitness has been overcome and an agency has intervened, the natural parent has an extremely difficult time subsequently demonstrating his fitness in a hearing to revoke a neglect decree. In other words, there is a presumption of parental fitness, but once a parent has been declared unfit, there seems to be a presumption of continuing unfitness.

32. The Model Adoption Act drafted by the U. S. Department of Health, Education, and Welfare, provides for the voluntary termination of parental rights regardless of the availability of satisfactory placement. *See* Children's Bureau, U. S. Dept. of Health, Education, and Welfare, Legislative Guides for the Termination of Parental Rights and Responsibilities and the Adoption of Children 12–13 (1961).

33. While these terms are stated as a child's needs, they also represent social values. It is safe to say that as values, they are shared by a majority

of the population in the United States. But the sharing of these values and the priorities given to them may be quite different depending upon class, race, religion, and other factors. It is possible, for example, that groups in our society place the highest priority on morality, while others may give that value the lowest priority. For a discussion of these values in the context of child custody matters, *see* S. Katz, *Community Decision-Makers and the Promotion of Values in the Adoption of Children*, 38 The Social Service Review 26 (1964). For an application of these value categories to other family problems, *see* W. Weyrauch, *Informal and Formal Marriage— An Appraisal of Trends in Family Organization*, 28 U. Chi. L. Rev. 88 (1960).

34. *See* N. Pacht, *Support of Dependents in the District of Columbia: Part I*, 9 How. L. J. 20, 36–38 (1963).

35. Hunter v. State, 10 Okla. Crim. 119, 134 P. 1134 (1913).

36. Osborn v. Weatherford, 8 Div. 356 (Ala.), 170 So. 95, 96 (1936).

37. *See* Porter v. Powell, 79 Iowa 151, 44 N.W. 295 (1890); Crain v. Mallone, 130 Ky. 125, 113 S.W. 67 (1908); Holland v. Beard, 59 Miss. 161, 42 So. 360 (1881); State v. Thornton, 232 Mo. 298, 134 S.W. 519 (1911); Geary v. Geary, 102 Neb. 511, 167 N.W. 778 (1918); Garlock v. Garlock, 279 N.W. 337, 18 N.E.2d 521 (1939). *See also* S. Jones, *The Problem of Family Support: Criminal Sanctions for the Enforcement of Support*, 38 N. C. L. Rev. 1, 13 (1959); Pacht, *supra*, note 34 at 21.

38. *See, e.g.*, State v. Waller, 90 Kan. 829, 136 P. 215 (1913).

39. These are often found in child neglect statutes. *See, e.g.*, Alaska Stat. § 11.35.010 (1962); Ariz. Rev. Stat. Ann. § 13–801 (1956); Colo. Rev. Stat. § 22–2–1 (1963); Ind. Ann. Stat. § 10–815 (1956); Md. Ann. Code art. 27 § 88(b) (1957); Mass. Gen. Laws Ann. ch. 273, § 1 (Supp. 1965); Ohio Rev. Code Ann. § 2151.99(B) (1963); Wis. Stat. § 947.15 (1961).

40. *See, e.g.*, Watts v. Steele, 19 Ala. 656, 54 Am. Dec. 207 (1851); *In re* Estate of Weisskopfs, 39 Ill. App. 2d 380, 188 N.E.2d 726 (1963); Fruen v. Fruen, 228 Minn. 391, 37 N.W.2d 417 (1949); Libby v. Arnold, 161 N.Y.S.2d 798 (N.Y. City Com. Rel. Ct. 1957).

41. *See, e.g.*, Rogers v. Rogers, 93 Kan. 114, 143 Pac. 410 (1914); Huffman v. Hatcher, 178 Ky. 8, 198 S.W. 236 (1917); State v. Bell, 184 N.C. 701, 115 S.E. 190 (1922).

42. *See, e.g.*, Commonwealth v. Kirk, 212 Ky. 646, 279 S.W. 1091 (1926); Greenman v. Gillerman's Estate, 188 Mich. 74, 154 N.W. 82

(1915); Worthington v. Worthington, 212 Mo. App. 216, 253 S.W. 443 (1923). *See also* Jones, *supra*, note 37, at 12, 13.

43. *In re* Seiferth, 309 N.Y. 80, 127 N.E.2d 820 (1955) (hair lip and cleft palate); *In re* Hudson, 13 Wash. 2d 673, 126 P.2d 765 (1942) (congenital arm deformity); *In re* Tuttendario. 21 Penn. Dist. 561 (Q.S. Phila. Co. 1911) (rachitis).

44. *See, e.g.*, Greenspan v. Slate, 12 N.J. 426, 97 A.2d 390 (1953).

45. People *ex rel.* Wallace v. Labrenz, 411 Ill. 618, 104 N.E.2d 769 (1952); State v. Perricone, 37 N.J. 463, 181 A.2d 751 (1962). For a discussion of parental obligations in other health-related areas, *see In re* Carstairs, 115 N.Y.S.2d 314 (N.Y. City Dom. Rel. Ct. 1952) (mental health); People v. Pierson, 176 N.Y. 201, 68 N.E. 243 (1903) (pneumonia).

46. State v. Perricone, 37 N.J. 463, 480, 181 A.2d 751, 760 (1962).

47. *Id.* at 473–4, 181 A.2d at 757.

48. Ford v. Ford, 109 Ohio App. 495, 167 N.E.2d 787 (1959).

49. Calogeras v. Calogeras, 163 N.E.2d 713, 720 (Ohio Juv. Ct. 1960). It has been stated that the most important factors in determining a father's liability for the expenses of a child's education are the father's ability to pay and the child's capacity for further education. Pincus v. Pincus, 197 A.2d 854 (D.C. Ct. App. 1964); Hoffman v. Hoffman, 210 A.2d 549 (D.C. Ct. App. 1965). *See also* Commonwealth v. Rice, 206 Pa. Super. 393, 213 A.2d 179 (1965); O'Brien v. Springer, 202 Misc. 210, 107 N.Y.S.2d 631 (Sup. Ct. 1951); Commonwealth v. Decker, 204 Pa. Super. 156, 203 A.2d 343 (1964).

50. L v. N, 326 S.W.2d 751, 755 (Mo. 1959).

51. Courts have generally stated that it is outside the province of the law to regulate religious activities in the home. *See, e.g.*, Abington School Dist. v. Schempp, 374 U.S. 203 (1963); Lynch v. Uhlenhopp, 248 Iowa 68, 78 N.W.2d 491 (1956); Wojnarowicz v. Wojnarowicz, 48 N.J. Super. 349, 137 A.2d 618 (ch. 1958); Paolella v. Phillips, 27 N.Y. Misc. 763, 209 N.Y.S.2d 165 (Sup. Ct. 1960); People *ex rel.* Sisson v. Sisson, 271 N.Y. 285, 2 N.E.2d 660 (1936); Hackett v. Hackett, 78 Ohio L. Abs. 485, 150 N.E.2d 431 (Ct. App. 1958).

2

The process of public intrusion

Public intrusion into the parent-child relationship occurs in response to child neglect. Broadly speaking, child neglect occurs when the expectations of parenthood that are dominant in our culture are not met. From a legal perspective, child neglect connotes a parent's conduct, usually thought of in terms of passive behavior, that results in a failure to provide for the child's needs as defined by the preferred values of the community.

In this context, child neglect should be distinguished from child abuse. Perhaps the key to distinguishing the two is the element of deliberateness. From a legal perspective, child abuse connotes a parent's or custodian's active and usually intentional behavior which causes physical injury to his child. The conduct is usually deliberate, calculated, consistent, and often torturous. Because child abuse usually is evidenced by some discernible physical damage, such as broken bones, scars, or burns, it is more apparent and more easily discovered than child neglect.

Abusive conduct frequently takes the form of excessive physical punishment inappropriate to the occasion. In legal terminology, child abuse may encompass the torts of "assault" and "battery." An illustration of a case of child abuse treated in terms of assault and battery is *Gillett v. Gillett*.[1] A description of the abusive conduct is included in the appellate court opinion:

Plaintiff Sharon [8 years old] and her older sister Inette were doing the supper dishes; plaintiff was drying; she dropped a dish and it broke; defendant [stepmother] came in from the yard, and

22

according to Inette, got very upset, started yelling and screaming and swearing at Sharon, hit her in the back with her doubled fists; Sharon ran into the bedroom and defendant followed, hitting her on the way and in the bedroom; at that place Sharon was between two beds with her face to the wall, crying and screaming, and defendant kept hitting her in the back with her doubled fists sideways.

The injury which the stepmother inflicted on the eight-year-old child resulted in internal bleeding, probably caused by a ruptured spleen. In order to prevent the child from bleeding to death, both her spleen and kidney were removed. Clearly, the stepmother overreacted to the dropping of the dish. Her behavior should be compared with what might be a normal parental reaction: generally spontaneous, indirect, impulsive, and often, from the parent's perspective, loving.

Child neglect, on the other hand, is usually manifested in a more passive context, often exhibited by a seeming indifference toward a child and an inability to carry out the expected roles of parenthood. For the purpose of the present discussion, child neglect and child abuse will therefore be separated. The need for, and the significance of, the separation in this chapter is also based on the fact that, while all American jurisdictions have enacted statutes and codified procedures for the legal handling of abuse cases, this is not true for child neglect.

PROFILE OF THE NEGLECTING PARENT

Before discussing the process of public intrusion into the parent-child relationship, some general characteristics of parents *reported* as neglecting their children should be presented. The word "reported" is italicized because it is important to make clear that the knowledge we have about "neglecting parents" results from cases that have been discovered by someone and reported to a community agency. There is no way of knowing precisely how many parents neglect their children so long as our society protects the privacy of large numbers of families, particularly those in the middle and upper classes. This does not mean that middle- and upper-class parents do not neglect their children. Rather, because our society does not, as a practical matter, have the same standards for middle- and upper-class parents that it tries to enforce on the lower classes, child neglect proceedings are primarily instituted against lower-class parents.

Permanent or temporary parental abandonment of a child by leaving it with a neighbor is thought to be neglectful if it involves a poor parent and an equally poor neighbor. Indeed, in Massachusetts a person who is unrelated by blood or marriage who permanently cares for another's child in his home may be fined if he fails to obtain a license for operating a foster home.[2] Rudimentary requirements of due process of law—notice of a hearing and an opportunity to be heard at the hearing—to remove the child from the neighbor's home may not be enforced; they may even be denied.[3] Illinois specifically provides that child abandonment, even if the child is cared for by another, is a felony.[4] Conviction carries with it the penalty of imprisonment for at least one year. It seems clear, however, that middle- and upper-class parents who leave their children in the care of nursemaids or place them in private boarding schools, failing to visit them for long periods of time, would not be regarded by the community as felons. Moreover, the community does not regard parents of children who use drugs or run away to the East Village or Haight-Ashbury as neglectful even though their anguished questions of "where did we go wrong" are read in the press. In most instances community officials will categorize events that occur in middle- and upper-class areas as "social problems," not cases of individual parental neglect.

A profile of parents reported as neglecting their children can be drawn. Several sociological studies, all focusing on the identification of the neglecting family, agree in their conclusions.[5] The most striking feature of neglecting parents is the level of poverty in which they live. By almost any economic scale, these parents are poor. Not surprisingly, a high proportion are supported by either private or governmental welfare funds.[6] Substandard housing, lack of good health and educational facilities, and little opportunity for recreational diversions appear to be the standard way of life. These parents are indeed part of the "other America."[7]

Beyond this, the poverty of neglecting parents often causes them to attempt temporary escapes from the misery of their existence. Thus, alcoholism, drug use, and sexual promiscuity are common. This in turn often results in poor health, erratic employment, chaotic home life, and transient living.

> When life demands action, they cannot act—they have learned little from their parents but modes of escape. The most typical responses to reality problems were to deny them, to run away from them and to submit passively to the consequences. There is in all this what amounts almost to an abnegation of living, an acceptance of defeat so complete that action becomes irrelevant. Defeatism is a spiritual poison that is passed on to the children, one that is too often encouraged by their experience in the community.[8]

Closely related to this way of life is the high incidence among neglecting families (sometimes over 50 percent) of households headed by a single parent, generally the mother.[9] Separation by a spouse through desertion, divorce, or an initial illegitimate relationship are all factors leading to this phenomenon.[10]

Although poverty and family structure are contributing factors in child neglect, many families living marginally rear their children according to accepted community standards. Neglecting parents, however, tend to have additional problems. They are often characterized by a history of deviant behavior as viewed by the community at large, although within their own subculture their conduct may reflect the norm. Many neglecting fathers, for example, have criminal records. Neglecting parents tend to exhibit a form of indifference toward their children and indeed toward the total community. They tend to be socially isolated, ostracized from the larger community. They rarely join organizations. They tend to have little contact with either friends or relatives. They are, in the truest sense of the word, alone.

Beyond the social problems attached to poverty, neglecting

parents tend to have serious personal difficulties. They are
likely to lack both emotional maturity and the ability to adjust
to and cope with their environment. Many can neither accept
their roles as parents nor as spouses.[11] Often they have lacked
positive role models, since they themselves may have been the
products of neglecting parents. They tend to suffer from psychological disorders, often exhibiting psychotic behavior.

We saw their immaturity in their childlike, pleasure-seeking,
irresponsible, impulsive behavior. We noted the crisis-to-crisis, un-
planful inability to learn from experience. We observed that children
were neglected because their needs were secondary to the adults'
own gratifications. We recognized the impaired perception of reality
and the faulty judgment which such distortion caused. We were
struck by the misery and all-pervading failure which surrounded
the total life experience of these impulse-ridden persons. They are
at odds with the whole world. All their relationships, within and
outside the family, operate in an atmosphere that at various times
includes hostility, suspicion, aloneness, futility, frustration, and rage.
But under the bravado of "leave me alone" we found an abysmal
sense of unlovability and low self-esteem.[12]

The portrait of the neglecting parent that emerges from the
various studies, then, is bleak. Neglecting parents are the dis-
advantaged whose lives are hollow. They are not part of the
American dream, with its great emphasis on upward striving.
Neglecting parents, like so many of the very poor, are desper-
ate, lonely, and withdrawn individuals. They are socially rejected. Some are physically abusive—that is, purposely hostile
or intentionally destructive—toward their children. But not all
neglecting parents are necessarily abusive. Rather, they tend to
exhibit an appalling lack of care, as witnessed by such events
as prolonged and repeated periods of parental desertion and a
failure to meet their children's immediate and basic health
needs. The great American notion of parental indulgence is not
part of their value system. Indeed, they have little to give their
children, both in terms of material things and emotional
strengths. This results from their own inability to participate in

the economic processes in society, their own feelings of inadequacy, and society's reluctance to bear the responsibility for effectively meeting their needs. Because of their plight in society and the low esteem in which the community holds them, neglecting parents have difficulty in passing on to their children the social values which the dominant culture deems desirable. And when society's expectations are not met, questions of parental fitness and alternative parents may be raised.

We have divided the process of public intrusion into these families into four stages: the *report* of the event thought to be neglectful, agency *investigation* of the event, the *challenge* to the parental right to custody, and the *state intervention* itself. This breakdown results not from any specific statutory scheme, but rather from general practice. This chapter will focus on the first three stages of public intrusion, leaving for Chapter Three a discussion of state intervention.

THE REPORT

The process of public intrusion into the parent-child relationship usually begins with an individual's decision to report what he perceives as child neglect.[13] The report may be made by a neighbor, relative, school teacher, social worker, landlord, police officer, physician, nurse, or hospital administrator to a public or private social service agency, to a law enforcement agency such as the local police, or directly to the courts. One community agency not equipped to handle a neglect case may report the neglect to another more appropriate community agency. Frequently, one parent may report the other, especially where the parents are separated or having other domestic difficulties. Many of the reports are made anonymously. For the most part, the decision not to report is a "low-visibility" decision —that is, while the report of a neglectful event may be reviewed by an agency, there is no practical way to either control or review an individual's decision not to report. In states that make the reporting of neglect mandatory, a criminal sanction attaches to the failure to report, if that is discovered.

As we have stated, several types of agencies may receive

child neglect reports. Within a given community, private voluntary child protective agencies (existing in ten states),[14] child
welfare divisions of a state or county welfare department,[15]
the local law enforcement agency,[16] or a court[17] may receive
these reports from time to time. The hour at which the reports
are made, the degree of immediate harm to the child which the
report indicates, the identity of the complainant, and other
facts may all influence the choice of agency as well as the
initial response of that agency. At the same time, variations in
the handling of neglect reports exist from state to state and
indeed from community to community and agency to agency
within a community. Some agencies equipped to handle reports
proceed on their own, while others may act as conduits, referring reports to agencies specifically designed to handle neglect
matters.

It should be added that the decision to report instances of
neglect to an agency may relate more to economic, ethnic, or
personal factors than to legally recognized standards. Indeed,
the reports may be used by a separated spouse to continue and
compound marital difficulties, by a neighbor trying to get a
fellow neighbor jailed or evicted from a housing project, or
among relatives and neighbors to generally resolve personal
antagonisms.

As mentioned earlier, the reporting of child neglect that results in public intrusion is a phenomenon found primarily,
though not exclusively, among the urban lower classes. The reasons for this are complex. But it may be conjectured that central
to the issue of intrusion is family visibility. The poor are visible
because their lives are public. The lower classes utilize community resources such as public welfare funds, public health
services, emergency rooms of hospitals, and outpatient departments of hospitals and clinics. Their personal affairs, their
personal appearances and those of their children, and their
everyday living activities are subject to scrutiny.

On the other hand, middle-class Americans living in the suburbs lead a more private life than the lower classes in the cities.
The middle-class suburbanite usually lives in a single-family
house which is much more private than a multiple-unit apart-

ment building. It is often difficult to discover what is occurring in a neighbor's house surrounded by a spacious lawn; it is easy to detect what is happening behind the adjoining wall.

Furthermore, a psychological isolation is found in middle-class suburbs that may not be present to the same extent in lower-class urban areas. This does not mean that lower-class urban areas are entirely free from this kind of estrangement. An alienation does exist in urban areas. Urban people are transient; they are neither likely to develop roots nor to sustain relationships with neighbors. For our purposes, however, it is important to stress the difference in attitudes that city and suburban people have toward their neighbors. Middle-class residents tend to live under the impression that their neighbors are fit for their parental roles. The idea of family privacy and the bias in favor of parental fitness which is found in the suburbs may not be held by lower-class urban residents or by the individuals, officials, or agencies that serve them. Indeed, while it might be in poor taste for a neighbor in the suburbs to call the police to intrude in a neighbor's family dispute, it is common for police to be called to quell family fights and make arrests in lower-class urban areas. Furthermore, police in suburban areas tend to view their role with respect to involvement in domestic matters as passive, whereas urban police are more likely to treat domestic quarrels as routine matters for active intervention.

AGENCY INVESTIGATION

Once a report of the allegedly neglectful event has been made to an agency, an investigation usually takes place according to established agency procedures. Interviews with the child, the parents and neighbors, the person who made the report, and a visit to the child's home may well be part of the initial investigation.

Furthermore, agencies check their records and inquire of other agencies whether there are other reports on the parents or whether the parents have been previously involved with the agency. At the same time, some agencies may attempt to weed

out those cases which do not on their face appear to warrant
the full investigatory resources of the agency. Insufficient information in the initial report, a strong agency suspicion of
ulterior motives on the part of the person reporting, and the
limited resources of most agencies may all play a role in these
decisions.

When an investigation does take place, it usually is conducted by the receiver of the report. In the majority of cases,
few problems will be encountered by the investigating agency
since it usually has access to the situation through the agreement of the party being investigated. This agreement may be
the result of a generally receptive and responsive parent or the
result of the subtle pressures that an agency, because of its
power position in the community, can bring to bear upon
parents. Where access may be limited, some welfare and health
agencies may use the police department to conduct the initial
on-the-scene investigation.[18] The police would then report back
to the agency, which might conduct additional investigations.

Upon completion of the agency's investigation, it must decide
whether to proceed further with the case. Where the investigation has not revealed facts which in the agency's mind are sufficiently harmful to the child to warrant further action, the
matter may be dropped entirely. On the other hand, if the
agency is a social service one, it may at this point decide to
make its caseworker, homemaker, or other workers and services
available to the family.[19]

The Mitchell family illustrates a case which was both referred to and resolved by a private child protective agency
within its own institution.

The Mitchell family

The Mitchell family was referred to a child protective agency
by the social service department of a large urban hospital
where the children received outpatient medical care. Both
parents, each thirty years old, were described as being infantile
and depressed and suffering from financial and severe marital
problems. Mr. Mitchell drank heavily and spent a great deal of
time away from his family. Mrs. Mitchell was in outpatient

psychiatric treatment at the hospital, and the family was being visited weekly by a local visiting nurse because of the children's slow physical development. Martha, who was twenty-one months old, was born eleven months prior to the marriage. Ann was twelve months old at the time of referral. Mrs. Mitchell was experiencing great difficulty in caring for and feeding the children and performing her housekeeping duties. The house was dirty and messy, and the children were grossly undernourished and retarded in physical and emotional development.

Mrs. Mitchell was verbally abusive toward both children, frequently ridiculing them and referring to them not by name but be the impersonal "it." The hospital discovered through X rays that Ann had suffered a fractured skull; the circumstances surrounding this injury were never explained, although Mrs. Mitchell had been known to strike Martha with a wooden spoon. The parents were not receptive to the agency referral and displayed anger and resistance toward the referring physician and social worker. The child protective agency accepted the referral on the basis of the neglect and abuse which had occurred, and the fear expressed by the mother's psychiatrist that her self-control might at any time break down completely.

Interviews with Mr. and Mrs. Mitchell revealed that both parents grew up in families in which the identification and sex roles were reversed, the mothers played the dominant role in both families while the fathers were the more passive, acquiescing partners. Also, both Mr. and Mrs. Mitchell were severely deprived as children; their respective families were not prosperous financially, and they both were emotionally deprived and unstimulated in their formative years. As a result, the Mitchells were both insecure in their own identification and confused in their roles as husband and wife, father and mother. Mrs. Mitchell, in an unsuccessful attempt to feel more powerful and important, in many ways threatened her husband's masculinity. He, in turn, became abusive toward her. Mrs. Mitchell consequently directed her hostility and anger toward Martha, whom Mrs. Mitchell viewed as a burden and the cause of many of her problems. An additional frustration and source

of conflict was Mr. Mitchell's employment and low income. He
was employed as a clerk in an art supply store; he disliked his
work and had a poor relationship with his employer. Also, his
income was low and the family was able to acquire only the
bare necessities of life. Although Mr. Mitchell frequently spoke
of finding other employment, he never showed the motivation
to do so. His excessive drinking, late hours away from his
family (apparently an escape from the pressures of family
responsibility), and a poor sexual relationship were further
sources of conflict, as was Mrs. Mitchell's being housebound
with the two children.

The accumulation of these problems created a situation which
was detrimental to the children. Mr. Mitchell's frustration, insecurity, and role confusion restricted his positive interaction
with his daughters, as did his frequent escapes through liquor
and separation. Mrs. Mitchell's depressed state resulted in poor
physical care of the home and children. Her own identity problem resulted in a confusing identification model for her daughters, and her anxiety, anger, and aggressiveness resulted in the
physical and verbal abuse described earlier. However, the caseworker felt that this family could be salvaged and perhaps re-
habilitated by appropriate agency services without removal of
the children from the home.

The parents were seen weekly in joint interviews for eight
months, after which Mr. Mitchell refused to participate in
treatment because, although he had found the sessions helpful
in understanding himself, he felt he had to learn his obligations
and responsibilities on his own. Although the female caseworker
was at times threatening to his masculinity, he did gain some
insight into his own behavior and his interaction with his wife.
He was seen only occasionally after this time. Mrs. Mitchell
remained in casework treatment for another fourteen months.
These supportive interviews helped Mrs. Mitchell gain understanding of her behavior and the patterns of her marital conflicts with her husband. She gained awareness of their mutual
insecurity and identification problems, and learned to compro-
mise without feeling that she was constantly "giving in" to her
husband. Communication between the parents gradually im-

proved and Mrs. Mitchell learned to be less threatening to her husband, thus relieving much of the tension between them. The caseworker also helped Mrs. Mitchell to enroll Martha in nursery school—and the agency helped finance this move— which not only relieved pressure from Mrs. Mitchell but also provided added stimulation and socialization for the child. The family also moved to a new apartment which was a great improvement over their previous residence. Both parents seemed less depressed in this new environment, and Mrs. Mitchell allowed and requested the child protective agency caseworker to continue visits.

The case was closed two years after the referral with generally improved conditions, as seen from the agency's perspective, and the cessation of the children's need for protection. Although the marital relationship continued to be less than ideal (with Mr. Mitchell still occasionally drinking in excess and remaining out of the home with friends), many improvements were observed. The marital difficulty was relieved and Mr. Mitchell's abuse of his wife had ceased. Mrs. Mitchell's neglect of her children had ceased; they were being provided adequate care and feeding and were progressing more normally. Mrs. Mitchell's housekeeping ability had greatly improved, and she was gaining gratification from her newly found social contacts. Martha's involvement in nursery school was both encouraging her development and relieving her mother's anxiety.

A final service to this family occurred a year after the case was closed. Mrs. Mitchell called the child protective agency and asked for help with Martha, who was becoming increasingly jealous of Ann and was constantly teasing her. Mrs. Mitchell was referred to a family counseling agency and was assisted in contacting them, because the problem was family-oriented rather than requiring the protection of neglected children.

In cases different from the Mitchell family, however, an agency may believe that its resources are insufficient to deal with the problem and refer the family to another local agency. A child protective agency, for example, may find that the family problems are primarily financial, with the neglectful

event being merely a manifestation of poverty, such as inadequate housing, insufficient food, clothing, and the like. In these
instances, referral to the public child welfare department that
deals primarily with meeting financial needs of children might
be the extent of the original agency's intrusion into the family.
Or a public child welfare agency may receive the initial report
and, after conducting an investigation, may find that the family's problems may be traced to the mother's having insufficient
information about children's health matters and the availability
of community health services. Here the agency could simply
refer the family to a local public health agency or arrange for
a home visit by a visiting nurse.

Furthermore, an agency may feel that it cannot deal with the
matter because it lacks the legal authority to make binding its
decisions—that is, the state has not endowed it with the power
to compel a parent to accept its services. Nor has an agency the
legal authority to reorganize a parent-child relationship by
making custodial change, even if it feels that a parent has so
violated his duties as to make continuation of his parental role
detrimental to his child. Illustrative of an agency's decision to
invoke the legal process for a custodial change is the case of the
Smith family.

The Smith family

A visiting nurse referred the Smith family, residents of a lower-
middle-class urban community, to the children's protective
service agency. The family included Mr. and Mrs. Smith (ages
thirty-one and twenty-seven, respectively) and their four children: Elizabeth (eight), Amy (four), Anne (three), and
Michael (three months). Another child had died of a respiratory
ailment at the age of three months. Mr. Smith was a laborer
who received a low salary inadequate to meet the family's
needs. Primarily as a result of his wife's spending sprees, Mr.
Smith was in debt. Mrs. Smith had a history of mental illness.

Mr. and Mrs. Smith were physically abusive to one another—
Mrs. Smith on several occasions assaulted Mr. Smith with a
knife. Unable to control or tolerate his wife's behavior, Mr.
Smith often left home. In the evening, he would either lock

himself in his bedroom or go out to a bar. Several times he packed his clothes and left, only to return in a few hours. He showed little affection toward the children (other than Elizabeth) and did not assist Mrs. Smith in their care.

The Smith children were frequently left alone and were often locked out of the house during rain and snow storms. Furthermore, they were not provided with adequate medical advice for serious illnesses. Mrs. Smith was irrationally fearful of doctors and hospitals, firmly believing that her baby's death resulted from his being used as a "guinea pig" by medical officials. The younger girls were frequently locked in separate rooms and harnessed to their beds all day. As a result of this isolation, they exhibited primitive behavior and had difficulty using language. They were not toilet trained, and their clothes were usually soaked with urine and caked with feces. Mrs. Smith did not allow them to feed themselves and was abusive to them when they cried.

Elizabeth was sent to school each day in dirty clothes; she experienced great difficulty in relating to peers and frequently battled with other children. She was disruptive in the classroom, she wandered about, spoke out at inappropriate times, and constantly demanded her teacher's attention. She was unable to concentrate on her studies. Upon returning home, she was either locked outdoors or in her room. She was jealous of and abusive toward her younger siblings.

Mrs. Smith also had great difficulty relating to her three-month-old son Michael, offering him no physical or emotional comfort. She hardly ever held him, she medicated him so that he would sleep, and, like the girls, locked him in a room by himself. Furthermore, she fed him with a nipple punctured with so many holes that he could not control the amount or speed of intake. Consequently, Michael suffered from severe cramps, to which Mrs. Smith reacted by forcing more food into him.

In an attempt to keep the family together, the Smiths were provided with social services to improve their care of the children. Mrs. Smith was encouraged to seek psychotherapy for her personal conflicts as an outpatient at a local hospital and continued to receive caseworker services from the child protective agency for her problems relating to the children. She was also provided with homemaker services. Mr. Smith was seen regularly by the caseworker in an attempt to help him gain insight into his functioning as father and husband. Amy was enrolled in a nursery school class for problem children, and Anne was visited several days a week by a special-education teacher.

Although the children showed immediate improvement, it became readily apparent that Mrs. Smith was not progressing in resolving her personal conflicts: as soon as the homemaker was not present, she continued to physically and emotionally abuse the children. It was thus decided in a joint conference between the psychotherapist, the caseworker, and the nursery school teachers that placement of the children outside the home was necessary for their protection. Both parents refused to agree to a voluntary placement. Mr. Smith, although recognizing the need for placement, could not bring himself to sign the necessary papers, while Mrs. Smith threatened to kill the children before she would allow them to be taken from her home.

Ten months after referral, the caseworker presented the Smith family to the District Court by signing a Care and Protection Petition alleging that the children were not receiving necessary physical and educational care and that the parents were unable to provide it for them. An arraignment, held that day in Juvenile Session, was attended by the children, the parents, the attorneys representing each parent and the children, a social worker from the Division of Child Guardianship, a court probation officer, and the Children's Protective Service caseworker. Following testimony by the caseworker, the court awarded temporary custody of the children to the Division of Child Guardianship. On the same day the children were placed by that agency in foster homes. Both the Division of Child Guardianship caseworker and the probation officer were ordered to conduct independent investigations of the family situation and to report with recommendations in one month.

When the reports were received, the court determined that permanent custody of the children should be placed with the

Division of Child Guardianship, and the children were placed that same day. The court's decision was made solely on the basis of the two reports. The Children's Protective Service case was closed shortly thereafter with the children in the custody of the Division of Child Guardianship. The Division assumed all responsibility for providing the needed services to both parents and children.

An agency's decision to seek court authority is based on factors which are difficult to isolate. Besides the child's welfare, factors that might be influential are: the agency's or a staff member's relationship with the court and the possibility of the claim's success; the identity of the child's parents and their community position and influence; and the agency's view of its own position and its regard for preserving its reputation in the community.

CHALLENGE

The agency's decision to invoke the judicial process which questions the parental right to custody, and ultimately may result in state intervention into the parent-child relationship, is an event we have labeled "challenge." A parent may view any agency's activity as a challenge to his parental right to custody. Under our scheme, however, a "challenge" exists only after an agency (or an individual) has decided to invoke the judicial process.

In order to bring the challenge, the agency must look to specific child neglect statutes (discussed in the next chapter), welfare codes, or juvenile or family court acts. These codes include procedures designed to examine both the validity of the neglect charge and the disposition of the allegedly neglected child. Some jurisdictions treat these issues separately; others treat them as intimately connected.[20] The child neglect procedure is designed to minimize or eliminate the traditional accusatory nature of judicial proceedings, which focus on notions of guilt or blame.[21] In child neglect proceedings, the court must decide what disposition of the case will promote the child's best interests. Money damages are not awarded. Neither

parents nor agencies are fined or jailed.[22] For all practical purposes, the proceedings are meant only to decide who should
have power over a child.

Child neglect proceedings, like other child custody matters,
do not fall easily into either of the traditional classifications—
civil and criminal—of the law. They are usually designated
with names such as *In re Anonymous, In re the Welfare of John*
or *In re John,* giving the illusion of a case which does not involve opposing or conflicting parties. But behind the name of
the case are litigants, usually parents and agencies, each making a claim to the court for the care, custody, and control of
the child. Beyond the two private litigants, found in any civil
dispute, child neglect cases involve a further party—the state.
Unlike criminal matters, however, where the state is an actual
party to the case, the state in neglect proceedings is represented
by the court itself, and consequently maintains alliance with
neither the petitioner nor the parent. Rather, the court, following its historical role in matters relating to children, views itself
as the protector of the child, who is assumed too young to
protect itself.

Despite the non-adversary orientation of neglect proceedings,
a parent may often view them as a battle because of the stakes
involved: the possible loss of a child and the stigma of being
labeled a "neglecting parent." Furthermore, a parent may view
the state's attempt to interfere with his custodial rights as judicial or executive harassment intended to force him to conform
to the state's standards. Or he may view it as a punishment, not
for what he has failed to provide his child, but for his low
social position.[23]

The petition

A petition or motion in an appropriate court charging that a
child is neglected or is within the court's jurisdiction begins the
formal legal process that challenges a parent's right to the care,
custody, and control of his child. The legal mechanisms that
may eventually lead to state intervention are often initiated
long after a parent's first contact with a community agency. As
previously noted, an agency usually initiates the court action

only after it has attempted to resolve the family problems itself. If, on the other hand, a private individual initiates the process, the time between discovery of neglect and the challenging of the parent's custodial rights may be short indeed. A private individual might resort to the court process immediately upon suspecting the neglectful event, thus avoiding any report to a social service or law enforcement agency, traditionally the intermediate step in the intervention process.

The petition, authorized under a specific statute, may be referred to by a variety of labels such as a "neglect" petition, a "care and protection" petition, or a petition alleging specific jurisdiction. It typically requires the child's name, residence, often its age, the names of the parents or other custodians, their residence, and the facts of the alleged neglectful event. However, provision is usually made for the filing of a petition where the facts of the neglectful event are unclear, leaving to the court and other officials the burden of investigating the facts needed to establish child neglect.[24]

Court investigation

Courts, as well as community agencies, may order an investigation into an alleged neglectful event. These court investigations, authorized by statute in many states, may not differ substantially from agency investigations. Indeed, in at least one jurisdiction, an agency investigation may be used by the court in lieu of its own study.[25] Court investigations, however, may serve different functions from those conducted by agencies.

Court investigations may be ordered upon the court's receiving knowledge of a neglectful event,[26] or after a petition is filed.[27] In the case of the former, these investigations are designed to determine whether sufficient evidence exists to warrant judicial inquiry into the parent-child relationship. The timing in these cases allows the reports to be used as screening devices to ascertain whether the court should issue a petition. When a court investigation is ordered after the formal filing of a petition, it serves as a judicial fact-finding measure, as well as being useful for determining the disposition of a case.[28]

The procedures for a court investigation, like so many of the

specific procedures in neglect cases, may vary widely from jurisdiction to jurisdiction. (Divergence in handling cases may even
occur from court to court within a jurisdiction, depending upon
the statutes in effect, the judge receiving the petition, and the
history of the case prior to its reaching court.) Some jurisdictions, for example, make the judicial decision to investigate
discretionary;[29] others make it compulsory.[30] Some require investigation into the child's social and family environment,[31]
some into his physical and psychological health,[32] and others
into the family's history and other related factors.[33] Many
merely suggest an investigation, leaving to the investigator's
discretion the focus and depth of the inquiry.[34] Court and probation officials are used as investigators in many states;[35] some
jurisdictions require state welfare and social service departments to conduct the studies.[36] In instances where parental
resistance may be expected, the police department may be
utilized.

The hearing

After a petition has been filed and a court investigation has
occurred, the next likely step in the process leading to state
intervention is the issuance of a summons to various parties
directing them to appear at a hearing. The petitioner, the child,
his parents or custodians, sometimes his foster parents,[37] and
an agency involved with the case may all be required to be present. Hearings in neglect cases are likely to be scheduled shortly
after the issuance of a petition, allowing only enough time for
the parties to receive the summonses. One state in fact grants
specific priority status to neglect cases,[38] thus eliminating delays
often found in court dockets.

Hearing procedures vary from jurisdiction to jurisdiction.
Generally, however, the hearings are informal and private. Unlike criminal proceedings, which are governed by strict rules of
evidence, neglect hearings tend to allow for wide-ranging inquiries beyond the specific allegations of neglect. Various jurisdictions, however, do limit and control neglect hearings in
several ways. Connecticut, for example, provides that no hearing "shall be held in a room regularly used for the transaction
of criminal business."[39] That state also allows the judge to

confer with the child at neglect hearings, treating the interviews as privileged communications.[40] Although few other jurisdictions make specific statutory references to the privileged communication issue, the Connecticut practice seems widespread.

In almost all states neglect hearings appear to require the presence of the child at some stage in the court process, although some jurisdictions specifically exclude the child from the hearing.[41] The age of the child and the fact that some information elicited in the hearing might have a damaging effect on him are factors influencing the judicial decision to exclude the child from the hearing.

The function of the neglect hearing is to determine the validity of the facts alleged in the petition and, in many jurisdictions, to determine the appropriate disposition of the case—for example, whether there should be any custodial changes or parental supervision. In some states, the dispositional function is performed in a second hearing, leaving to the first inquiry the sole question of determining whether neglect exists.[42] Many jurisdictions give wide discretion to the judge, allowing him to make whatever disposition he deems will advance the child's best interests.[43] Others limit the judge's discretion to actions short of legally terminating the parent-child relationship.[44]

Most neglect hearings proceed on the assumption that there are no opposing sides, that all parties share in a common desire to promote the child's welfare. At the same time, however, practical analysis makes it clear that the desire to advance a child's best interests can take several forms, thus raising legitimate conflicting interests. Realizing this, many states have provided specific statutory provisions for counsel not only for parents, but also for children.[45] Traditionally, however, the judge has assumed the role of protector of the child's interests, and consequently many states have not felt it necessary to specifically allow for the appointment of legal counsel for children in neglect hearings or other child custody disputes.

SUMMARY

Child neglect, that event which may prompt the public to look into the affairs of parents, is mainly a lower-class phenomenon.

In part this results from the fact that the lower classes, visible and often unable to successfully delegate their parental responsibilities, are discovered depriving their children of "basic human needs" and are consequently reported to officials. Middle- and upper-class parents, on the other hand, may be irresponsible in their personal affairs, ignore their children, and abandon them to boarding schools, grandparents, or friends. But society does not scrutinize these families. It merely labels them "eccentric," "arty," or "jet setters" and generally leaves them free from legal intrusion. Thus, it should be stressed that child neglect is a value-loaded concept clearly based on class factors.

That neglecting parents are generally poor is a statement of fact. The conclusion should not be drawn, however, that economics alone is the determining factor. Many poor people in both urban and rural environments rear their children according to accepted standards as defined by the dominant culture. They may accomplish this alone or with financial support from others. These parents may provide their children with a warm, affectionate, and secure relationship, passing on to them positive attitudes toward a society that may have rejected the parents.

The point is that neglecting parents are generally lacking in areas beyond economics. Their psychological makeup prevents them from fulfilling their parental role. To use a popular phrase, neglecting parents suffer from "personality problems." This may result from a family history that includes inadequate parental role models, or from an inherent inability to survive in a society that is filled with external pressures and hostility. The lack of both money and psychological strengths results in unstable home lives, erratic employment, transient living, emotional numbness, and indifference toward their children. Neglecting parents live marginally and secluded from others, but not so secluded as to escape official intrusion into their lives.

Public intrusion usually consists of four stages: the report, the investigation, the challenge, and the state intervention. Sometimes, of course, the process may be abbreviated; that is, a step or two may be omitted. But typically the process begins when community agencies receive reports about neglectful parents. These may come from a number of sources, some reliable, others not. Moreover, what constitutes neglect is difficult to define, since neglect is not readily apparent save in the most severe cases, such as starvation or abandonment. And even if a definition were simple, it is likely, because of our society's discrimination, that it would be unevenly interpreted.

When viewing the process of public intrusion, the immense amount of discretion that is available outside the judicial process is striking. It is on the basis of its own investigation that an agency decides to challenge a parent's right to custody. It should be clear that agencies have great powers if they choose to use them. They need the force of law to impose supervision on an unwilling parent or to remove a child from the physical custody of its parents. They can seek the aid of courts to support them in their decision in these instances.

The procedures used to challenge a parent's right to custody, with a few isolated exceptions (such as not providing an opportunity for a foster parent to be heard at a hearing to determine her foster child's custody, and the lack of a specific provision for free counsel for indigent parents and children), have the earmarks of fairness. Whether fairness exists in practice—that is, whether judges administer the procedural aspects of child neglect statutes in a just manner—is quite another matter, and only an empirical study of the lower courts would provide the answer.

The next chapter will examine the guidelines that determine when the state should intervene into the parent-child relationship and will discuss judicial interpretation of the substantive laws of neglect.

NOTES

1. 168 Cal. App. 2d 102, 335 P.2d 736 (1959). For a description of child abuse statutes in relation to "neglect" legislation, see note 13 *infra*.

2. Mass. Acts of 1954, ch. 646, § 4 reads: "Any person, other than a relative by blood or marriage, who, for hire, gain or reward, receives or has under his care or control any child under sixteen years of age, of whom he is not the legal guardian, for purposes of giving such a child

a home, or for board or for adoption, shall be deemed to maintain an independent foster home for children unless such child was placed in his care by the department, or a public or private social agency which has been authorized by the department to place children under sections fourteen to twenty-two, inclusive. Within two days after receiving such a child, such persons shall give written notice to the department of the date and the terms upon which such child was received, with the name, age and birthplace of the child, name and address of its parents, and the name and address and relationship of the person from whom the child was received. Within two days after the discharge or adoption of such a child, the person shall give written notice to the department in the form prescribed by the department.

"§ 5. No person shall maintain an independent foster home for children unless such person has been issued a permit therefor by the department."

3. A recent case, James v. McLinden, Civil No. 13127 (D. Conn., filed May 23, 1969), illustrates this fact. See Appendix, p. 151.

4. Ill. Ann. Stat. ch. 23, § 2359 (1968).

5. R. Mulford & M. Cohen, Neglecting Parents: A Study of Psychosocial Characteristics (Children's Division, American Humane Association, 1967); H. Riese, Heal the Hurt Child (1962); L. Young, Wednesday's Children (1964).

6. The Mulford & Cohen study, *supra* note 5, at 6, showed the median family income for neglecting families to be $75 per week, with 30 percent of the group studied receiving some form of public assistance. The Young study, *supra* note 2, at 69, showed 128 out of a group of 300 (43 percent) receiving assistance, and 78 out of 95 (82 percent) in another group living on incomes of $400 per month or less.

7. M. Harrington, The Other America, 133–37 (1962).

8. Young, *supra* note 5, at 36.

9. This is not to suggest that the lower-class matriarchal family is not doing a reasonably good job. *See* H. Kay & I. Philips, *Poverty and the Law of Child Custody*, 54 Calif. L. Rev. 717, 736–37 (1966); G. Myrdal, An American Dilemma 930–35 (rev. ed. 1962); W. Weyrauch, *Dual Systems of Family Law: A Comment*, 54 Calif. L. Rev. 781, 789 (1966).

10. Riese, *supra* note 5, at 123–27.

11. Mulford & Cohen, *supra* note 5, at 7.

12. E. Philbrick, Treating Parental Pathology through Child Protective Services 7–8 (Children's Division, American Humane Association, 1960). *See also* E. Pavenstedt, *A Comparison of the Child-Rearing Environment of Upper-Lower and Very Low-Lower Class Families,* 35 American Journal of Orthopsychiatry 89, 94–95 (1965). Dr. Pavenstedt, in describing "low-lower class" families, states: "The outstanding characteristic in these homes was that activities were impulse-determined; consistency was totally absent. The mother might stay in bed until noon while the children also were kept in bed or ran around unsupervised. Although families sometimes ate breakfast or dinner together, there was no pattern for anything. The parent, incensed by the behavior of one child, was seen dealing a blow to another child who was closer. Communication by means of words hardly existed. Directions were indefinite or hung unfinished in mid-air. . . . As the children outgrew babyhood, the parents differentiated very little between the parent and child role. The parents' needs were as pressing and as often indulged as were those of the children."

13. Reporting of child neglect is mandatory in those states that have included "neglect" in the child abuse reporting statutes. All jurisdictions have enacted statutes which require the mandatory reporting (usually by physicians, nurses, hospital administrators, social workers, etc.) of child abuse and specific procedures for the receipt and handling of these reports. These statutes are based upon a Model Act, developed by the Children's Bureau of the U. S. Department of Health, Education, and Welfare. Sec. 2 of that Act provides as follows: "Any physician, including any licensed doctor of medicine, licensed osteopathic physician, intern and resident, having reasonable cause to suspect that (a) child under the age of _____ (the maximum age of juvenile court jurisdiction) brought to him or coming before him for examination, care or treatment has had serious physical injury or injuries inflicted upon him other than by accidental means by a parent or other person responsible for his care, shall report or cause reports to be made in accordance with the provisions of this Act; provided that when the attendance of a physician with respect to a child is pursuant to the performance of services as a member of the staff of a hospital or similar institution he shall notify the person in charge of the institution or his designated delegate who shall report or cause reports to be made in accordance with the provisions of this Act."

The states that have added neglect to the instances covered in § 2 (above) are: Ala. Code tit. 27, ch. 4, § 21 (1967); Alas. Stat. § 11.67.070(1) (1965); Ark. § 42–802 (1965); Ses. Laws of Hawaii, Act. 261 § 2 (1967); Idaho Code § 16–1641 (1965); Ill. Ann. Stat. ch. 23 § 2042 (Smith-Hurd 1968); Iowa Code Ann. § 235A.3 (1965); Kan. Stat. Ann. § 38–717 (1965); Md. Ann. Code art. 27, § 11A(c) (1963); Minn. Stat. Ann. § 626.554(2) (1965); Mont. Rev. Code Ann. § 10–902 (1965); Nev. Rev. Stat. § 200.502 (1965); N.M. Rev. Stat. Ann. § 571.26 (1965); N.Y. Pen.

Code § 483–d (McKinney 1964); N.C. Gen. Stat. § 14–318.2 (1965);
Ohio Rev. Code Ann. § 2151.421 (1966); Okla. Stat. Ann. tit. 21, § 846
(1966); Tenn. Code Ann. § 37–1202 (1966); Tex. Civ. Stat. art. 695c–2
(1965); Utah Code Ann. § 55–16–2 (1965); Va. Code § 16.1–217.1
(1968); Wash. § 26.44.030 (1965); W.Va. Code § 49–6A–2 (1965). For
an analysis of abuse legislation, see B. Daly, *Willful Child Abuse and State
Reporting Statutes,* 23 Miami L. Rev. 283 (1969); M. Paulsen, G. Parker,
& L. Adelman, *Child Abuse Reporting Laws—Some Legislative History,*
34 Geo. Wash. L. Rev. 482 (1966); M. Paulsen, *Child Abuse Reporting
Laws: The Shape of the Legislation,* 67 Colum. L. Rev. 1 (1967).

14. Where private child protective agencies (social work staffs specifically developed to work with parents to help them meet their children's
needs within their own home) exist, they are usually organized as Societies
for the Prevention of Cruelty to Children. These organizations tend to be
located in the eastern part of the United States. They vary from large
statewide agencies offering a full range of protective services to smaller
groups handling a limited caseload in specific parts of a state. Where these
agencies exist, they remain outside the actual governmental and formal
channels of the official statutory procedures for handling neglect cases. At
the same time, however, they play an important part in the neglect case,
often acting as the recipient of reports and often initiating court action.
Through these activities, informal ties with "official" bodies and groups
(e.g., police, probation officers, judges, state welfare departments, etc.)
often develop and directly influence the neglect cases. For a discussion of
protective services, *see* A. L. Sandusky, Protective Services, in Encyclo-
pedia of Social Work 579 (H. L. Lurie ed. 1965).

15. All states have public welfare departments, some organized on a
statewide basis, others organized on a city, county, or local basis. Most of
these departments have child guardianship or child welfare divisions which
serve nationally as the backbone of the agencies involved in social welfare
work with children. Usually these agencies are authorized specifically by
the state child neglect statutes to handle casework, foster home placement,
and other matters relating to neglect cases. The size of funding, com-
petence of the staff, and work performed by child welfare departments,
however, vary considerably from one state to another. The training, experience, and particularly the orientation of the staff or department all
influence the work and direction of these agencies in neglect cases. For
an analysis of the various welfare departments in handling child matters
see Child Protective Services (Children's Division, The American Humane
Association, 1967). This publication offers a comprehensive analysis of the
coverage of the departments within each state. Included are the extent of
geographical coverage within a state, the sources from which complaints
are received, information concerning the staffing and training of the departments, and other factors gathered from a field survey.

16. For a brief analysis of the present role and a suggestion for the future role of law enforcement agencies in dealing with child protective matters, *see* R. Myran & L. Swanson, Police Work with Children (1962). *See also,* V. Carey, J. Goldfarb, & M. Rowe, The Handling of Juveniles from Offense to Disposition, Volumes 1 & 2 (U. S. Department of Health, Education, and Welfare) dealing with police handling of juvenile delinquents.

17. In many jurisdictions, the practice appears to be that when the initial report is made to the juvenile court, referral to the welfare department is standard procedure before additional court action is initiated. Here the statutes govern whether investigations are conducted at this point by the court and the actual immediate action upon the petition.

18. It should be noted that in some cases the opinion of the investigator will be that the child should be removed from the home immediately. In these cases, statutes usually grant emergency authority to local police departments to take such action. The Idaho statute expresses the seriousness of this action and appears to set some reasonable limits upon it: "A child may be taken into custody by any peace officer without warrant only when he is seriously endangered in his surroundings and prompt removal appears to be necessary for his immediate protection." Idaho Code § 16–1633 (1963). Other statutes appear to grant the court discretion for the placement of a child pending the hearing and disposition of his case, but this determination is made only after the actual initiation of the court's proceedings and the filing of a petition.

19. This summarizes the investigatory process. In discussing private child protective agencies, one author has broken the process down further, focusing on specific functions of investigations. He sees the initial investigation as a fact-finding procedure which attempts to confirm or negate the original report or complaint. If evidence to confirm the original report is available, additional investigations occur to determine the extent of immediate danger to the child. Furthermore, the investigation serves to isolate the harm which may have already resulted to the child from the parental behavior and to assess the likelihood of future damage if the child continues in its present environment. This last function appears to be more relevant to dispositional aspects of the case as opposed to initial determinations concerning the complaint's validity. V. De Francis, Fundamentals of Child Protection—A Statement of Basic Concepts and Principles in Child Protective Services (The American Humane Association, 1955).

20. Alabama, for example, allows the court to determine whether the child comes within the statutory definition of neglect, and if the question is answered affirmatively, to then "make and enter such judgment and orders for his custody, discipline, supervision, care, protection and guar-

dianship, as, in the judgment of the court, will properly conserve and protect the welfare and best interests of such child." Ala. Code tit. 13, ch. 7, § 351 (1958). This two-step approach of first examining the neglect charge on statutory grounds, then examining the disposition, appears to represent the majority view in this country.

Some states, however, clearly interweave the two decisions: the finding of neglect and the disposition of the child. The courts are allowed to determine whether state interference in the family is in the best interest of the child without a specific and separate preliminary finding of neglect. See, e.g., Colo. Rev. Stat. Ann. § 22-1-1 (1963) and Mass. Ann. Laws, ch. 119, § 26 (1965).

21. The "intent" sections introducing several of the neglect and juvenile court statutes in this category, especially those written within the past few years, clearly express the idea that "the best interests of the child" should be the overriding guide rather than punitive measures against parents. For example, the recently enacted Minn. Stat. Ann. § 260.011 (Supp. 1969) begins: "The purpose of the laws relating to juvenile courts is to secure for each minor under the jurisdiction of the court the care and guidance, preferably in his own home, as will serve the spiritual, emotional, mental, and physical welfare of the minor and the best interests of the state; to preserve and strengthen the minor's family ties whenever possible, removing him from the custody of his parents only when his welfare or safety and protection of the public cannot be adequately safeguarded without removal; and, when the minor is removed from his own family, to secure for him, custody, care and discipline as nearly as possible equivalent to that which should have been given by his parents. The laws relating to juvenile courts shall be liberally construed to carry out these purposes."

22. Criminal sanctions may be imposed for child neglect, e.g., Ill. Ann. Stat. ch. 23 § 2361 (Smith-Hurd 1968); Reynolds v. State, — Ind. —, 260 N.E.2d 793 (1970) overturned the conviction of a mother charged under an Indiana statute recently amended to make child abandonment a felony.

23. There may be some basis in fact to this claim if child neglect proceedings are primarily instituted against persons in the lower classes.

24. Alabama, for example, allows simply an averral that the child is neglected, dependent, or delinquent and in need of the care and protection of the state, e.g., Ala. Code tit. 13, ch. 7. See 352(2) (1958); Ohio Rev. Code Ann. § 2157.27 (1968); Pa. Stat. Ann. tit. 11, § 246 (1965). Although not specifically allowing an averral of neglect, Wisconsin provides that if facts normally required in the petition are not known or cannot be

ascertained, the petition may still be adequate although it merely states that fact, *e.g.,* Idaho Code § 16.1628 (Supp. 1969); Wis. Stat. Ann. § 38.20 (1957).

25. R.I. Gen. Laws § 14–1–10 (1956).

26. *E.g.,* Kan. Stat. Ann. § 38.816 (Supp. 1968); R.I. Gen. Laws § 14–1–10 (1956); Wis. Stat. Ann. § 48.19 (1957). *See also* Idaho Code § 16–1628 (Supp. 1969) requiring both a preliminary investigation before the petition is filed, and § 16–1636 requiring a further investigation prior to disposition of the case. In New York the probation service is authorized to investigate with the specific aim of adjusting and thus sorting out suitable cases before the petition is filed. N.Y. Family Court Act § 333(a) (McKinney 1963).

27. *E.g.,* Conn. Gen. Stat. Ann. § 17.66 (1958); Mass. Ann. Laws ch. 119 § 24 (1965); Minn. Stat. Ann. § 260.151 (Supp. 1969). *See also* Ind. Stat. Ann. § 9–2814 (1956), which requires that a probation officer carry on an investigation after the complaint is filed, but before a summons is issued.

28. Although an investigation after the filing of the petition is most often a general fact-finding measure, it may serve a more specific purpose as well. Montana, for instance, uses its investigation to determine whether the parents of the child live within the appropriate county and whether the parents can afford to pay the cost of taking care of the child in a foster home. Mont. Rev. Code Ann. § 10–506 (1968).

29. *E.g.,* Kan. Stat. Ann. § 38.817(a) (Supp. 1968); Minn. Stat. Ann. § 260.151 (Supp. 1969).

30. *E.g.,* Idaho Code § 16–1636 (Supp. 1969); Ind. Stat. Ann. § 9–2814 (1956); Mass. Ann. Laws ch. 119 § 24 (1965); R.I. Gen. Laws § 14–1–10 (1956); Wis. Stat. Ann. § 48.19 (1957).

31. *E.g.,* Conn. Gen. Stat. Ann. § 17–66 (1958); Ind. Stat. Ann. § 9–2814 (1956); Kan. Stat. Ann. § 38.816(1)(b) (Supp. 1968); Minn. Stat. Ann. § 260.151 (Supp. 1969); R.I. Gen. Laws § 14–1–10 (1956).

32. *See* Conn. Gen. Stat. Ann. § 17–66 (1958) and Minn. Stat. Ann. § 260.151 (Supp. 1969), both of which are not mandatory but at the discretion of the court.

33. *E.g.,* Ind. Stat. Ann. § 9.2814 (1956) and R.I. Gen. Laws § 14–1–10 (1956).

34. *E.g.*, Mass. Ann. Laws ch. 119 § 24 (1965); Minn. Stat. Ann. § 260.151 (Supp. 1969); Wis. Stat. Ann. § 48.19.

35. *E.g.*, Ind. Stat. Ann. § 9–2814 (1956); Kan. Stat. Ann. § 38.816 (1)(b) (Supp. 1968). *See also* Minn. Stat. Ann. § 260.151 (Supp. 1969), which allows either a probation officer or the county welfare board to carry out the investigation, and Wis. Stat. Ann. § 48.19 (1957), which allows anyone designated by the court to carry on the investigation.

36. *E.g.*, Idaho Code § 16–1628, 16–1636 (Supp. 1969) and Mont. Rev. Code Ann. § 10–506 (1968).

37. Unless the statute specifically enumerates the parties to be given notice and an opportunity to be heard at the hearing, foster parents would have to argue their standing to participate in the hearing under a general category such as "persons having control of the child." Conn. Gen. Stat. Ann. § 17–61 (1958). *See* James V. McLinden, *supra*, note 3.

38. Minn. Stat. Ann. § 260.021(2)(3) (Supp. 1969).

39. Conn. Gen. Stat. Ann. § 17–67 (1958).

40. *Id.*

41. Generally the exclusion of the child is discretionary with the court. *E.g.*, Idaho Code § 16–1635 (Supp. 1969); Mass. Ann. Laws ch. 119 § 26 (1965); Minn. Stat. Ann. § 260.155(2) (Supp. 1969); Ohio Rev. Code Ann. § 2151.35 (1968).

42. N.Y. Family Ct. Act § 344–345 (McKinney Supp. 1967).

43. *E.g.*, Colo. Rev. Stat. Ann. § 22–1–6 (1963) and Me. Rev. Stat. Ann. tit. 22 § 3792, 3793 (1964).

44. *E.g.*, Minn. Stat. Ann. § 260.191 (Supp. 1969). *See also* Idaho Code § 16–1638 (Supp. 1969), which allows a rehearing on termination of parental rights only after a three-month period from the date of the court's original decree.

45. *E.g.*, Cal. Wel. & Inst. Code § 679 (West 1966); Minn. Stat. Ann. § 260.155(2) (Supp. 1969); N.Y. Family Ct. Act § 249 (McKinney 1963); Ohio Rev. Code Ann. § 2151.35 (1968); Wis. Stat. Ann. § 48.25 (1957). It has been suggested that the New York law be modified to require counsel for the parents, but not require representation for children. This recommendation is based on the theory that since the focus in a New York

neglect proceeding is on the conduct of the parents, their rights need paramount protection. An empirical study conducted by the *Columbia Journal of Law and Social Problems* revealed that in 1966, 76 percent of all respondents (parents) in neglect cases of the Kings County (Brooklyn) Family Court did not have counsel at any hearing. Under the New York law, parents not provided with counsel are required to be notified of their right to counsel. N.Y. Family Ct. Act § 343(a) (McKinney 1963). Comment, *Representation in Child-Neglect Cases: Are Parents Neglected?*, 4 Columbia Journal of Law and Social Problems 230 (1968).

3

State Intervention

State intervention, as we use the term, is the judicial decision to intrude into the family in the interest of making an adjustment in the parent-child relationship. To understand this concept, we should recall the community's expectations of parenthood, especially the notion that basic elements of privacy and autonomy or—stated less legally—of intimacy surround the parent-child relationship. By imposing some kind of social service, the mere judicial act of ordering a state agency to supervise a parent in his parental role is intervention. In theory, it is as much an invasion into the exclusivity of the family as the judicial decision to terminate the parent-child relationship.

The question of when, why, and to what extent state intervention occurs cannot be answered in the abstract. Too many factors must be considered to allow a simple answer. Nor is there an easy response to the question of standards for deciding intervention. The kind of standards used may depend on the identity or, more specifically, the professional identification of the person setting the guidelines for and the purpose of the intervention. This point warrants more than a cursory reference. Therefore, before proceeding with a discussion of the legal framework in which state intervention operates, we shall discuss the extralegal standards governing therapeutic interference with the custodial rights of parents.

THERAPEUTIC ASPECTS

Few child-development specialists would argue with the law's assumption that a child is best reared in his own biological family.[1] "Best" is here used synonymously with "ideally." Our culture considers the ideal parents for a child to be his biological mother and father. They are the ones who have at least the *potentiality* for carrying on the healthiest parent-child relationship. "Potentiality" is an important qualification because some biological parents may in fact be entirely ill equipped by virtue of personality makeup, lack of emotional resources, intellect, or life-style to continue a parental relationship without intervention.

Mr. and Mrs. Dorwin exemplify this kind of parent. They were reported to a child protective agency in a large metropolitan city. They had moved to the city from a farming community. Mrs. Dorwin, who was twenty-eight years old, had been reared in a poverty-stricken rural area. She had completed six years of formal education. Her family had lived in a shack without electricity or plumbing. Both her father and sister had been hospitalized several times because of mental illness.

Mr. Dorwin was thirty-one years old; he was raised in an urban area of a predominantly rural state. Because of his mother's mental illness and his father's alcoholism and abusive treatment of his children, Mr. Dorwin and his brothers and sisters lived with and were raised by a relative. Mr. Dorwin completed eight years of formal education. An auto mechanic, he had a criminal record for drunkenness and assault and battery on his wife and children. He seldom worked steadily. The Dorwins were married when Mrs. Dorwin was six months pregnant.

Mr. and Mrs. Dorwin had moved into an attractive, well-kept apartment, later to be evicted for nonpayment of rent and causing damage to the residence. The walls of their present apartment were dirty, with large holes where plaster had been removed. The floors were uncared for; garbage and feces were spread throughout the rooms. The house had a strong urine odor. The five Dorwin children (ages ten, nine, seven, five, and four), were dirty, poorly clothed, and malnourished. Frequently they were seen begging in the streets for scraps of food. Neighbors reported that the children were often left alone at night or with an alcoholic uncle as a baby sitter. Often the children slept on sodden mattresses without sheets. Sometimes they all slept in the same bed with their mother. Neighbors said that the parents frequently swore at their children. The children themselves said they were afraid of their father, who often struck them in the head with his fist. The children were also witness to physical battles between their parents.

The children were absent from school between fifty and sixty days during the year. When they did attend, they were dirty. Their peers rejected them. They had few playmates. Frequently they were without money for lunch or for recreational activities. Teachers reported that they fell asleep in class. Although they exhibited average intelligence on standard psychological tests, they consistently failed in school. David (age seven) was sent home from school after seven days because he, like his sisters Donna (age five) and Sonia (age four), was not toilet trained and could not control himself in the classroom. The three older children had severe visual problems, but the Dorwins never followed through with an ophthalmologist's recommendation for treatment. Nor did the Dorwins cooperate with a physician who was treating Donna for a painful bowel disease that could have been cured by their supervising a simple program of diet and medication for the girl.

Clearly, the Dorwins failed to protect their children and to meet their basic human needs. More than deficiencies in environmental conditions is involved. Their behavior indicates a pronounced lack of concern, care, and interest in their children's healthy growth and development. Blood ties do not compensate for these deficiencies.

It is not difficult to find other examples of biological parents apparently unconcerned about their children's welfare. Studies have been made which document bizarre, heinous, and shocking activities of biological parents who fail to protect their children from harm. Young reports cases of children who have been "accidentally" burned because of lack of care, of unsupervised children who have drunk kerosene, and of children suffering from severe malnutrition.[2] All such cases make the point clearly: A biological parent's potentiality for providing the healthiest parent-child relationship may never be realized. Others may perform the task better.

From a mental health point of view, a healthy parent-child relationship may be defined as a mutual interaction between adult and child, biologically related or not, in which the adult provides the child with affection, stimulation, and an unbroken continuity of care.[3] This definition is misleading if it gives the impression of absolutes or that a recipe for a healthy parent-child relationship will include a certain amount of each ingredient without regard for the basic endowment of the parents and the needs of the child. The healthy parent-child relationship is one in which the child's individual emotional and physical needs and the parent's ability to fulfill these special needs are in approximate harmony.[4] Stated another way, a healthy parent-child relationship may be viewed in terms of a fairly balanced equation of the continuing needs and demands of the child with the necessary continuity of attention, protection, stimulation, and nurture by its parent.

To behavioral scientists dealing with children in a therapeutic context, the parent's major responsibility is to further the child's emotional and physical well-being so that whatever his endowments, he will have the "best available opportunity to fulfill his potential in society as a civilized human being."[5] In other words, the parent's job is to make a positive contribution toward his child's overall healthy development. Other goals, such as the achievement of a specific religious identification, a particular political belief, or a high intellectual capacity, may be relevant or important in individual cases for maintaining good health, but in the hierarchy of values, sound physical health and emotional stability have the highest priority. Indeed, these other goals may depend on emotional ties. Therapeutic intervention is justified, then, when the emotional or physical health of the child is threatened.

Some might suggest that this prescription, which demands positive activity of parents, and at certain developmental stages the activity of one parent more than the other, goes too far; that it might be more correct not to assign positive tasks to parents, but to merely require that they not interfere with the normal processes of growth. This approach presupposes an unusually strong and malleable human organism whose development is

difficult to retard or damage. We recognize that each individual
may have unique qualities, some with the potential for growth
undisturbed by internal and environmental stresses. However,
we think of infants and children as helpless and dependent
human beings whose survival depends on adults and an adult
world. Without therapeutic intervention, children's psyches may
be damaged early, leaving scars which may emerge off and on
throughout their lives.

THE LEGAL FRAMEWORK

The judicial decision to intrude into a family, in the main, rests
on legal standards formulated by a legislature and interpreted
by courts. From a governmental perspective, state intervention
is meant to be a response to parental failure. We should keep in
mind, however, that parental failure in a legal context may be
broader in scope than—and sometimes entirely different from—
parental failure as defined in a therapeutic context. The process
leading to court intrusion is complex and often involves factors
other than parental neglect of a child's health.

Sometimes the process of public intrusion may be concerned
with an aspect of a parent's behavior that is difficult to tie to
his or her relationship with the child. Indeed, in both court
cases and welfare agency dispositions, instances can be found
in which the intervention has apparently nothing to do with a
parent's responsibility to the child. For example, in 1968 the
penalty a mother on public welfare in Minnesota had to pay
for writing bad checks was the termination of her legal relationship with her children.[6] In 1970 the public welfare agencies in Massachusetts indicated that the child of a welfare
recipient who "mismanages" his or her financial affairs may be
removed from its home and placed with others.[7]

Legislative and judicial responses
The legal standards that form the basis for judicial intervention
into the parent-child relationship are generally found in the
same group of statutes referred to in the discussion of the
challenge in Chapter Two. These neglected or dependent child

statutes, enacted in all jurisdictions, provide a direct basis for intervention.[8]

Neglect statutes, in many respects, incorporate a community's view of parenthood. Essentially, they are pronouncements of unacceptable child-rearing practices. Some neglect statutes, however, go further. They amount to punitive regulations of adult behavior and are used to control what a community defines as deviant conduct, the usual area for the criminal law.

Standards for intervention in neglect statutes vary greatly, thus making classification difficult. The following list of provisions found in these statutes will reveal the divergent definitions of a neglected or dependent child. All of them are negative in approach, specifying what is undesirable and merely leaving to inference what is desirable. Neglect or dependency may occur:

1. When a child lacks parental care because of its parent's fault or its parent's mental or physical disability.[9]
2. When a parent refuses or neglects to provide for a child's needs.[10]
3. When a parent has abandoned a child.[11]
4. When a child's home, by reason of neglect, cruelty, or depravity of its parent, is unfit.[12]
5. When a parent refuses to provide for a child's moral needs.[13]
6. When a parent refuses to provide for a child's mental needs.[14]
7. When a child's best interests are not being met.[15]
8. When a child's environment, behavior, or associations are injurious to it.[16]
9. When a child begs, receives alms, or sings in the street for money.[17]
10. When a child associates with disreputable or immoral people or lives in a house of ill repute.[18]
11. When a child is found or employed in a bar.[19]
12. When a child's occupation is dangerous or when it is working contrary to the child labor laws.[20]
13. When a child is living in an unlicensed foster home or

has been placed by its parents in a way detrimental to it or contrary to law.[21]

14. When a child's conduct is delinquent as a result of parental neglect.[22]

15. When a child is in danger of being brought up to lead an idle, dissolute, or immoral life.[23]

16. When a mother is unmarried and without adequate provision for the care and support of her child.[24]

17. When a parent, or another with the parent's consent, performs an immoral or illegal act before a child.[25]

18. When a parent habitually uses profane language in front of a child.[26]

A typical neglect statute

A number of neglect statutes seem all-encompassing. They refer to activities of parents as well as children. They also are concerned with environmental conditions of child rearing. One example is the Indiana statute. Enacted in 1907, the statute has remained basically unchanged since then. Indiana defines a neglected child as:

any boy under the age of sixteen (16) years or any girl under the age of seventeen (17) years, who has not proper parental care or guardianship; or who habitually begs or receives alms; or who is found living in any house of ill-fame, or with any vicious or disreputable persons; or who is employed in any saloon; or whose home, by reason of neglect, cruelty or depravity on the part of its parent or parents, guardian or other person in whose care it may be, is an unfit place for such child; or whose environment is such as to warrant the state, in the interest of the child, in assuming its guardianship.[27]

At first glance the Indiana statute may seem archaic and its references to environmental conditions old-fashioned. "Begging or receiving alms," for example, may seem to be a nineteenth-century expression; but whatever the label, the activity still exists. As the agency report on the Dorwin children stated, "Frequently they were seen begging in the streets for scraps of food." Other conditions, such as "living in any house of ill-fame, or with any vicious or disreputable person," are not uncommon, especially in urban areas and among lower-class children. One may also think of communal living among some counter culture groups.

Statutory words such as "neglect," "cruelty," and "depravity," and phrases such as "unfit place" or "whose environment is such as to warrant the state, in the interest of the child, in assuming its guardianship," cannot be easily or mechanically defined. Like "cruelty" or "abusive conduct" as grounds for divorce and separation, these standards for intervention are subjective. From the legislative perspective, they are designed to give a local judge, who is close to the family situation and knowledgeable about the community, discretion in interpretation and application. The effect is to make these standards subject to a judge's personal biases about sex, religion, and race, his own attitudes toward child-rearing practices, and his own feelings toward parents, adult males, adult females, and children.[28]

"Cruelty" and "abusive conduct" have been mentioned as similarly subjective grounds for divorce and separation. The analogy to the reorganization of the husband-and-wife relationship, however, must be made with caution. When these grounds are used in reorganization proceedings brought by the aggrieved spouse—that is, the person who is, or feels to be, hurt—the court must first determine whether the other spouse's cruel and abusive acts fall within the state's standards for decreeing the divorce or separation. But the crucial issue is the aggrieved party's subjective response to the other spouse's conduct: ". . . what is experienced as cruelty by one may not be felt as cruelty by another."[29]

In child neglect, however, the judge, by virtue of *parens patriae*, has the freedom and perhaps the responsibility to use his own subjective views. It is the judge's notion of "neglect" or "depravity" that is most important. He evaluates the evidence; he decides its weight. It is *his* subjective response that is important. Judges, again by virtue of *parens patriae*, are supposed to be endowed with unique insight into the best interests of the child. Less important, and often irrelevant, is the child's own feelings toward its parents or toward environmental conditions.

The law has not yet formally recognized in its procedure a child's competency to express its own feelings or to know its own best interests, save in isolated instances.[30]

Minnesota and Idaho statutes

By delineating more sharply among the various standards used in determining neglect and by adding categories not found on the list on pp. 57–58, the neglect statutes of Minnesota and Idaho stand out as unique. By introducing the concepts of emotional neglect of the child and the psychological health of the parent, both state statutes make a dramatic shift from tradition. The Minnesota statute defines a neglected child as one:

(a) Who is abandoned by his parent, guardian, or other custodian; or

(b) Who is without proper parental care because of the faults or habits of his parent, guardian, or other custodian; or

(c) *Who is without proper parental care because of the emotional, mental or physical disability, or state of immaturity of his parent, guardian or other custodian; or*

(d) *Who is without necessary subsistence, education or other care necessary for his physical or mental health or morals because his parent, guardian or other custodians neglects or refuses to provide it; or*

(e) Who is without the special care made necessary by his physical or mental condition because his parent, guardian or other custodian neglects or refuses to provide it; or

(f) Whose occupation, behavior, condition, environment, or associations are such as to be injurious or dangerous to himself or others; or

(g) Who is living in a facility for foster care which is not licensed as required by law, unless the child is living in the facility under court order; or

(h) Whose parent, guardian, or custodian has made arrangements for his placement in a manner detrimental to the welfare of the child or in violation of law; or

(i) Who comes within the provisions of subdivision 5 [juvenile delinquency provision], but whose conduct results in whole or in part from parental neglect. (Emphasis added.)[31]

The Idaho statute defines "neglect" as a situation where:

1. the child lacks parental care necessary for support or education as required by law, or
2. the child lacks parental care necessary for his health, morals and well-being, or
3. the child has been abandoned as defined in this act for a period less than one (1) year.[32]

At the same time, the statute gives the court jurisdiction over any child:

a. Who is neglected, abused, or abandoned by his parents or other legal custodian, or who, being an orphan, is homeless; or
b. *Whose behavior indicates social or emotional maladjustment;* or
c. Whose environment or associations are injurious to his welfare. (Emphasis added.)[33]

The Idaho statute defines "emotional maladjustment" as

the condition of a child *who has been denied proper parental love, or adequate affectionate parental association, and who behaves unnaturally and unrealistically in relation to normal situations, objects and other persons.* (Emphasis added.)[34]

The difference between the Minnesota and Idaho categories and the typical provisions mentioned earlier is readily apparent. The typical provisions define neglect mainly in terms of physical harm, moral deprivation, and deficiencies in environmental conditions. They operate on what we may call a "first" or an "apparent" level: that which can be seen or felt, or which seems to have an easily definable causal connection between act or omission and damage or the likelihood of damage to the child. They do not concern themselves with the emotional impact of the conduct or event on the child. In reaching the second level, the Minnesota and Idaho statutes add a new dimension. They require a judge to measure the strengths and weaknesses of the parent's relationship with the child. The judge must deal with both the parent's feelings and conduct toward the child. Thus, these statutes recognize not merely the child's physical condition, but rather the totality of its well-being.

In this respect the Minnesota and Idaho statutes reflect the thinking of modern mental health specialists. Some specialists, for example, have stated that the emotional well-being of children is more important than their physical health. As Bowlby has said:

> A child may be ill-fed and ill-sheltered, he may be dirty and suffering from disease, he may be ill-treated, but, unless his parents have totally rejected him, he is secure in the knowledge that there is *someone* to whom he is of value and who will strive, even though inadequately, to provide for him until such time as he can fend for himself.[35]

Other authors have suggested that removal of a psychologically damaged child from its home may be more imperative than removal of a physically deprived child.[36] The belief is that if parents of the physically deprived receive supportive help (usually financial) through social services, they will be able to provide for the child's physical needs while maintaining their emotional ties and the necessary unbroken continuity of the relationship.

OBSERVATIONS ON STATUTORY RESPONSES

It seems clear that even the most detailed neglect statute, through phrases such as "unfit home" or "improper environment," would probably be termed "broad" or even "vague" in areas other than family law. As mentioned earlier, the legislative purpose behind the broad language appears to be to allow judges wide discretion in deciding neglect cases. Presumably local judges have a knowledge of community resources as well as information about the area which they can call upon in the disposition of a case. At the same time, juvenile and domestic relations judges are considered "closer" to the issues in any given case and to generally reflect local community attitudes and values.

Unfortunately, the attitudes and values reflected by these judges are not always consistent with the judicial role. The following colloquy occurred in a California Juvenile Court:

THE COURT: Don't you know that things like this are terribly wrong? This is one of the worst crimes that a person can commit. I just get so disgusted that I just figure what is the use? You are just an animal. You are lower than an animal. Even animals don't do that. You are pretty low.

I don't know why your parents haven't been able to teach you anything or train you. Mexican people, after 13 years of age, it's perfectly all right to go out and act like an animal. It's not even right to do that to a stranger, let alone a member of your own family. I don't have much hope for you. You will probably end up in State's Prison before you are 25, and that's where you belong, any how. There is nothing much you can do. . . .

Apparently, your sister is pregnant; is that right?

THE MINOR'S FATHER: Yes.

THE COURT: It's a fine situation. How old is she?

THE MINOR'S MOTHER: Fifteen.

THE COURT: Well, probably she will have a half a dozen children and three or four marriages before she is 18.

The County will have to take care of you. You are no particular good to anybody. We ought to send you out of the country—send you back to Mexico. You belong in prison for the rest of your life for doing things of this kind. You ought to commit suicide. That's what I think of people of this kind. You are lower than animals and haven't the right to live in organized society—just miserable, lousy, rotten people.

There is nothing we can do with you. You expect the County to take care of you. Maybe Hitler was right. The animals in our society probably ought to be destroyed because they have no right to live among human beings. If you refuse to act like a human being, then, you don't belong among the society of human beings.

[Counsel]: Your Honor, I don't think I can sit here and listen to that sort of thing.

THE COURT: You are going to have to listen to it because I consider this a very vulgar, rotten human being.

[Counsel]: The Court is indicting the whole Mexican group. . . .

The Court ought to look at this youngster and deal with this youngster's case.

THE COURT: All right. That's what I am going to do. The family should be able to control this boy and the young girl.

[Counsel]: What appals [sic] me is that the Court is saying that Hitler was right in genocide.

THE COURT: What are we going to do with the mad dogs of our society? Either we have to kill them or send them to an institution or place them out of the hands of good people because that's the theory—one of the theories of punishment is if they get to the position that they want to act like mad dogs, then, we have to separate them from our society.

Well, I will go along with the recommendation. You will learn in time or else you will have to pay for the penalty with the law because the law grinds slowly but exceedingly well. If you are going to be a law violator—you have to make up your mind whether you are going to observe the law or not. If you can't observe the law, then, you have to be put away.[37]

Broad statutes nevertheless provide a means of allowing parental behavior a wide degree of variance. Until society reaches the point of determining the exact "formula" for molding "ideal" or "normal" citizens, and unless total uniformity among our citizens is desired, there does not appear to be any clear basis for preferring one particular form of child rearing over another and permitting intervention for deviation from that mode. At the same time, however, neglect statutes recognize that "neglectful" behavior can also vary, and thus cannot be easily or specifically defined. Behavior cannot be deemed "neglectful" in and of itself, but only as it affects the child. The broad neglect statutes allow judges to examine each situation on its own facts. They thus eliminate the need and perhaps the tendency to search for specific behavior upon which to "pin" the charge of neglect. As one juvenile court judge noted:

> The neglect statutes are concerned with parental behavior not as behavior per se, but only and solely as it adversely affects the child in those areas of the child's life about which the statutes have expressed concern. Each child embodies his own unique combination of physical, psychological, and social components; no child has quite the same strengths or weaknesses as another or exactly the same relationship with his family. The parental failure which markedly damages one child might leave another quite untouched. This interaction between the child and his family is the essence of a neglect situation, the imponderable which defies statutory constraints.[38]

But, as broadness enhances discretion, it also provides the judge with the means for making wide-ranging value judgments which may go unchecked because of the absence, in many instances, of a written opinion and the paucity of cases which are appealed. It is the nonspecific statute which provides the judge with a vehicle for imposing on others his own preferences for certain child-rearing practices and his own ideas of adult behavior and parental morality. These statutes and the cases which have been decided under them sometimes appear to be a means of policing the poor, especially parents on public welfare, and other parents, often young, who do not conform either in dress, life-style, or child-rearing practices to dominant middle-class norms. Here the interests of the child become secondary to the desire to punish, thus subverting child protection, the basic philosophy behind the neglect laws.

Another aspect of neglect statutes is their effect upon child protective and child welfare agencies, whose power they often serve to enhance. If a social agency is well established, has the support and confidence of the community, and appears to be performing at a high level, it is likely that a judge will respect both its administrative procedures and recommendations. Consequently, when the agency comes before a court and petitions it to commit a child to its care, the judge might be more inclined to listen closely and give more credence to the agency's testimony than he would to an individual petitioner. In fact, the legal presumption in favor of parental fitness might recede as a result of a series of unarticulated, informal presumptions mirroring the agency's recommendations. The very fact that an agency decides to bring a case before the court might even in and of itself create a presumption favoring the agency's claim of parental neglect. Or a judge might merely assume that the agency, through staff, resources, and training, is better equipped than his court to determine these matters. Here there would be a de facto delegation of power to the agency despite a clear legislative grant of power to the courts, and despite the fact that such a delegation might prove unconstitutional if it were appealed to a higher court. A Washington judge said:

> We are convinced that the professional personnel of the King County Youth Service Center and the State Department of Public Assistance, as a result of their training and experience, are well aware of, and are significantly guided and influenced by, a policy which recognizes the social or all-round desirability of leaving a child, if reasonably possible, in the custody of its natural parents. Furthermore, we believe these professional personnel are oftentimes more competent, or at least better trained and more experienced, in the matter of family relationships and problems than most judges and lawyers. In mentioning these considerations and adverting to certain understandable "presumptions," emotional tendencies, and the reluctance of most people to intervene in family affairs, it should be implicit that we will not indulge in any presumption of inevitability or omniscience in favor of juvenile court determinations. Instead, the need is for cautious and, insofar as possible, objective evaluations at all official levels dealing with child welfare matters. However, we are confident that petitions to have a child made a ward of the state are usually resorted to only in the absence of any other rational, practicable solution to the particular problem involved.

Matters of child custody by their very nature present extremely difficult problems to trial and appellate courts, particularly when a natural parent is striving to maintain custody of an offspring in the face of persuasive indications or allegations of dependency or delinquency status. However, the judicial decision making process still must function and operate in specific instances in the troublesome child custody area as well as in others, reflecting, of course, hopefully insofar as humanly possible, objective evaluation of the facts, the applicable social standards, and the legal issues presented.[39]

Finally, it should be noted that the absence of a right to a jury trial in neglect cases—a right guaranteed in most cases involving community standards and the freedom of an individual—increases the danger of almost unbridled judicial discretion. Most neglect cases, like most delinquency cases,[40] are tried before a single judge. The danger is that a case's outcome will depend on the view of one man rather than on the possibly varying views of many.

Conclusions

Among the neglect statutes in the United States, those of Minnesota and Idaho are unique. By adding considerations of the emotional health of the child and parents to the scope of judicial inquiry, they illustrate the apparent deficiencies of most other neglect statutes. Yet the other statutes are not necessarily incomplete. If judges interpret words such as "neglect," "cruelty," or "depravity" to include situations relating to the mental health of the child and parents, it would not be essential to specifically recognize "emotional neglect" in the statute.[41] If, however, judges read the statutes restrictively—that is, looking merely to their literal meaning—then the statutes are indeed in need of reform, as this example shows:

> In its definition of the words "neglected child" the Legislature has carefully, expressly, and explicitly defined and limited the jurisdiction which it has conferred upon the juvenile court with respect to neglected children. Whenever that court undertakes, on the score of neglect, to supervise the care and custody of a child who is not "destitute or homeless, or abandoned," etc., it is merely an intermeddler, and its order is a nullity.

> *   *   *

> According to the record under review, the juvenile court of Jackson county did not find the existence of any specific condition which

would have placed the child, Margaret Marty, within the statutory
classification of a "neglected child," nor did it find generally that she
was a "neglected child" within the statutory definition thereof. It
merely found that "Margaret Marty is neglected." The information
by which the proceeding was initiated charged "that she is in the
custody of her mother, Olive B. Marty, who neglects and fails to
properly care for said Margaret Marty." The court may have used the
word "neglected" in the same sense in which it was used by the
informant. But, whether it did or not, its finding of mere neglect, to
which nothing can be added by intendment, falls far short of "desti-
tute or homeless, or abandoned, or dependent upon the public for
support," etc., the conditions specified in the statute.[42]

It is thus highly desirable that legislative recognition be given
to "emotional neglect" as an independent legal standard. This
view is a result of experience showing a judicial reluctance to
carve out categories of neglect that are not clearly provided
for in the statute itself. Specific statutory reference to mental
health would provide the needed "peg" upon which to hang a
finding of emotional deprivation. Because we have not yet
acquired sufficient knowledge about normal and abnormal child
development, it is not suggested that an elaborate or detailed
definition of "emotional neglect" be frozen into a statute.
"Actually, we are learning only gradually what exactly *not* to do
with *what kind* of children at *what* age."[43]

Of course, merely listing "emotional neglect" as a standard
for intervention will not cure neglect statutes. Nor will it necessarily revolutionize the handling of child neglect cases. It was
in Minnesota, with its statutory provision recognizing emotional disability, that a mother was subjected to termination
proceedings for writing bad checks.[44] And in Maryland, with a
similar provision in its neglect statute, a child was removed
from its mother merely because it was in a home with other
illegitimate children.[45] The recognition of mental health as a
relevant factor, however, will open up an avenue of judicial
inquiry that takes cognizance of the complexity of individuals
and the unreliability of depending exclusively on "conduct-
based" or "event-based" classifications.[46]

OBSERVATIONS ON JUDICIAL RESPONSES

A search of appellate reports for judicial responses to child neglect reveals striking findings. Given the large number of children reported as neglected and placed in foster homes,[47] the number of appellate cases is quite low. Apparently the great bulk of neglect cases are handled within social welfare agencies exclusively. When parental rights are challenged in a lower or trial court, the issues are resolved, usually summarily, for reasons already discussed.[48] Appeals to higher courts are not frequent. For a parent to appeal a neglect case, he needs a certain amount of sophistication even to know that appellate review exists. Then he must have the funds for legal fees or be aware of the availability of community legal services. Or a community agency must become interested in his case.

Research into appellate reports also reveals that only a small number of cases decided under neglect statutes have been concerned with issues of physical harm or emotional deprivation. The vast majority of older appellate cases concern parents who failed to provide medical care for their children, who attempted to raise their children in unpopular religions, or whose behavior involved questions of parental morality or offended dominant community standards.[49] This is not to say that cases involving instances of physical and emotional neglect are not now appearing with greater frequency in appellate reports.[50] Some cases have been litigated under neglect statutes, while others have been litigated under criminal law and tort law. For example, many cases categorized under the heading of parental immunity for tort liability concern parents who use their disciplinary authority to brutalize or deprive their children.[51]

Recent appellate cases dealing with parental morality reveal a discernible trend. Appellate judges appear increasingly unwilling to employ neglect laws to impose their middle-class mores upon families and to punish a parent's undesirable conduct unless that conduct can be shown to result in damage to the child.[52] The fact is significant, however, that someone or some agency challenged parental rights on the basis of alleged parental immorality, and that a lower or trial court used a neglect law to punish the parents by removing their children from custody. For even though the trend referred to appears on the appellate level, the same may not be true on the trial level. Indeed, agencies and trial courts may still be imposing their own prejudices and values on parents while ostensibly remedying a neglect situation. Unfortunately, with our highly selective legal reporting system, it is very difficult to know the nature of neglect cases resolved in the lower courts. In the absence of a written opinion on the trial level, a case is invisible for purposes of legal research.

In re Cager,[53] three Maryland cases decided together, dealt primarily with one provision in that state's neglect statute and will serve to illustrate the point. In *Cager*, the State's Attorney brought an action under Art. 26, § 52 of the Maryland Code to test the provision in that state's neglect law that defines a neglected child as one who is living in a home "which fails to provide a stable moral environment." The statute provides:

> In determining whether such a stable moral environment exists, the court shall consider, among other things, whether the parent, guardian, or persons with whom the child lives
> (i)   Is unable to provide such environment by reason of immaturity, or emotional, mental or physical disability;
> (ii) Is engaging in promiscuous conduct inside or outside the home;
> (iii) Is cohabiting with a person to whom he or she is not married;
> (iv) Is pregnant with an illegitimate child; or
> (v)   Has, within a period of twelve months preceding the filing of the petition alleging the child to be neglected, either been pregnant with or given birth to another child to whose putative father she was not legally married at the time of conception, or has not thereafter married.

The principal question before the court was whether three illegitimate children were "neglected" and should be removed from their home because they were living with at least one illegitimate sibling and thus in an unstable moral environment. In deciding that the children *were* neglected, the lower court judge wrote:

Most first illegitimate children we think are the result of a mistake. . . . The second time around we think represents a lack of judgment and demonstrates an unstable moral attitude on the part of the mother. We think for her to continue to conduct herself in such a way as repeatedly to bring illegitimate children into her household, reflects a weakness in her character, and a demonstrable view of morals on her part, that is inconsistent with the minimum moral standard the community requires. And the reason therefore, that by her deliberate knowing course of conduct in engaging in sexual relations with men, that produce illegitimate children, she has demonstrated in the most forceful and irrefutable way that she either does not care for the views of society on morals, or caring, is unable to conform her conduct to their minimum standards.

We have no difficulty concluding that the words unstable moral environment relate or were intended to apply to a situation where a mother had had a series of illegitimate children such as these mothers had in these cases. And that such a series of illegitimate children constitutes on the part of the mother neglect of each of the children involved.

Neglect concerns itself not only with the physical aspects of the children's lives, but with their moral and spiritual existence as well. That it is impossible for a mother of less than independent wealth to care for three or four or seven or eleven or twelve illegitimate children on the slender means provided her by the welfare department, we think is axiomatic. That it is virtually impossible for a mother who continues to have illegitimate children by a series of fathers, that it is impossible for such a woman to provide the moral training and the spiritual counseling that ought to surround the nurture of children of tender years so they will not themselves fall into the difficulties that she has fallen into. . . .[54]

The decision was based solely upon the finding that a home with more than one illegitimate child was "an unstable moral environment" within the statutory definition.

As the appellants brief stated in commenting upon the lower court's decision:

In imposing this condition [more than one illegitimate birth] the court was obviously far more interested in the vast sociological and moral problems of our times, as it viewed them, than in determining where the best interests of the children would lie under a statute designed and intended to protect children. . . .

. . . Neither the inherent powers of an Equity Court nor its powers of *parens patriae* allow an imposition by the court of its own ideas of policy and morals.[55]

The appellate court determined that the lower court's finding should be reversed. In concluding that to meet the state's standards for determining neglect, more must be shown than simply the finding of more than one illegitimate child in the home, the court stated:

> Being pregnant with an illegitimate child or having given birth to an illegitimate child within twelve months of the filing of the petition alleging the child to be neglected are two factors to be considered under the statute, "among other things," as indicating neglect, but they cannot alone and automatically be found to be indicators of that fact. The "other things" the court is directed to consider in determining whether there is or is not a stable moral environment must include the factors previously enumerated in § 52 (f), pertinent to the particular case. Furthermore, that section does not make explicit as a test of neglect the fact that two illegitimate children of a mother live with her and we do not find such a test reasonably or fairly implicit in the statute as a sole determinant.
>
> It is clear that the ultimate consideration in finding neglect which will serve as a basis for removing a child from its mother's custody is the best interest of the child.[56]

One judge dissented. He argued that a mother's giving birth to a series of illegitimate children was sufficient evidence that the home over which she presides is so devoid of order and of good moral example that the children must be benefited by their removal. He felt that the legislative framers of the neglect standards intended cases of this kind to be handled by removal. He wrote:

In my opinion, the trial court correctly interpreted the Maryland statute, and its findings were supported by the record. The record does not indicate to me that the present cases were "instituted not to serve and perpetuate the best interests of the children but rather impermissibly to use the children as pawns in a plan to punish their mothers for their past promiscuity and to discourage them and other females of like weaknesses and inclinations from future productivity" as is indicated in the majority opinion. On the contrary, the record indicates to me that the removal of the children from a home in which a stable moral influence does not exist is definitely for the best interests of those children so that, in the words of the Report of the Commission on Illegitimacy, the children will not be permitted "to live in homes where promiscuity and nonconforming patterns of family life become the accepted standards of living for the children to emulate." If as a peripheral benefit of this primary legislative policy to benefit the illegitimate children, promiscuous parents are led to abandon their immoral life, the public interest is advanced to that extent. This, however, is not the primary purpose of the institution of the present case.[57]

While the Maryland statute construed in *Cager* is unique, the attitudes implicit in its enactment, the decision of the lower court, and the appellate dissent undoubtedly appear elsewhere in the country. In other courts, moreover, the situation may be even worse. Where no statute dealing specifically with illegitimacy and neglect exists, decisions based upon these factors may appear disguised in the general and often vague language of neglect decisions, and no specific basis for appeal is available.

A recent California case, for example, involved similar attitudes about adult morality, but with a more typical statute. In *In re Raya*,[58] a welfare agency brought an action under the provision of 600 (a) of the California Welfare and Institutions Code to have two children declared wards of the state and removed from the custody of both their parents. Sec. 600 (a) of the California Welfare and Institutions Code reads in part:

Any person under the age of 21 years who comes within any of the following descriptions is within the jurisdiction of the juvenile

court which may adjudge such person to be a dependent child of
the court:

(a) Who is in need of proper and effective parental care or control
and has no parent or guardian, or has no parent or guardian
willing to exercise or capable of exercising such care or control,
or has no parent or guardian actually exercising such care or
control.

The children's parents were separated in 1960 and each was
living with, but not married to, another person. The two children had lived with their mother and her paramour for seven
years subsequent to the separation and had not had contact
with their natural father since that time. In fact, both children
considered their mother's paramour as their father.

Each of the children's parents wished to remarry, but the cost
of a divorce prevented them from seeking one. In 1967 a legal
aid office began to pursue a divorce for the parents. In his
prayer for divorce, the father alleged that the mother was "a fit
and proper person to have custody of the children." A probation report stated that the children were healthy and were receiving good parental care. The house in which they lived was
adequate. They seemed to be leading happy, normal lives.

The lower court found that the parents' cohabitation with
their paramours was in and of itself sufficient evidence of improper and ineffective parental care. The court ordered the
children removed from their mother's custody. They were first
placed with their grandmother, who was later found to be unfit
because she was living with a man not her husband, and then
removed and placed in an institution.

The appellate court reversed the lower court's decision, concluding that the children should not be removed. It recognized
the competing interests of the child and the parents in custody
cases, and stated that parental rights to custody should be disturbed only in extreme cases of improper and ineffective parental care. *Raya*, said the court, did not present facts of such
an extreme nature. Indeed, by refusing to find evidence of ineffective parental care, the appellate court showed tolerance for

the parents' way of life. In a compassionate plea for understanding their plight, the court wrote:

> There was no debate but that poverty had played a major
> role in producing the home situation which evoked the wardship.
> Adequately financed couples can afford divorce. Many take the step
> nonchalantly, quickly severing their marriages in jurisdictions which
> invite such business and changing mates with great readiness. The
> children of quickie marriages and quickie divorces need never find
> themselves in homes characterized by a permanent liaison such as
> Mrs. Raya's. For centuries the law has termed such liaisons meretri-
> cious or adulterous. Perhaps, in this day of casually created and
> broken marriages, the label should be applied with less readiness
> when poverty is a prime factor in producing the relationship. There
> is a danger here of imposing standards adapted to the well-to-do,
> who can usually pay for the forms of legitimacy, and ill-adapted for
> the poor, who frequently cannot. Attempts to apply across the board
> standards to rich and poor alike may avoid a theoretical discrimina-
> tion and create a practical one.

      ✻   ✻   ✻

     If abstract legal propositions fail to decide concrete cases,
abstract moral dogmas accomplish even less. The safest moral guides
for the courts are those crystallized in the statutes and case law. In
determining whether the evidence supported an adjudication of Mrs.
Raya's parental incapacity, the court neither excuses nor condemns.
It simply decides that in these particular circumstances the finding
of parental incapacity was unjustified by the facts.[59]

A more blatant example of an agency's attempts, sanctioned
by a lower court, to impose certain moral views on an adult
through the use of neglect laws can be found in a case decided
by the Missouri Supreme Court, *State v. Greer*.[60] The statute
involved defined a neglected child as "any child under the age
of seventeen years, who is homeless or abandoned, or who
habitually begs or receives alms, is found living in any house
of ill-fame; or with any vicious or disreputable person, or who

is suffering from depravity of its parents, or other person in whose care it may be."[61] The case was instituted by a prosecuting attorney and involved a baby only three months old. The allegation was that the child was "suffering from the depravity of its mother," and the prayer was for the child's being declared "neglected." Essentially, the evidence against the mother was drawn from the testimony of a sheriff and two state troopers, who stated that the mother had twice been seen in taverns drinking beer, that she was twice present in a car when the operator was arrested for traffic violations, and that two or three times a week she went out, leaving her child in the care of the child's grandmother. The appellate court summarized the evidence against the mother in the following manner:

> Summarizing, we find here a baby girl, just a few months old, who was concededly adequately housed, fed, clothed and attended, personally and medically. The child's mother visited taverns sometimes but there was no effort to show these places were of illrepute unless the name "tavern" so implies. Her alleged misbehavior there was drinking beer, but not excessively. The child was born out of wedlock, and the mother had dates. The child's mother and grandmother are poor. For some reasons not explained, dependency child aid was "cut off."[62]

The lower court's decision was reversed on appeal. The appellate court based its decision on the presumption that the best interests of a child are to be found in the home of its natural parent. The court wrote:

> We accord full deference to the trial judge on disputed matters of evidence but we believe the testimony offered showed neither depravity of the mother, nor that the child was "neglected" within the purview of our juvenile laws. Although such proceedings are properly conducted in a summary manner and even though it is possible the trial judge possessed extraneous information as to the merits of this controversy, still affirmative evidence of the required facts must appear on record. We cannot and will not on appeal magnify this evidence by surmise or conjecture and thereby deprive

a natural mother of the custody of her child and prepare the way to place that child with strangers.[63]

One other observation should be made on the handling of neglect cases by the courts. This is where a parent attempts to regain custody of his child after it has been placed in foster care through a court process.[64] The facts of the appellate cases usually involve a parent who because of financial plight voluntarily relinquishes his child to an agency, then tries to regain custody after his economic conditions improve. Another situation is where a court has declared a child neglected and a parent attempts to have the neglect order revoked after he has overcome his alleged deficiencies. In both instances it seems fair to say that a parent has a difficult time regaining custody, both on the trial and appellate level. The presumption in favor of parental fitness seems no longer in force once a finding of neglect has been entered, even though a subsequent attempt is made by the parent to have it revoked.

In re Neff[65] illustrates this last group of cases. In *Neff* a mother asked a Pennsylvania court to revoke a juvenile court order entered nine years before that had committed her four children, then ages ten, nine, eight, and six, to a private sectarian child welfare institution to which the children's father paid a monthly fee for support. This commitment was ordered two years after the same court had adjudged the children neglected. At that time, they were placed with the public child welfare department, which in turn placed them in foster home care. The first neglect proceeding took place two weeks before the parents were divorced. Subsequent to the commitment to the private institution, both parents remarried. Both frequently visited the children.

The trial court revoked the commitment order as to the oldest child, a nineteen-year-old college student. The court refused to revoke the order as to the other three children, even though two of them specifically stated that they preferred to return to their mother. This ruling was upheld by the appellate court.

The appellate court's decision to deny the mother's request

and to continue the institutional placement that had been in force for nine years seemed to be based on an assumption that the institution was better able to provide the children with strict discipline and economic security. The court reached its decision without reference to the intangible factors favoring placement in a family setting. Instead, the court focused almost exclusively on financial considerations. Nowhere in the majority opinion is there a discussion of the continued existence of neglect, supposedly the issue at hand. Rather, the court engaged in a comparative analysis of the two settings. The court wrote:

[The children] would undoubtedly enjoy a greater freedom at the home of their mother than they have at the Methodist Home. We are not at all convinced, however, that greater freedom would improve their welfare. Much of the juvenile delinquency present today may be traceable to the enlarged freedom of youth. Some people firmly believe that juvenile delinquency could be reduced by a greater discipline and stricter supervision. Be this as it may, this record convinces us that these children have not been unduly restricted and that they have received a fine religious training which certainly will stand them in good stead in days to come. . . .

Our conclusion in this case is largely based (as it was in the court below) upon the brief that the mother and her present husband do not fully appreciate the enormity of the expense necessary to keep four children in high school and college at the same time. The mother and her present husband have annual gross earnings of $12,700.00. The husband receives $5,000.00 from his present employment at Curtis-Wright and $3,200.00 retirement pay as an army officer and the mother receives $4,500.00 from her employment. The mother intends to give up her employment to take care of the children if they are awarded her. This will reduce their gross annual income to $8,200.00 a year. It costs approximately $1,200.00 a year to keep Barbara in college, thus reducing the annual income to $7,000.00 a year. Out of this the two adults must live and then find money to put three more children through high school and college. With costs as they are today, this will be a very difficult thing to do. The failure to do all or any of it will seriously affect the best welfare of the children. If they remain at the Home they will be adequately provided for and their college training will be assured.[66]

Three judges dissented. All agreed that the conditions present nine years before no longer existed and that the mother's claim for custody should be granted. They stated that the evidence revealed that the mother's home was adequate and the atmosphere wholesome. One judge quoted another Pennsylvania case: "No matter how competent and sympathetic the treatment of a child in an institution may be, it cannot be compared with the loving care received in a normal family life. Only in a totalitarian government do we find the philosophy that 'efficient institutional care' is considered preferable to normal family life."[67]

Three judges recognized the difficulty of regaining custody. They viewed the outcome in the case as a penalty to both the mother and her children. One judge wrote:

> As I view it, the order before us is not only contrary to the Juvenile Court Law, supra, but is fair to no person. It is not fair to the mother who seeks to have custody of her children; it is not fair to these young people who seek the experience of living in a home instead of an institution; it is not fair to those who operate and support the institution which is looking after these children whose parent is willing and able to look after them; and it is not fair to the taxpayers of Pennsylvania who are paying for the education of children whose mother lives in an expensive home in New Jersey.

> * * *

> It is natural that these children should prefer their mother's home to an institution, however excellent the latter may be. They have emphatically expressed their preference. I think that to deny their request is in the nature of the imposition of punishment upon these unfortunate children, who were brought into juvenile court, not as delinquents, but as neglected children. They do not deserve the stern treatment which they have received at the hands of the law. Their plea to be released from an institution in order to reside in their mother's home is entitled to a more sympathetic ear than the courts have given it.[68]

Conclusions

These cases reveal the prevailing attitudes of legislatures, social service agencies, trial courts, and appellate courts toward neglect. The legislative, administrative, and judicial processes may reflect divergent views. It would appear that the judicial process, particularly on the appellate level, can sometimes provide the needed restraints on abuses in the other institutions. Although in many cases lack of funds precludes a party from resorting to the appellate courts, these courts do sometimes provide the community with an effective and much-needed check on legislatures, welfare agencies, and lower courts. This is not to say that appellate courts are always the haven for families who have been separated by agencies and trial courts. The majority opinion in *In re Neff* illustrates this well.

SUMMARY

The process of public intrusion, beginning with a report to a social service agency about neglecting parents, may eventually lead to court intervention. The judicial response that results in making an adjustment in the parent-child relationship is the event we call "state intervention."

Neglect statutes form the legal basis for intervening in the normally private and intimate parent-child relationship. Rather than defining the state's expectation of parenthood in positive terms, reflecting accepted teachings in child development—a concern for affection, stimulation, and an unbroken continuity of care—these statutes are written in negative terms. They are drafted with a view toward directing judicial inquiry toward conduct or events thought to be undesirable, rather than toward positive indices of a wholesome parent-child relationship.

Typically, neglect statutes do not adequately recognize the emotional components of the parent-child relationship. Only Idaho and Minnesota elaborate on these essential features. But no matter how archaic or enlightened a neglect statute is on its face, the important consideration is how it is construed in the courts. Neglect statutes consist of words and phrases which are often purposely vague so as to give lower court judges who are close to community affairs wide discretion in interpretation. Indeed, many of the phrases have meaning only through interpretation. "Proper care," for example, may be interpreted to mean the mere fulfillment of a child's need for food, shelter, clothing, and health, all on a minimal level. Or, at the other extreme, it may be interpreted to assure that a child is given the opportunity to achieve his educational potential. The point is that by using their discretion in interpreting and applying statutory guides for intervention, judges have enormous power to establish, administer, and reorganize families according to their own values, biases, and prejudices. Sometimes lower court judges have to correct injustices done to families by welfare agencies. Unfortunately, in some cases the injustice is compounded by a lower court, leaving correction to an appellate court.

As stated earlier, state intervention results in an adjustment in the parent-child relationship. By "adjustment" we mean quite simply a change, whether temporary or permanent, in the normally private relationship. If, for example, a judge decides that the evidence before him, including the agency's report and the testimony of other interested parties (usually parents), is not sufficient to prove neglect and therefore dismisses the case, there has been no state intervention. No judicial adjustment has been made in the parent-child relationship. But if a judge decides that sufficient evidence of neglect is present, then he must think of an appropriate remedy. When social welfare agencies are involved, they may play an important role in recommending a disposition. They might recommend that the court allow the child to return to its parents under the supervision of the agency. The change in the relationship in this case would be the intrusion of an agency, by way of supervision, in the otherwise private affairs of the family. Or an agency may request that it be awarded temporary custody of the neglected child with the power to place the child in foster care until the neglectful conditions have been remedied by the parents themselves, or until the agency has equipped the parents for their parental responsibilities as defined by the agency. (It should be said that once intervention of this kind occurs, parents may have difficulty in reclaiming their child and resuming a normal relationship with it.) Finally, the agency may recommend that it be awarded permanent custody (later to have parental rights terminated) with the power to place the neglected child in an adoptive home.

The next two chapters will focus on foster care and adoption. Both are meant to be alternatives to natural parents who, according to standards in neglect statutes, have failed.

NOTES

1. See Note, *Alternatives to "Parental Right" in Child Custody Disputes Involving Third Parties*, 73 Yale L. J. 151 (1963).

2. L. Young, Wednesday's Children (1964).

3. *See, e.g.*, A. Freud, *Psychoanalytic Knowledge and Its Application to Children's Services*, in 5 The Writings of Anna Freud: 1956–1965, 469 (1969). "The best interests of a child are served, according to our point of view, by all measures which promote his smooth progression toward normal maturity. The latter, in its turn, depends above all on the coincidence of three factors; on the free interchange of affection between child and adult; on ample external stimulation of the child's inborn, internal potentialities; and on unbroken continuity of care."

4. Dr. Albert Solnit takes the position that "the healthy development and adjustment of child, parents, and family connote a concordance of [the] best interests of [the] child and other members of his family, a mutuality of child and parent." A. J. Solnit, Speech before the American Orthopsychiatric Association, San Francisco, California, April 13, 1966.

5. J. Goldstein, *Psychoanalysis and Jurisprudence*, 77 Yale L. J. 1053, 1076 (1968).

6. *See In re* Welfare of Karren, 280 Minn. 377, 159 N.W.2d 402 (1968).

7. Letter from Robert F. Ott, Commissioner of Massachusetts Department of Public Welfare, to Welfare Service Offices, March 20, 1970.

8. Neglect statutes are concerned with children whose parents fail to provide sufficiently for their child's welfare. Dependent child statutes involve children without parents or guardians who are in need of parental

care and supervision. These categories, however, are not uniform. In fact, some jurisdictions draw no distinction between neglect and dependency; other jurisdictions do not use these terms at all.

9. *See, e.g.,* Mass. Gen. Laws Ann. ch. 119 § 24 (1969); Minn. Stat. Ann. § 260.15 (Supp. 1970); Ohio Rev. Code Ann. § 2151.03 (Baldwin 1969); Pa. Stat. Ann. tit. 11 § 243 (1965); Utah Code Ann. 55–10–64 (Supp. 1969); Wash. Rev. Code Ann. § 13.04.010 (1962); Wis. Stat. Ann. § 48.13 (1957).

10. *See, e.g.,* Ala. Code tit. 13 § 350 (1959); Colo. Rev. Stat. Ann. § 22–1–1 (1964); D.C. Code Ann. § 11–1551 (1966); Fla. Stat. Ann. § 39–01 (1961); Idaho Code Ann. § 16–1626 (Supp. 1969); Kan. Gen. Stat. Ann. § 38–802 (1964); Mich. Stat. Ann. § 27–3178 (598.2) (Supp. 1970); Minn. Stat. Ann. § 260.015 (Supp. 1970); Mo. Ann. Stat. § 211.031 (1962); N.J. Stat. Ann. § 9.6–1 (1960); Ohio Rev. Code Ann. § 2151.03 (Baldwin 1969); Pa. Stat. Ann. tit. 11 § 243 (1965); Utah Code Ann. § 55–10–64 (Supp. 1969); Va. Code Ann. § 16.1–158 (Supp. 1970); Wis. Stat. Ann. § 48.13 (1957).

11. *See, e.g.,* Ala. Code tit. 13 § 350 (1959); Colo. Rev. Stat. Ann. § 22–1–1 (1964); Conn. Gen. Stat. Ann. § 17–53 (Supp. 1969); D.C. Code Ann. § 11–155 (1966); Fla. Stat. Ann. § 39.01 (1961); Ga. Code Ann. § 24–2408 (Supp. 1969); Idaho Code Ann. § 16–1626 (Supp. 1969); Ill. Ann. Stat. ch. 23 § 2360 (Smith-Hurd 1968); Ind. Ann. Stat. § 9–2806 (1956); Kan. Gen. Stat. Ann. § 38–802 (1964); Mich. Stat. Ann. § 27.3178 (598.2) (1962); Minn. Stat. Ann. § 260.015 (Supp. 1970); N.J. Stat. Ann. § 9:6–1 (1960); N.M. Stat. Ann. § 13–9–2 (1968); N.Y. Family Court Act § 312 (McKinney 1963); Ohio Rev. Code Ann. § 2151.03 (Baldwin 1969); Okla. Stat. Ann. tit. 11 § 243 (1965); R.I. Gen. Laws Ann. § 14–1–3 (1970); Utah Code Ann. § 55–10–64 (Supp. 1969); Vt. Stat. Ann. tit. 33 § 632 (Supp. 1969); Va. Code Ann. § 16.1–158 (Supp. 1970); Wis. Stat. Ann. § 48.13 (1957).

12. *See, e.g.,* Ala. Code tit. 13 § 350 (1959); Cal. Wlf. & Instns. § 600 (West 1966); Colo. Rev. Stat. Ann. § 22–1–1 (1964); Fla. Stat. Ann. § 39.01 (1961); Ill. Ann. Stat. ch. 23 § 2360 (Smith-Hurd 1968); Ind. Ann. Stat. § 9–2807 (1956); Md. Ann. Code art. 26 § 52 (1966); Mich. Stat. Ann. § 27.3178 (598.2) (1962); Mont. Rev. Code Ann. § 10–502 (1968); N.M. Stat. Ann. § 13–9–2 (1968); Okla. Stat. Ann. tit. 10 § 1101 (Supp. 1969); R.I. Gen. Laws Ann. § 14–1–3 (1970); Wash. Rev. Code Ann. § 13.04.010 (1962).

13. *See, e.g.,* Conn. Gen. Stat. Ann. § 17–53 (Supp. 1969); Idaho Code Ann. § 16–1625 (Supp. 1969); Mass. Gen. Laws Ann. ch. 119 § 24 (1969); N.J. Ann. Code art. 26 § 52 (1966); Mich. Stat. Ann. § 27.3178 (598.2)

(1962); Minn. Stat. Ann. § 260.011 (Supp. 1970); N.J. Stat. Ann. § 9:6–1 (1960); Ohio Rev. Code Ann. § 2151.03 (Baldwin 1969); Pa. Stat. Ann. tit. 11 § 243 (1965); Utah Code Ann. § 55–10–64 (Supp. 1969).

14. *See, e.g.,* Conn. Gen. Stat. Ann. § 17–53 (Supp. 1969); D.C. Code § 11–1551 (1966); Fla. Stat. Ann. § 39.01 (1961); Minn. Stat. Ann. § 260.015 (Supp. 1970); Ohio Rev. Code Ann. § 2151.03 (Baldwin 1969); Pa. Stat. Ann. tit. 11 § 243 (1965); Utah Code Ann. § 55–10–64 (1969); Wis. Stat. Ann. § 48.13 (1957).

15. *See, e.g.,* Colo. Rev. Stat. Ann. § 22–1–2 (1964); Ind. Ann. Stat. § 9–2807 (1956); Mont. Rev. Code Ann. § 10–501 (1968); Ohio Rev. Code Ann. § 2151.04 (Baldwin 1969); Va. Code Ann. § 16.1–158 (Supp. 1970).

16. *See, e.g.,* Ala. Code tit. 13 § 350 (1959); Conn. Gen. Stat. Ann. § 17–53 (Supp. 1969); D.C. Code Ann. § 11–155 (1966); Fla. Stat. Ann. § 39.01 (1961); Ga. Code Ann. § 24–2408 (Supp. 1969); Idaho Code Ann. § 16–1626 (Supp. 1969); Kan. Gen. Stat. Ann. § 38–802 (1964); Md. Ann. Code art. 26 § 52 (1966); Me. Rev. Stat. Ann. tit. 22 § 3792 (1964); Minn. Stat. Ann. § 260.015 (Supp. 1970); Mo. Ann. Stat. § 211.031 (1962); Ohio Rev. Code Ann. § 2151.03 (Baldwin 1969); R.I. Gen. Laws Ann. § 14–1–3 (1970); Va. Code Ann. § 16.1–158 (Supp. 1970); Wis. Stat. Ann. § 48.13 (1957).

17. *See, e.g.,* Ala. Code tit. 13 § 350 (1959); Colo. Rev. Stat. Ann. § 22–1–1 (1964); Ill. Ann. Stat. ch. 23 § 2360 (Smith-Hurd 1969); Ind. Ann. Stat. § 9–2807 (1966); Mont. Rev. Code Ann. § 10–501 (1968); N.M. Stat. Ann. § 13–9–2 (1967); R.I. Gen. Law Ann. § 14–1–3 (1970).

18. *See, e.g.,* Colo. Rev. Stat. Ann. § 22–1–1 (1964); D.C. Code Ann. § 11–1551 (1966); Fla. Stat. Ann. § 39.01 (1961) (under Delinquency); Ill. Ann. Stat. ch. 23 § 2359 (Smith-Hurd 1951); Ind. Ann. Stat. § 9–2807 (1956); Mich. Stat. Ann. § 27–3178 (598.2) (1962); Mont. Rev. Code Ann. § 10–501 (1968); N.M. Stat. Ann. § 13–9–2 (1967); Ohio Rev. Code Ann. § 2151.03 (Baldwin 1969); Pa. Stat. Ann. tit. 11 § 243 (1965); R.I. Gen. Laws Ann. § 14–1–3 (1970) (under Wayward); Wash. Rev. Code Ann. § 13.04.010 (1962).

19. *See, e.g.,* Fla. Stat. Ann. § 39.01 (1961) (under Delinquency); Ind. Ann. Stat. § 9–2807 (1956); Mich. Stat. Ann. § 27.3178 (598.2) (1962); Wash. Rev. Code Ann. § 13.04.010 (1962).

20. *See, e.g.,* Ala. Code tit. 13 § 350 (1959); D.C. Code Ann. § 11–1551 (1966); N.J. Stat. Ann. § 9:6–1 (1960); Pa. Stat. Ann. tit. 11 § 243 (1965); R.I. Gen. Laws Ann. § 14–1–3 (1970).

21. *See, e.g.,* Md. Ann. Code art. 26 § 52 (1966); Minn. Stat. Ann. § 260.015 (1969); N.J. Stat. Ann. § 9:6–1 (1960); Ohio Rev. Code Ann. § 2151.04 (Baldwin 1969); Wis. Stat. Ann. § 48.13 (1957).

22. *See, e.g.,* Minn. Stat. Ann. § 260.015 (1969); Wis. Stat. Ann. § 48.13 (1957).

23. *See, e.g.,* Wash. Rev. Code Ann. § 13.04.010 (1962).

24. *See, e.g.,* Mich. Stat. Ann. § 27.3178 (598.2) (Supp. 1970).

25. *See, e.g.,* N.J. Stat. Ann. § 9:6–1 (1960).

26. *See, e.g.,* N.J. Stat. Ann. § 9:6–1 (1960).

27. Ind. Ann. Stat. § 9–2806 (1956).

28. In *In re* Douglas, 164 N.E.2d 475 (Ohio Juv. Ct. 1959), an Ohio Juvenile Court judge quoted W. S. Gilbert in commenting on the parents involved in a neglect case: "Husband twice as old as wife, argues ill for married life." The mother was sixteen and the father was thirty-two years old at the time of their marriage. In describing the couple, the judge wrote: "It should be recalled that this court had the dubious privilege of seeing and hearing the witnesses who testified in this matter. Some of them are well, and unpleasantly, known to the court as the result of criminal charges against them. Without going any further into the details of the testimony, it is sufficient to say that this court must necessarily conclude that both Mr. and Mrs. Douglas have been guilty of serious marital misconduct; that Mr. Douglas is a conscienceless, selfish monster, whose main interest in the children is to use them as clubs to beat his wife into submission; that Mrs. Douglas is without either morals or good sense, and is also more concerned with gratifying her desires of the moment than the welfare of her children."

29. J. Katz, *Family Law and Psychoanalysis—Some Observations on Interdisciplinary Collaboration,* 1 Fam. L. Q. 69, 73 (1967).

30. It is not uncommon in child custody proceedings following divorce for a judge to question a child regarding his preference for a custodian. Some state statutes specifically refer to a child's wishes as a factor to be considered in making a custodial disposition. *See, e.g.,* Ariz. Rev. Stat. Ann. § 8–101 (1956); Cal. Civ. § 225 (1954); Okla. Stat. Ann. tit. 10 § 60.11 (1966). *Cf.* N.D. Cent. Code § 30–10–10 (1960) and Utah Code Ann. § 75–13–13 (1953) which allow children of certain ages to choose their custodians under certain conditions. Cases are collected in Annot., 4

A.L.R.3d 1396 (1965). *But see* Flanagan v. Flanagan, — Ill. App. 2d —, 259 N.E.2d 610, 612 (1970): "The presence and participation of children in [divorce] litigation . . : can be and generally is a very traumatic experience for them and the litigants. Their participation is not to be encouraged nor permitted if the Chancellor believes he has sufficient evidence to make a judgment that is in their best interest." Most states require the consent of a child, if over a certain age (usually twelve), to his own adoption.

31. Minn. Stat. Ann. § 260.15 (Supp. 1970).

32. Idaho Code Ann. § 16–1626 (Supp. 1969).

33. *Id.* It would seem that provisions of this sort, if literally applied, could result in many middle-class parents being found to have neglected their children.

34. *Id.*

35. J. Bowlby, Maternal Care and Health 68 (1950).

36. *See, e.g.*, E. Smith, Reading in Adoption 6 (1963).

37. Record, In the Matter of a Minor (Cal. Super. Ct., Santa Clara County, Juv. Div., Sept. 2, 1969).

38. T. Gill, *The Legal Nature of Neglect*, 6 N.P.P.A.J. 1, 5 (1960).

39. Todd v. Superior Court, King County, Juvenile Court, 68 Wash.2d 587, 590–591, 414 P.2d 605, 607–608 (1966).

40. Whether the right to a jury trial in delinquency cases is constitutionally required is presently a subject of controversy. The United States Supreme Court in the landmark case of *In re* Gault, 387 U.S. 1 (1967), did not decide this question. The trend in the state decisional law is against recognizing this constitutional right. *See* Annot., 100 A.L.R.2d 124 (1965). However, the question is before the United States Supreme Court in *In re* Burrus, 275 N.C. 517, 169 S.E.2d 879 (1969), *cert. granted*, 90 S. Ct. 1379 (1970) (No. 1544, Misc.).

41. Even though a neglect statute may not specifically provide for an inquiry into the emotional health of a parent or his child, judges may interpret other statutory standards to require this consideration. *See, e.g.*, Kennedy v. State Dept. of Pensions and Security, 277 Ala. 5, 166 So.2d 736 (1964) ("best interests of the child"); Todd v. Superior Court, King County Juvenile Court, 68 Wash.2d 587, 414 P.2d 605 (1966) ("unfit home").

42. State *ex rel.* Dew v. Trimble, 306 Mo. 657, 673–674, 269 S.W. 617, 622 (1925).

43. E. Erikson, *Growth and Crises of the Healthy Personality,* Psychological Issues, vol. 1, no. 1, monograph 1, 1959, at 50, 71, cited in Goldstein, *Psychoanalysis and Jurisprudence, supra* note 4, at 1076.

44. *See In re* Welfare of Karren, *supra,* note 5.

45. *See In re* Cager, 251 Md. 473, 248 A.2d 384 (1968) discussed *infra* at pp. 70–73.

46. *See* Goldstein, *supra* note 4, at 1076.

47. *See* p. 90 *infra.*

48. *See* pp. 37–41 *supra.*

49. *See, e.g.,* M. Sullivan, *Child Neglect: The Environmental Aspects,* 29 Ohio St. L. J. 85 (1968).

50. See cases collected in P. Dodyk, M. Sovern, C. Berger, W. Young, & M. Paulsen, Cases and Materials on Law and Poverty, 1011–1091 (1969); O. Ketcham & M. Paulsen, Cases and Materials Relating to Juvenile Courts 165–240 (1967).

51. Cases are collected in Annot., 19 A.L.R.2d 423 (1951).

52. *But see In re* Anonymous, 37 Misc.2d 411, 412–413, 238 N.Y.S.2d 422, 423–24 (1962): "Statutes often define in general terms. Decisional law particularizes and refers to a given set of facts. The statutory definition of neglect, therefore, being in general terms, has resulted in a dearth of cases reported; and the tendency has been to leave it to the Judge in a particular case to make his own decision as to whether or not there is neglect, based upon the particular and unique set of facts in the case at bar. It therefore has developed upon the courts to establish the moral standards to be followed by persons to whom is entrusted the care and custody of children. And never has there been a greater need for the courts to maintain a high level of moral conduct than exists today. This court intends to give more than lip service to the principle that the fabric of our society is composed of the family unit and when the family unit is damaged, the fabric of society suffers. Our courts will continue to insist upon a high level of moral conduct on the part of custodians of children, and will never succumb to the 'Hollywood' type of morality so popular today, which seems to condone and encourage the dropping of our moral

guard. We have not yet reached the point where, when parents who have tired of each other's company, may be free to seek other companionship with complete disregard of the moral examples they are setting for their children. This is the crux of the case at bar.

"The record is replete with credible testimony to the effect that the respondent mother, living in an apartment house with her five small children separated from the petitioner father, frequently entertained male companions in the apartment and in the presence of the children. In fact, on occasion, these male companions not only spent considerable parts of the day there but ate meals with her and the children, and, on at least one occasion, one of them spent the night with the respondent and, in fact, slept with her, to the knowledge of the children. On another occasion, she took the children to an airport to meet a boy friend and brought him back to the apartment, where he spent parts of several days. This conduct would be culpable under any circumstances, but was particularly culpable because only a year ago, this court in another similar proceeding for neglect between the same parties, found her to have neglected the children and temporarily deprived her of custody, and only returned them to her upon the condition that, when the children were in her custody '[t]hey are not to be subjected to the influence of any boy friend or male companion of the mother.' Therefore the respondent in this proceeding cannot be heard to complain that, she didn't think she was doing anything wrong."

53. 251 Md. 473, 248 A.2d 384 (1968). *See* Appendix, p. 155.

54. *In re* Cager, 251 Md. 473, 498–9, 248 A.2d 384, 398–9 (1968).

55. Brief for Appellants at 11–12, *In re* Cager, 251 Md. 473, 248 A.2d 384 (1968).

56. *In re* Cager, 251 Md. 473, 479, 248 A.2d 384, 388 (1968).

57. *Id.* at 499, 248 A.2d at 399.

58. 255 Cal. App.2d 260, 63 Cal. Rptr. 252 (1967).

59. *Id.* at 267–8, 63 Cal. Rptr. at 256–7.

60. 311 S.W.2d 49 (1958).

61. Mo. Ann. Stat. § 211.310 (1959).

62. State v. Greer, 311 S.W.2d 49, 52 (1958).

63. *Id.*

64. *See* Note, *The Custody Question and Child Neglect Rehearings,* 35 U. Chi. L. Rev. 478 (1968).

65. 187 Pa. Super. 79, 142 A.2d 499 (1958). *See* Appendix, p. 185.

66. *In re* Neff, 187 Pa. Super. 79, 83–4, 142 A.2d 499, 501–2 (1958).

67. *Id.* at 87, 142 A.2d at 503.

68. *Id.* at 88–9, 142 A.2d at 504.

4

Foster Care

When a court separates a child from its biological parents and awards custody to a child welfare agency, the agency usually places the child with foster parents. Eventually, it is thought, the child will be reunited with its biological parents and the natural family relationship reestablished. Since there has been no judicial termination of all the biological parents' rights, both the court and the agency view the disposition as temporary and the legal rights of the natural parents are held in abeyance.[1]

Approximately 200,000 neglected children live with foster families in the United States in any given year.[2] While behavioral scientists have developed a sociological profile of foster care as an institution and a psychological and socioeconomic portrait of foster parents,[3] the legal implications of the foster family setting have received scant consideration. This chapter will deal with these implications.

INSTITUTIONAL ORIGINS AND COMMON LAW BACKGROUND

Little is known about the origins of foster care. Although foster-age was practiced among the Anglo-Saxons, the Welsh, and the Scandinavians, the institution reached its peak of development in ancient Ireland.[4] An examination of the Irish institution reveals a sharp contrast between it and its modern counterpart. Fosterage in ancient Ireland was based on a voluntary contract between natural parents and foster parents, both usually members of the upper class.[5] The goals of the institution were to provide a means of training children and, by forming close bonds between families, to promote social cohesion.[6] Social status was the controlling factor in fosterage. In addition to determining the fee that natural parents were to pay the foster parents,[7] social status determined the legal obligations that attached to the network of relationships established, as well as the nature of the food, clothing, training, and discipline the child was to receive.[8]

Foster care, as the term is generally used today, is quite different from the ancient Irish institution. It is an agency-supervised placement for children, generally from the lower and lower middle classes, whose natural parents are unable to provide them with proper care and who are therefore provided with substitute parents, most often recruited from the lower middle class.[9] Since foster care is theoretically a temporary arrangement, it is generally an alternative to institutional care, with the child receiving the advantages of a family setting[10] and the state benefitting economically.[11]

A foster parent is one who, although not legally related to the child by direct parental blood ties, nor decreed a parent in formal adoption proceedings, assumes the role of a parent. This status most commonly arises when a court awards guardianship and custody of a child to a child welfare agency which in turn delegates the parental role to persons chosen by the agency. Less commonly, foster status may arise in other ways. For example, a court may award guardianship and custody to persons other than the natural or adoptive parents, such as when a divorce court awards custody of a child to an aunt rather than to either of the spouses. Or it may arise as a result of persons who, because of legal defects in an adoption decree, are legally only adoptive parents. Finally, a person may be considered a foster parent if he or she cares for another's child through a formal or informal arrangement or by voluntarily caring for a foundling.

In these situations, the legal rights and duties of foster parents are determined by the common law doctrine of *in loco parentis*. Under this doctrine, persons holding themselves out as parents are held to similar, and often the same, standards as natural parents.[12] Courts use the *in loco parentis* doctrine to impose on foster parents the same responsibilities as natural parents with respect to providing their children with proper health, education, and an environment conducive to the development of sound moral character.

Unless specifically decreed by a court, the parental right to legal custody does not attach to foster parents. In other words, foster parents seem to have more duties than rights. This statement, however, may be misleading, for foster parents do in fact enjoy the right to custody without benefit of the label. A *de facto* custodial interest develops in a foster parent when the foster relationship continues over a period of time. Courts are reluctant to interfere with this interest, and when they attempt to interfere, the foster parent is generally notified and given an opportunity to appear and defend his or her interest.[13] A continuing foster relationship, if secure and orderly, is typically protected against even a natural parent's unreasonable intrusion.[14] A natural parent who wishes to interfere with the foster parent relationship (established in ways other than through court or agency intervention) must, as any other individual, carry the burden of proving the foster parent's unfitness, as well as the burden of showing that the child's needs will be best served by a change in the custodial arrangement.[15]

Under certain conditions, a foster parent may terminate the relationship with a foster child. The most important of these conditions is that the foster parent must intentionally perform a positive act—which ordinarily implies obtaining the consent of all parties in interest—severing all aspects of the relationship.[16] Announcing a decision to terminate the relationship while continuing to live with the child is insufficient.[17] A foster parent may not choose to honor the right to enjoy companionship, for example, and fail in the duty to provide support.[18]

The fact that a person has only a foster relationship with a child will ordinarily not relieve him of the obligation to provide financial support. In enforcing a foster parent's support duty, courts have held that persons acting in the role of natural parents assume the duties of natural parents.[19] Foster parents, therefore, may be required to reimburse those who undertake to support their foster children.[20]

CONTRACTUAL ASPECTS OF THE FOSTER PARENT-CHILD RELATIONSHIP

A distinction must be drawn between the legal implications of the foster parent-child relationship that emerge from the common law doctrine of *in loco parentis* and the foster parent-child relationship created by agencies under court authority. The status of the individual chosen by an agency to become a foster parent hinges on whether the agency deems him to be an employee or whether he is a person simply selected by the agency to perform the function of a foster parent. Foster parents most commonly are not considered employees, but rather are persons unconnected with the agency's organization. Their rights and duties are determined by a placement contract, a standard-form agreement whose provisions are drafted by the agency and acquiesced in by the foster parents. The provisions of the contract normally supersede the common law doctrine of *in loco parentis*.

A further distinction should be drawn between the ostensible expectations of the foster parent-child relationship and the contractual basis which establishes it. As the Child Welfare League of America *Standards for Foster Family Care Service* states:[21]

The ultimate objectives of foster family care should be the promotion of healthy personality development of the child, and amelioration of problems which are personally or socially destructive.

Foster family care is one of society's ways of assuring the well-being of children who would otherwise lack adequate parental care. . . .

Foster family care should provide, for the child whose own parents cannot do so, experiences and conditions which promote normal maturation (*care*), which prevent further injury to the child (*protection*), and which correct specific problems that interfere with healthy personality development (*treatment*). Foster family care should be designed in such a way as:

to maintain and enhance parental functioning to the fullest extent;

to provide the type of care and services best suited to each child's needs;

to minimize and counteract hazards to the child's emotional health inherent in separation from his own family and the conditions leading to it;

to make possible continuity of relationship by preventing replacements;

to facilitate the child's becoming part of the foster family, school, peer group and larger community;

to protect the child from harmful experiences;

to bring about his ultimate return to his natural family whenever desirable and feasible.

These expectations should be compared with the harsh legalistic language in a representative foster care contract:[22]

In consideration of being accepted as foster parents by the Agency we agree as follows:

1. The child placed with us will be accepted by us as a member of our family, and will receive our affection and care as foster parents. The Agency will furnish a monthly board payment, payable at the end of each month. At the time of placement, we will be notified of the specific rate for the child placed with us.

The Agency will provide for the child's clothing, medical and dental expenses.

We will be reimbursed for certain other expenditures made, as described in the Foster Parents' Manual, provided they have been previously authorized by the Agency.

2. We will notify the Agency of any change or plans for change in our own life, which may affect the child placed with us. This will include, but is not limited to vacation plans, illnesses, job changes, moving, and any change in the composition of our family.

3. We will notify the Agency immediately if the child placed with us becomes ill, and we will comply with the Agency's arrangements for medical and dental care.

4. We are aware that the Agency has the responsibility for making plans with regard to the child's relationship with his or her own relatives. We will cooperate with the arrangements made by the

Agency worker for visits between the child and his or her own relatives.

5. We acknowledge that we are accepting the child placed with us for an indeterminate period, depending on the needs of the child and his family situation. We are aware that the legal responsibility for the foster child remains with the Agency, and we will accept and comply with any plans the Agency makes for the child. This includes the right to determine when and how the child leaves us, and we agree to cooperate with the arrangements made toward that end.

6. Should we find ourselves unable to continue giving foster care to the child placed with us, we will notify the Agency promptly, and will cooperate with the Agency in making the change of placement as easy as possible. For this reason, we will give the Agency as much time to make such change as is needed, unless our situation is emergent.

As can be seen from the provisions set forth above, the stated goals of foster care, centering on the welfare of the child, the quality of the foster parent-child relationship, and the preservation of the natural parents' interests, are neither stated nor implied in the contract.

Because of the ambiguities inherent in the attempt to reconcile the goals of foster care programs with the provisions in placement contracts, conflicts inevitably arise between the agency and the foster parents. In resolving these disputes, the agency often asserts the provisions of the contract in support of its position and in opposition to the foster parents' assertion that they are furthering the very goals which foster care programs ostensibly seek to promote. Thus, disputes between agencies and foster parents raise grave doubts as to whether the best interests of the child are the paramount consideration in foster care programs, as well as whether foster parents are, in fact, viewed as "one of the crucial human resources for the care of children who must leave their own homes."[23]

The process by which these disputes are resolved and the considerations that bear upon their resolution are illustrated by the following two cases, *In re Jewish Child Care Association*[24] and *In re Alexander.*[25]

The case of Laura

The history of Laura, the five-and-a-half-year-old whose custody
was at issue in the New York case of *In re Jewish Child Care
Association*, resembles that of many other children similarly involved in the struggle of foster parents to make permanent their
relationship with their foster children over the objections of
placement agencies. When Laura was thirteen months old, she
was placed by the Jewish Child Care Association, a foster care
agency, with Mr. and Mrs. Sanders, a childless couple in their
thirties. Laura's mother, who was eighteen years old and unwed,
had been unable to care for the baby at birth and had voluntarily placed her with the New York City Department of Welfare, which transferred the child's custody to the Jewish Child
Care Association (hereafter referred to as the Agency).

At placement, the Sanderses were required to sign a document in which they accepted the standard conditions of foster
care.[26] Among other things, the couple promised to give Laura
affection and care, to follow the Agency's regulations regarding
the boarding arrangement and any illnesses or changes in the
family situation, and they agreed to cooperate with the Agency's
plans for continuing a relationship with the child's natural
mother. If the couple became unable to continue as foster
parents, they promised to work with the Agency in making an
orderly transition to another placement. The Sanderses acknowledged that they were accepting Laura for an indeterminate
period and were aware that the legal responsibility for the child
remained with the Agency.

During the first year after placement, the Sanderses spoke
with the Agency about adopting Laura. They were told that
adoption was not possible and were asked to help the child
understand her relationship to her natural mother. The child
had seen her natural mother once during the first year of placement. During the second year of foster care, the Sanderses again
mentioned their desire to adopt Laura. The Agency refused to
consider the proposal and required the couple, as a condition
for keeping the child, to sign a statement acknowledging that
they had the child only on a foster home basis. The Sanderses
persisted in their efforts to adopt Laura, unsuccessfully seeking

approval from the child's natural mother, grandmother, and other relatives. When the Sanderses requested permission to take Laura with them on an out-of-state vacation, the Agency refused, asserting that the child should be returned to her natural mother during that time. Laura, then four years old, had lived with the Sanderses for three years and had seen her natural mother only twice. She was not to see her mother again until the litigation over her custody began.

The Sanderses' constant efforts to adopt Laura, along with the Agency's belief that the couple had become too emotionally attached to the child, prompted the Agency to demand Laura's return. The couple refused and the Agency brought a writ of habeas corpus to obtain the child's release from the Sanderses' home. From the perspective of the foster parents, the Agency's decision to seek the writ was potentially beneficial for various reasons. It allowed the Sanderses to bypass administrative remedies and to obtain an immediate judicial review of the Agency's decision denying request for adoption. Considering their strained relations with the Agency, the Sanderses' chances for administrative relief would probably have been slim. Furthermore, since a habeas corpus proceeding is a method by which a court may explore the question of the child's welfare[27] beyond the narrow issue of the legal right to custody,[28] the fact that the Agency was Laura's legal guardian did not place it in a significantly advantageous position.

In the trial court proceedings to determine whether Laura's "best interests" would be served by a custodial change, the testimony was focused on the effect the proposed change would have on the child's natural mother as well as on the child's own physical and emotional well-being. The line of questioning at the trial seemed to be based on the assumption that the goal of the proceedings was to determine how Laura's needs could best be secured in light of the natural mother's inability to raise the child.

The trial judge heard testimony from the foster parents, representatives of the Agency, the Department of Welfare, and a psychiatrist. The Agency acknowledged that the Sanderses had taken good care of the child and were providing her with a comfortable home environment. However, it claimed that, because of the great love of the foster parents for the child, Laura should be removed from their custody and placed in a "neutral environment" where foster parents would be called "aunt" and "uncle" instead of "mother" and "father" and where "there would not be this terrible pull on the child between her loyalty to her foster parents and her mother."[29] In other words, the Agency did not claim that the foster parents were depriving the child of love, but rather that they were indulging her with too much love. The effect of their indulgence on the child, the Agency urged, was a strain on her relationship with her natural mother.

A large part of the trial consisted of the interrogation of a psychiatrist called by the foster parents. In his testimony, he analyzed the effect of a custodial change on Laura's emotional development. In his opinion, the Sanderses' love for the child had positive rather than damaging emotional effects; indeed, Laura's removal from her foster parents would be detrimental to her emotional growth. He stated that latency was a critical period in a child's development and that, at Laura's age, she needed the security of the sustained relationship with her foster parents.

The trial judge apparently either was not sufficiently convinced by the psychiatric testimony or was persuaded by the Agency's argument that the child was becoming too attached to her foster parents, thus threatening her "relationship" with her natural mother. He decided to remove Laura from her foster parents and to allow the Agency to regain custody and place her in a "neutral environment."[30] After the intermediate appellate court affirmed the decision of the trial court,[31] the Sanderses appealed to the New York Court of Appeals, which held in favor of the Agency in a split (4–3) opinion.[32]

In the New York Court of Appeals' opinion, there is a discernible and major shift in emphasis from that found in the lower court's opinion. The trial court viewed the "best interests of the child" doctrine in terms of securing Laura's health needs in light of her natural mother's situation. The New York Court of Appeals interpreted "the best interests of the child" in terms of preserving the continuity of biological family loyalty.

To the majority of the Court of Appeals, the fact that the Sanderses were Laura's foster (rather than natural or future adoptive) parents was crucial. The court perceived foster parenthood as something less than full parenthood. By showing "extreme love," "affection," and "possessiveness" and by acting more like natural than foster parents, the Sanderses, in the court's estimation, had gone beyond the limits of their role as set out in the placement agreement. In essence, what the majority took as conclusive—namely, the "vital fact . . . that Mr. and Mrs. Sanders are not, and presumably will never be, Laura's parents by adoption,"[33]—was the very issue the court was to decide.

The court stressed its concern for preserving the natural ties between Laura and her mother. "[I]n considering what is in Laura's best interests," the court wrote, "it was not only proper, but necessary . . . to consider the facts in terms of their significance to Laura's eventual return to her own mother."[34] And later the court stated:

What is essentially at stake here is the parental custodial right. Although Child Care has the present legal right to custody . . . it stands, as against the Sanders, [*sic*] in a representative capacity as the protector of Laura's mother's inchoate custodial right and the parent-child relationship which is to become complete in the future.[35]

Finally, in its concluding remarks, the court crystallized its views on the best interests of the child as follows:

[T]he more important considerations of the child's best interests, the recognition and preservation of her mother's primary love and custodial interest, and the future life of the mother and child together are paramount.[36]

In addition, the court in *Child Care* was concerned with three considerations, all interrelated (but not necessarily related to the best interests of Laura): the preservation of the natural mother's rights; the sanctity of the placement contract; and the maintenance of the Agency's prestige and authority in the community. In the final remark of his opinion for the Court of Appeals, Chief Judge Conway came to grips with these issues. While the interests of Laura and her natural mother (but apparently not those of the foster parents) were of significant importance, what was paramount was the integrity of the law, as manifested in the child placement contract and in a private agency's administrative decisions. In order to maintain authority, these administrative policies had to be affirmed and the child placement agreement enforced: "[T]he program of agencies such as Child Care . . . may not be subverted by foster parents who breach their trust."[37]

The majority in *Child Care* was concerned with symbols: Judge Conway seemed compelled to preserve the sanctity of legal doctrines and, indirectly, the reputation of a community institution, since the Sanderses had been a threat both to the integrity and the stability of the placement contract[38] and to the prestige of the Agency. To allow Laura to remain with her foster parents would have been to reward persons who failed to fulfill their promises and who had undermined the Agency's decision.[39] It seems that by protecting community institutions, the court shifted its focus from Laura's welfare to other matters: on a jurisprudential level, it was the continuity of legal doctrine; on a practical level, it was the prestige of a social service agency.

Child Care represents a legal struggle between a long-standing and dominant community institution of high prestige and a couple performing a function with low social status.[40] As a consequence, the child's best interests—theoretically the guiding principle in child custody cases—were subverted. Laura experienced two placements in addition to the Sanderses in a two-year period subsequent to the decision.[41] The outcome in *Child Care* is thus in direct contradiction to the theories of those child development specialists who would avoid multiple placements[42] because "the greatest damage to healthy psychological development is instability—and the kinds of impediments that interfere with the process of identity formation."[43]

The case of Michael

Another illustration of the manner in which courts handle attempts by foster parents to adopt the children in their care is *In re Alexander*, a 1968 Florida case involving a two-year-old infant named Michael. Several days after he was born, a Florida Juvenile and Domestic Relations Court committed Michael to the Department of Welfare for subsequent adoption. Immediately after the Department was awarded custody, it placed the infant in the foster care of Mr. and Mrs. Alexander. As a condition of placement, the Alexanders were required to sign a Placement Agreement, stating, among other things, that they would not attempt to adopt the child.[44]

Mr. and Mrs. Alexander were a couple in their late forties who had served as foster parents for the Department on previous occasions. Their annual income was about $5,000. Mr. Alexander held both a full- and part-time job. They lived in a modest home, neat and well kept. Although Mr. and Mrs. Alexander had no natural children of their own, Mrs. Alexander had four sons, ages twenty-three, twenty-eight, thirty, and thirty-four, by her first marriage. None of Mrs. Alexander's sons had completed high school. All except the youngest seemed to be having difficulties of one kind or another. At the time of this proceeding, Mrs. Alexander was a grandmother.

Mr. Alexander refused to allow his wife to work outside the home. Mrs. Alexander stated that as a consequence, she was limited to child rearing as a means of occupying her time; otherwise she would feel "restless" as well as unproductive. The role of a foster mother provided her with an opportunity to satisfy her own needs, including her maternal needs, and at the same time meet her husband's demands.[45]

During the two years that Michael lived with the Alexanders, Mr. and Mrs. Alexander sought to obtain the approval of the Department to adopt him. They were told that adoption was not possible because of the Placement Agreement which stated that they would not try to adopt the child,[46] and they were requested to return Michael to the Department. On advice of their counsel, the Alexanders surrendered the infant and the

Department immediately placed him in another foster home. The Alexanders then sought the advice of another lawyer, and when he urged them to resume their adoption efforts, the case was heard in a court located in the same county as the Department.

At the trial court level, the case raised the issue of the power of the Department to exclude the Alexanders from adopting Michael. This question was framed in terms of the necessity of the Department's consent to the adoption and the extent to which the Placement Agreement was to be enforced. Ancillary to these considerations was the question of whether the child's best interests would be served by the adoption. The Department argued the case principally on the technical legal issues of contract and procedural law. It urged the enforcement of the placement agreement, seeking thereby to oust the court from jurisdiction over the case. Alternatively, it raised the unsuitability of the Alexanders as adoptive parents, pointing to the fact that they were older than most adoptive couples and that their financial situation was not as secure as the Department would demand. The Alexanders argued that the Department, through its contract with them, could neither deprive the court of its right and duty to determine the child's best interests nor withhold its consent to the adoption. They also argued that they were fit parents for Michael.

The trial court decided in favor of the Alexanders. In a brief opinion, it upheld their contention that a welfare department could not divest the court of its inherent power to determine the ultimate best interests of a child, even though, as a legal matter, the authority to deal with the child on a day-to-day basis had been delegated to the Department.[47]

Subsequent to the decision of the trial court, the case received wide publicity in the local papers.[48] Thus, when the Department ultimately appealed the case, it was faced not only with the necessity of overcoming legal obstacles, but also with the problem of strong local prejudice in favor of the Alexanders. The focus of the newspaper articles was naturally on the emotional aspects of the case. They stressed the personal qualifications of the Alexanders and their professed love for the child in contrast to the rigid bureaucratic position of the Department. The newspapers printed the opinions of local officials who portrayed the Welfare Department as cold blooded and "all knowing" and quoted a school principal as saying that "welfare workers had no concern for the welfare of children and their custody, and the only interest they have is in their rules."[49]

It is difficult to believe that these reports did not influence the appeals court when it decided to affirm the trial court by adopting its findings in toto.[50] Unlike some situations, for example *Child Care,* where the appeals court was removed physically and perhaps emotionally from local pressures, the appeals court in *Alexander* was located in the same community as the disputing parties—the Department, the foster parents, and the foster child.

The facts in *Alexander* represent the usual situation in cases where foster parents seek to adopt children placed in their care. However, because of the wide publicity given the case, it would not be fair to say that the court's disposition was truly representative. Nevertheless, it is possible to appraise the factors which probably influenced the decisionmaking process in both the court and the Department.

There are several aspects of the Department's handling of the case that violate basic precepts of child placement. Most importantly, the Department failed to implement the principle of continuity of care by immediately placing Michael in a permanent situation.[51] The Department knew when Michael was committed to it that the natural mother had given up all claims to the infant. Indeed, the court committed the infant to the Department for adoption. Nevertheless, instead of immediately seeking an adoptive couple for Michael, the Department placed him with the Alexanders, a couple chosen by foster care rather than adoption standards, and who were clearly informed that the arrangement was only temporary. It is difficult to understand why the Department chose this course of action, since none of the factors which would normally justify an interim placement prior to adoption—a child hard to place by virtue of its age or race, illness, legal complications, and so on[52] —was present in this case. Unfortunately, it is not uncommon for child welfare agencies to take this course of action and compound the error by allowing the temporary arrangement to continue indefinitely.

As was also the case in *Child Care,* the Department in *Alexander* used foster parents as boarding parents and was oblivious to the fact that emotional ties must inevitably develop between a child and its foster parents after years of living together. In each case the attachment should have been predictable. The Sanderses were a young childless couple eager to adopt a child; Mrs. Alexander was a woman known to have strong maternal needs. By resurrecting the Placement Agreement, the agencies in both cases sought to regain control over the situation and to give "law" precedence over normal human responses.

The result in *Alexander* is, or should be, more typical than that in *Child Care.* Theoretically, the court's role in child custody cases is that of *parens patriae.* As such, the court has a responsibility to make an independent examination of the facts to determine the best interests of the child. The courts in *Child Care* abdicated this responsibility and rested their decision on the Agency's findings. The courts in *Alexander,* on the other hand (if one disregards the possibility of publicity affecting their decisions), attempted at least to make an independent inquiry, and did not use the existence of the Placement Agreement as an excuse for failing to do so, as the courts in *Child Care* seem to have done. If the courts in *Child Care* and *Alexander* had affirmatively sought to promote the best interests of Laura and Michael, they would have balanced a fundamental principle of child development—continuity of care—against the alleged limitations as adoptive parents of the Sanderses—emotional overinvolvement—and the Alexanders—age and financial insecurity. Whether consideration of this principle would have altered the results in these cases is difficult to say, but a proper inquiry would at least have been made, and the responsibility of the courts to the children fulfilled.[53]

SUMMARY

In contrast to the ancient Irish institution of fosterage, which promoted social cohesion among upper class families, modern foster care is primarily a lower and lower middle class phenomenon which attempts to provide a substitute family for children whose natural parents have neglected them. With the placement of a child in a foster family, a network of complex relationships is established among the parties involved: the placement agency, the natural parents, the foster parents, and the child.

Unlike adoption, where a natural parent's legal ties to the child are completely severed, foster care is intended to be a temporary measure—a hiatus in the total relationship of a child with its natural parents which leaves the legal status of the foster parent and the foster child ambivalent. The intended temporary nature of foster care should be emphasized. From a theoretical perspective, foster care is designed to be a nonpermanent arrangement, and as a consequence, standards for choosing temporary custodians differ from those for permanent custodians. Experience has shown that to assume nonpermanence in foster care is unrealistic. Children placed in foster care remain in that status longer than is generally admitted by many placement agencies. Yet some agencies have not changed their conceptions about foster care or foster parents. They continue to hold foster parents and children in a state of limbo while jealously guarding biological ties. Their protection of the natural parent's rights often represents a misplaced loyalty and is sometimes simply a rationalization for the agency's own decisions.

The cases of *In re Jewish Child Care Association* and *In re Alexander* illustrate the seemingly inevitable trend toward long-term placements. In both cases the placements were intended to be temporary, although in *Alexander* the child was available for adoption when the Department gained guardianship and custody. In both cases, by allowing the foster parents to establish strong emotional ties with the foster children, the agencies required the foster parents to assume roles that were almost inherently contradictory. The Sanderses and the Alexanders were expected to be substitute parents, providing everything that natural parents should provide, but to do so without themselves forming emotional attachments.

Both cases also illustrate another inconsistent attitude taken by agencies toward foster parents. On the one hand, agencies ask that foster couples care for a neglected child as they would their own. On the other hand, agencies attempt to maintain ultimate control over the foster parent-child relationship, basing their authority on the fact that a court has committed a child to them. They emphasize that once a court has entrusted a child to their care, they are legally responsible for the child and answerable to the court. In practice, however, when a court grants the guardianship and custody of a child to an agency, the court neither oversees the process and standards by which the agency chooses foster parents, nor does it thoroughly or frequently review foster care placements.

Foster parents, however, are not as totally devoid of power as agencies sometimes assume. Not only does physical custody of a child give the foster parents certain legal advantages, but the doctrine of *in loco parentis* gives them something of a legal identity. A foster parent may be limited by a placement contract, but these contracts do not necessarily set the actual legal dimensions of his authority.

If foster care is used exclusively as a short-term living arrangement for a neglected child whose ultimate reunion with its natural parents is intended, it provides an agency, conscientiously seeking to promote the child's best interests, with an additional placement alternative to be used where natural care is temporarily undesirable and adoption inappropriate. When, however, foster care is used to provide a temporary home for a child eligible for adoption, it loses its unique properties and in fact often operates to defeat the child's best interests by breaking the continuity of care.

NOTES

1. Court intervention usually involves withdrawing a natural parent's custodial rights. While this does not disturb the reciprocal inheritance rights of the child and its natural parents, it does affect the child's rights under certain legislation. *See* E. duFresne, *The Rights of Foster Children to Financial Benefits of Foster Parents Under Federal Statutes,* 7 J. Fam. L. 613 (1968).

An interesting question is whether a natural parent could recover for the wrongful death of his natural child when that child is in the foster care of another as a result of court intervention. Or conversely, whether such a foster child could recover for the wrongful death of its natural parent.

2. S. Low, Foster Care of Children—Major National Trends and Prospects, U. S. Department of Health, Education, and Welfare, Children's Bureau 1–2 (1966). "An estimated 287,200 children were living in foster care throughout the United States on March 31, 1965, either in foster family homes served by social agencies or in child welfare institutions for neglected, dependent, and emotionally disturbed children. The rate of children in foster care was 4.0 per 1,000 children under 18 years of age in the U. S. population. This estimate does not include a large, but unknown, number of children living in 'independent' foster family homes who were placed by parents, relatives or others without the assistance of a social agency. Nor does it include a much smaller, but also unknown number of children placed directly in foster family homes by juvenile courts (a practice that occurs to a significant extent only in a few States) or placed by other agencies that do not report to the Children's Bureau.

º   º   º

"Assuming that the rate will continue to change in the direction and at the pace at which it was changing during the 1961–65 period, the number of children in foster care in 1975 is projected to be 364,000, a 27 percent increase over 1965 or an annual increase of about 2 percent. The 1975 rate is estimated at 4.7 per 1,000 children.

º   º   º

"The number of children in foster family homes on March 31, 1965, is estimated at 207,800, a rate of 2.9 per 1,000 children."

3. *See* D. Fanshel, Foster Parenthood (1966); E. Weinstein, The Self-Image of the Foster Child (1960); M. Wolins & I. Piliavin, Institution or Foster Family (1967); C. Babcock, *Some Psychodynamic Factors in Foster Parenthood* (pts. 1–2), 44 Child Welfare 485, 570 (Nov. 1965, Dec. 1965); D. Taylor & P. Starr, *Foster Parenting: An Integrative Review of the Literature,* 46 Child Welfare 371 (July 1967).

4. W. Hancock & T. O'Mahony, *Preface* to 2 Ancient Laws and Institutes of Ireland, *Senchus Mor,* Part II, XLVI (1869).

5. P. Joyce, 2 A Social History of Ancient Ireland 14 (1913).

6. *Id.* at 17.

7. Commission for Publishing the Ancient Laws and Institutes of Ireland, 2 Ancient Laws and Institutes of Ireland, *Senchus Mor* 151–5, Part II (1869).

8. *Id.* at 149–51.

9. *See* Fanshel, *supra* note 3, at 23–7, 54–7; Taylor & Starr, *supra* note 3, at 377–9.

10. *See* S. Provence & R. Lipton, Infants in Institutions 143–66 (1962).

11. It is well known that the cost of maintaining a child in an institution far exceeds the cost of maintaining it in a foster family. For example, in Massachusetts it costs approximately seven times more per week to maintain a child in an institution than in a foster family.

12. Schneider v. Schneider, 25 N.J. Misc. 180, 52 A.2d 564 (Ch. 1947).

13. *See In re* Adoption of Cheney, 244 Iowa 1180, 59 N.W.2d 685 (1953). *Contra,* James V. McLinden, Civil No. 13127 (D. Conn., filed May 23, 1969).

14. *See* Cummins v. Bird, 230 Ky. 296, 19 S.W.2d 959 (1929).

15. *See* State v. Knight, 135 So.2d 126 (La. App. 1961).

16. *See, e.g.,* Lewis v. United States, 105 F. Supp. 73 (N.D. W.Va., (1952); Leyerly v. United States, 162 F.2d 79 (10th Cir. 1947); Young v. Hipple, 273 Pa. 439, 117 A. 185 (1922).
The fact that a foster parent may terminate his relationship with his foster child more freely than either a natural or adoptive parent was used as the basis for applying less rigid standards for removing the foster child from the custody of its foster parents in State *ex rel.* Gilman, 249 Iowa 1233, 1238–39, 91 N.W.2d 395, 399 (1958): "The importance of the difference of the status of a natural or adoptive parent, on the one hand, and one merely standing in loco parentis, as in the case before us, is found in the fact that the defendant has made no attempt to adopt [his six-year-old foster child] during the several years he had custody of the child. He is still free to disavow his responsibility as a parent at any time. We do not say he has such an intent; but the right to do so and the possibility are there.
"Viewing the entire picture, we think the trial court was amply justified in holding that the best interest of the child requires that the defendant be permanently deprived of custody, and the boy sent to a child-placing institution. From there he may eventually be placed in the home of suit-

able adopting parents, where he will have not only food, clothing and shelter, and love and affection, but security, with freedom from constant shifting about and from the uncertainties and unfavorable influences to which he has heretofore been subjected."

17. *See* Capek v. Kropik, 129 Ill. 509, 21 N.E. 826 (1889); Schneider v. Schneider, 25 N.J. Misc. 180, 52 A.2d 564 (Ch. 1947).

18. That there is a duty to support under these circumstances is evident from public welfare law. The "man-in-the-house" rule, or, as it is sometimes called, the "substitute parent" policy, was stated in *People v. Shirley*, 55 Cal. 2d 521, 524, 360 P.2d 33, 34 (1961): "[U]nder regulations of the State Board of Social Welfare a stepfather living in the home is responsible for the support of the mother of a needy child unless incapacitated and unable to support. . . . A man living in the home assuming the role of spouse has the same responsibility as that of a stepfather for the mother and the needy children." *See also* N. Pacht, *Support of Defendants in the District of Columbia: Part I*, 9 How. L. J. 20, 36–38 (1963); J. tenBroek, *California's Dual System of Family Law: Its Origin, Development, and Present Status, Part III*, 17 Stan. L. Rev. 614 (1965).

19. *In re* Harris, 16 Ariz. 1, 140 P. 825 (1914); Howard v. Randolph, 134 Ga. 691, 68 S.E. 586 (1910); Faber v. Industrial Comm., 352 Ill. 115, 185 N.E. 255 (1933); Foreman v. Henry, 87 Okla. 272, 210 P. 1026 (1922); Rosky v. Schmitz, 110 Wash. 547, 188 P. 493 (1920); Ellis v. Cary, 74 Wis. 176, 42 N.W. 252 (1889). *See also In re* Adoption of Cheney, 244 Iowa 1180, 59 N.W.2d 685 (1953); Britt v. Allred, 199 Miss. 786, 25 So.2d 560 (1946); Hollis v. Thomas, 42 Tenn. App. 407, 303 S.W.2d 751 (1957); State *ex rel.* Gilroy v. Superior Court, 37 Wash. 2d 926, 226 P.2d 882 (1951).

20. *See* Rudd v. Fineberg's Trustee, 277 Ky. 505, 126 S.W.2d 1102 (1939).

21. Child Welfare League of America, Standards for Foster Family Care Service 6–7 (1959).

22. Cited in J. Goldstein & J. Katz, The Family and the Law 1021–22 (1965).

23. P. Hall, *Foreword to* D. Fanshel, Foster Parenthood v (1966).

24. 5 N.Y.2d 222, 183 N.Y.S.2d 65, 156 N.E.2d 700 (1959). *See* Appendix, p. 193.

25. 206 So.2d 452 (Fla. 1968). *See* Appendix, p. 210.

26. *See* note 22 and accompanying text.

27. *See, e.g.,* New York *ex rel.* Halvey v. Halvey, 330 U.S. 610 (1947); Berry v. Berry, 219 Ala. 403, 122 So. 615 (1929); Porter v. Chester, 208 Ga. 309, 66 S.E.2d 729 (1951); Heuvel v. Heuvel, 254 Iowa 1391, 121 N.W.2d 216 (1963). Even the matter of child support may be explored. *Cf.* Howarth v. Northcutt, 152 Conn. 460, 208 A.2d 540 (1965) with Buchanan v. Buchanan, 170 Va. 458, 197 S.E. 426 (1938); Pugh v. Pugh, 133 W.Va. 501, 56 S.E.2d 901 (1949). But some jurisdictions limit the court's inquiry on habeas corpus to the narrow issue of the legal right to custody. *See, e.g.,* May v. Anderson, 345 U.S. 528 (1953) (Ohio).

28. *See* New York Foundling Hosp. v. Gatti, 203 U.S. 429 (1906); Pukas v. Pukas, 129 W.Va. 765, 42 S.E.2d 11 (1947).

29. 5 N.Y.2d 222, 227, 156 N.E.2d 700, 702, 183 N.Y.S.2d 65, 68 (1959).

30. Jewish Child Care Ass'n v. Sanders, 9 Misc.2d 402, 172 N.Y.S.2d 630 (Sup. Ct. 1957), *aff'd,* 174 N.Y.S.2d 335 (App. Div. 1958), *aff'd,* 156 N.E.2d 700, 183 N.Y.S.2d 65 (Ct. App. 1959).

31. *Id.* The basis of the New York Supreme Court's opinion was as follows: "Respondents have, the court feels, become fond of the child to an extent which has resulted in an attempt by them to induce the mother to permit adoption by them; she has resisted these efforts and the conflict has resulted in this proceeding. The petitioner believes (quite correctly in the court's opinion) that it cannot suffer its established practice to be set at naught solely because respondents believe they can contribute more to the child's welfare than petitioner and the mother can. "The court does not believe that the best interest of this child will be served by the condonation of a disregard of their own obligations and agreements by the respondents, however well-intentioned they may be." Id. at 403, 172 N.Y.S.2d at 631.

32. 5 N.Y.2d 222, 156 N.E.2d 700, 183 N.Y.S.2d 65 (1959).

33. *Id.* at 229, 156 N.E.2d at 703, 183 N.Y.S.2d at 70.

34. *Id.* at 228, 156 N.E.2d at 703, 183 N.Y.S.2d at 69.

35. *Id.* at 229, 156 N.E.2d at 703, 183 N.Y.S.2d at 70.

36. *Id.* at 230, 156 N.E.2d at 704, 183 N.Y.S.2d at 71.

37. 5 N.Y.2d 222, 230, 156 N.E.2d 700, 704, 183 N.Y.S.2d 65 (1959).

38. *But see* note 45 *infra* and accompanying text.

39. Subsequent to this case, another dispute between foster parents and an agency arose. After much publicity, the agency relented and the child was allowed to remain with her foster parents. *See In re* St. John, 51 Misc.2d 96, 272 N.Y.S.2d 817 (Family Ct. 1966), *rev'd sub nom.* Fitzsimmons v. Liuni, 26 App. Div.2d 980, 274 N.Y.S.2d 798 (3d Dep't 1966), *commented on* in H. Foster & D. Freed, *Family Law*, 19 Syracuse L. R. 478, 479, 489–91 (1967); H. Foster & D. Freed, *Children and the Law*, 1966 Annual Survey of American Law 649, 660–61. *See* Appendix, pp. 212–246.

Apparently in response to the *Liuni* case, the New York State Legislature passed the following act: "Any adult husband and his adult wife and any adult unmarried person, who, as foster parent or parents, have cared for a child continuously for a period of two years or more, may apply to such authorized agency for the placement of said child with them for the purpose of adoption, and if said child is eligible for adoption, the agency shall give preference and first consideration to their application over all other applications for adoption placements. However, final determination of the propriety of said adoption of such foster child shall be within the sole discretion of the court, as otherwise provided herein." N.Y. Soc. Welfare Law § 383.3 (McKinney Supp. 1969).

40. D. Crystal, *What Keeps Us from Giving Children What We Know They Need?* 37 The Social Service Review 136, 137 (1953): "The plain fact is that foster-parenthood in our society—that is, being associated with a social agency for the purpose of rearing other people's children—evokes a series of negative associations in the mind of the public. . . . To be a foster-parent is to invite immediate practical questions from friends and neighbors as to economic motive, primarily, and in a sense to take on the stigma attached to being the recipient of 'welfare.' "

41. *See* Goldstein & Katz, *supra* note 22, at 1033–34.

42. A. Freud, *Psychoanalytic Knowledge and Its Application to Children's Services*, 5 The Writings of Anna Freud: 1956–1965, 468 (1969).

43. L. Rapoport, *Safeguarding the Child's Best Interests: A Discussion* (unpublished paper presented at the American Orthopsychiatric Association Meeting, San Francisco, April 13, 1966). *See also* A. Freud, *supra* Ch. 3, note 3.

44. The Placement Agreement stated simply, "No action for adoption or guardianship may be taken." Brief for Appellant, Appendix at 1.

45. *Id.* at 2–4.

46. The legal enforceability of a statement of this kind was at issue in *Adoption of McDonald*, 43 Cal.2d 447, 274 P.2d 860 (1954). In that case, foster parents signed an agreement with an adoption agency which included, among other provisions, a requirement that any request for adoption of the child placed with them had to be approved by the agency, and a stipulation that if after one year the agency was satisfied with the training of the child and the character of the foster parents' home, it would allow the adoption. The agreement further provided that the agency had the right to remove the child previous to legal adoption if at any time the circumstances warranted it. About eight months after the placement of the child, the foster father committed suicide. Later the agency demanded the return of the child. The foster mother refused to give up the child and petitioned a court for adoption without securing the agency's consent. The trial court granted the adoption, having concluded that the agency's consent was unnecessary.

One of the arguments which the agency made in its appeal to the California Supreme Court was that the foster mother was estopped from pursuing the adoption by virtue of the agreement she and her husband signed at the time of placement. Addressing himself to this argument, Justice Traynor wrote: "The [State] department [of Social Welfare] . . . has no power by regulation or otherwise to add to or detract from the rules for adoption prescribed in the Civil Code. . . . Thus, neither appellant, the department, the county agency, nor any private agency had the right by regulation or by agreement to deprive petitioner of the rights granted her by section 226 of the Civil Code to petition the court and have the court determine whether the petition should not be granted. If the department could give a licensed agency the right to control the adoption of a relinquished child, it could give such an agency the right to control the adoption of any child not subject to parental control. The statutory provisions governing adoption cannot be so circumvented.

"In a proceeding such as this the child is the real party in interest and is not a party to any agreement. It is the welfare of this child that controls, and any agreement others may have made for its custody is made subject to the court's independent judgment as to what is for the best interests of the child." *Id.* at 461, 274 P.2d at 868; *see also* Cal. Civ. Code § 224(n) (Supp. 1964).

47. *In re* Adoption, No. 155465–C (Fla. Cir. Ct., March 24, 1967). *See* Appendix, p. 204.

48. Tampa Times, May 3, 1967, at 2, cols. 1–8; April 28, 1967, at 4, cols. 3–7; April 27, 1967, at 2A, cols. 1–8; Mar. 29, 1967, at 3, cols. 1–8.

49. Tampa Times, May 1, 1967.

50. For a discussion of the effects of mass media on child custody deci-

sions, *see* S. Katz, *Community Decision-makers and the Promotion of Values in the Adoption of Children,* 38 The Social Service Review 26, 37–39 (1964).

51. "Adoptive home placement is an important approach in providing maternal care as early as possible. The need for a permanent home early in the child's life cannot be overemphasized. The trend toward adoptive placements in the early weeks of life is increasing and has many advantages both for the infant and for the adoptive parents." S. Provence & R. Lipton, Infants in Institutions 164 (1962).

52. *See* A. Freud, *Cindy,* in Goldstein & Katz, *supra* note 22, at 1051–53.

53. "Too often the courts have permitted themselves to become actors in a ceremony of official approval for whatever is being done or left undone for neglected children. Without sufficient or qualified staff to discover the needs of and the possibilities for children placed with foster agencies, the voluminous files loom larger than the child. The court is not made aware of the separation of siblings, the failure to work with the parents, and the failure to institute legal action on behalf of the child to free him for adoption and is given only a brief statement on why the child should be continued in placement. The lack of appropriate service by the social agencies, thus sanctioned and subsidized by court action, condemns countless children to emotionally arid lives." J. Polier, The Role of Law and The Role of Psychiatry 119 (1968).

5

Adoption

Practices similar to adoption have existed since the Biblical era. Although adoption as such has been recognized at law since Roman times, it was not a part of the English law because of the great importance the common law placed on blood ties in the inheritance of real property. Consequently, there is no common law of adoption, and the laws relating to adoption in the United States are purely statutory in origin.

The first American jurisdiction to enact legislation on adoption comparable to the modern form was Massachusetts, in 1851, although Louisiana and Texas, whose laws were strongly influenced by the Roman civil law, had recognized the practice earlier.[1] In those two states, the principal motivation behind the laws was the same as that behind their Roman counterparts: the providing of heirs. That motivation seems also to have been present generally in the other early statutes passed in the common law jurisdictions. In these statutes, however, the primary concern appears to have been to acknowledge and provide public records of private acts. Not until much later were the interests of the child considered by the legislatures.

Early judicial decisions in adoption matters reflected a concern for the child's welfare that was not apparent in adoption legislation of the same period. For example, a Massachusetts court observed in 1856 that "[adoption] is not a question of mere property, . . . the interest of the minor is the principal thing to be considered."[2]

As the emphasis in adoption has shifted from the inheritance of wealth toward social factors, the process of adoption has grown increasingly complex. Today public regulation of adoption—a process which little more than a century ago was not even afforded legislative recognition—is accepted as a matter of course. Concern over providing a neglected child with a family in which it will be fully integrated and be able to develop into a healthy and responsible adult has led to the intimate involvement of major community institutions, principally social service agencies and courts, in a formerly private matter.

This chapter will undertake to analyze the adoption process as it exists in the United States today, focusing in particular on questions relating to the termination of the rights of the natural parents and the selection process whereby the adoptive parent-child relationship is established.

TERMINATION OF NATURAL PARENTS' RIGHTS

Unlike the foster parent-child relationship, which is temporary in nature, the adoptive parent-child relationship is intended to be permanent and comes into existence only upon the absolute termination of the rights of the natural parents. This termination may be involuntary or may be with the consent of the natural parents, either implied or expressed.

Many states require that the natural parents give written consent to an adoption. Such consent must usually be acknowledged and appropriately witnessed. These requirements are designed to ensure that the natural parents are aware of the importance of the consenting act. The belief is that such formalities will probably help deter the natural parents from making a hasty and improvident decision, and will protect them from fraud, coercion, and overreaching. Some states require that the consent of a parent who is a minor must be accompanied by the consent of the minor's parents or guardian.[3] The District of Columbia[4] and several states,[5] however, take the position that minority is not a bar to consent.

Apart from those instances where adoption is predicated on the express consent of the natural parents, most jurisdictions recognize that there are some situations where express consent is not required. In those situations, consent is either implied on the basis of neglectful conduct on the part of the natural parent, or dispensed with entirely on the basis of conduct or occurrences which, while involuntary, have the same consequences toward the child as neglectful conduct.

Termination by implied consent

In some situations, even though the consent of the natural parents has been neither expressly given nor expressly dispensed with, the actions of the natural parent are construed as constituting implied consent to the adoption of the child. Although various terms have been used to describe this situation, the general term "abandonment" encompasses all of them. Abandonment has been variously defined as conduct of the natural parents renouncing the parental relationship,[6] "refusal to perform the natural and legal obligations of care and support,"[7] or the withholding of love, care, and the opportunity to display filial affections.[8] The courts have generally held that for conduct of the natural parents to constitute abandonment, it must be intentional.[9] Moreover, some jurisdictions have statutes which specify that conditions which can constitute abandonment must continue for a certain period of time before such a finding can be justified.[10]

The usual situation which results in a judicial finding of abandonment is where the parent leaves the child permanently or indefinitely in the care of others, making little or no effort to support it.[11] It is not necessary that the parent physically abandon the child. It is sufficient that his or her conduct indicate a total lack of interest in the child's welfare. As one court has stated:

> The mother did not, it is true, leave her child on a door step, but . . . [w]hen the appellant asserted that she did not want the baby and that she "wanted" to be done with the matter "as quickly as possible," when she did everything she could do to conceal the child's very birth, and herself hid behind a false name, and when thereafter she returned to Canada and for almost a year manifested not the slightest interest in the welfare of the child [her] . . . callous disregard for her child, [and] her complete indifference to how he was faring . . . constituted . . . abandonment. . . .[12]

Another court employed similar reasoning when a mother attempted to defeat the adoption efforts of the persons with whom she had left her illegitimate child. The record indicated that the mother had attempted unsuccessfully to abort the child; that when it was born she had lied about its relationship to her; and that subsequently she had placed it with others, visiting it only infrequently and still not disclosing its true identity. It was held that since she had abandoned the child, her consent to the adoption was unnecessary. The court caustically observed that the mother's "entire contact with the child [was] characterized by efforts to get rid of him."[13] She had pretended, said the court, that she "merely acted as an agent for some unknown parent in finding a refuge for the child."[14]

Abandonment has also been found to exist when a divorced parent deprived of custody has not exercised his visitation rights or made an effort to support the child. The courts have tended to treat this situation, evidencing a general lack of interest in the child's welfare, as an "abandonment."[15]

In some instances, a parent "abandons" the child but within a reasonable time thereafter resumes his or her parental duties. In these cases the courts have treated the parent's resumption of duties toward the child as repentance, and have revoked or terminated the abandonment,[16] at least where the repentance has been something more than a mere mental intent and has in fact been manifested in the resumption of parental responsibilities.[17]

Involuntary termination without consent

The most obvious situation that results in the involuntary termination of the natural parent-child relationship, without regard to the parents' either expressed or implied intention, is death. Others are incurable mental illness, life imprisonment ("civil death"), imprisonment for an extended period, and, in some instances, divorce.[18] Of these, only mental illness has given rise to a significant amount of litigation.

Most jurisdictions allow children of the mentally disabled to be adopted without their parent's consent[19] on the theory that a person suffering from mental disease is incapable of giving consent.[20] The constitutionality of such a statutory provision was passed on by the Illinois Supreme Court in *People ex rel. Nabstedt* v. *Barger*.[21] There the statute required that the parent's consent could be dispensed with if he or she had been mentally ill for a period of three years, and two qualified physicians selected by the court testified that the parent was not expected to recover in the foreseeable future.[22] The statute further authorized court appointment of a guardian *ad litem* to represent the parent and consent to the adoption. The Illinois court held that the Fourteenth Amendment's due-process-of-law requirement was not denied the parent by such a proceeding, even though the parent's relatives had not been given notice of its pendency, and even though there was a possibility that the parent might be restored to good health and reason but yet be unable to regain the custody and companionship of the child.

The statute sustained by the court in *Nabstedt* would seem to represent a satisfactory solution to one of the grave questions relating to the status of the mentally ill. Admittedly, it is unfair to a parent to give a court the power to take away the child when the parent might regain his or her health within a reasonable period of time. On the other hand, it is neither reasonable nor fair to an adoptable child to put it in an institution, in the temporary custody of relatives, or in foster care pending its parent's uncertain recovery from mental illness.

To protect the rights of a mentally ill parent, it would seem essential that the parental disability be hopeless or incurable. The problem is to determine the extent and duration of the natural parent's illness. To this end, a finding of incurability, based on some extended preexisting period of disability and corroborated by competent medical testimony as to its likely continuation, should be required. These limitations were met in *Nabstedt* through the testimony of court-appointed physicians and the statutory provision fixing the period of disability at three years. This approach is generally followed elsewhere,[23] although a few states[24] do not require an incurable affliction before dispensing with the consent of the mentally disabled parent.[25]

The *Nabstedt* case also illustrates another needed protection for the natural parent, namely, the appointment of a guardian, *guardian ad litem,* or "next friend," who acts for the parent to give or withhold consent.[26] Only with such a provision is the mentally ill parent assured of proper representation in the termination or adoption proceedings. Without such a provision all other protective devices, such as the incurable affliction requirement, could be rendered meaningless.

In its study of the mentally disabled and the law, the American Bar Foundation questioned the protection which adoption proceedings afforded natural parents afflicted with mental illness. It called for court-appointed counsel as one of several approaches to the problem.[27] However, this is a partial solution at best, since more than one party's interest is involved. Protection must be afforded not only the rights of the natural parents, but those of the child as well. An answer can be found only by balancing these representative interests and affording the maximum reasonable safeguards to the parents while bearing in mind the modern notion of adoption as a means of assuring the child's best interests.

Withdrawal of consent

Legislatures and courts have assumed a variety of positions regarding withdrawal of parental consent to an adoption.[28] At one extreme is the rule that consent, once given, is thereafter absolutely irrevocable unless fraud or duress can be shown.[29] At the other extreme are those cases which indicate that parental consent is absolutely revocable until the final decree of adoption is issued.[30]

Most American jurisdictions[31] now take a position between these two extremes.[32] Only Florida and Illinois appear to cling to the rule that consent is absolutely irrevocable.[33] Minnesota, formerly a leading jurisdiction in applying the absolute-right-of-revocation rule,[34] has embraced a discretionary rule by statute.[35] Other representative state statutes provide that parental consent, once given, "may not be revoked by the parents as a matter of right";[36] that the adoption petition may be granted without parental consent if such consent is withheld "contrary to the best interests of the child";[37] that the natural parents have sixty days after the giving of consent within which to seek the court's permission to revoke it;[38] and that consent is revocable in the discretion of the court until the interlocutory decree is issued.[39]

In evaluating the merits of these various positions, it must be remembered that here, as in other areas of adoption law, there are three parties involved—the natural parents, the adoptive parents, and the child—all of whose rights and well-being must be considered. While natural parents should have an opportunity to maintain their relationship with their child, to give them the absolute right to revoke consent at any time, or even within a limited time at their unrestricted election, would operate to the detriment of the parties involved in the adoption. With the threat of the natural parents' revocation hanging over the adoptive parents, a smooth transition to the adoptive parent-child relationship would be difficult and might have a detrimental effect on the adoptive parents' relationship with their adoptive child. Furthermore, the adoptive child might suffer as well, since shifts in environment stemming from the changes in the natural parents' position might cause serious psychological problems by disrupting the continuity of care. Finally, to give the natural parents an unfettered right of revocation, even for a limited time, could provide them with the power to choose between contesting sets of adoptive parents[40] or, conceivably, to extort money from the adoptive parents in return for a promise not to revoke consent.[41]

Illegitimacy

Illegitimacy presents a special situation. Generally, in the case of illegitimate children, the consent of the mother only[42] is required. Since paternal rights never attached to the father, there is no question of their termination. Rather, the question is whether the consent of a person to whom legal parental rights never attached should be required.

Statutes that dispense with the consent of the father constitute an exception to the general provision that both of the "living parents" of a child must consent to that child's adoption.[43] Failure to distinguish between the rule and the exception has led some courts into an erroneous position regarding the central problem in this area—the situation where a child is legitimatized *after* the previously unmarried mother has given her consent to its adoption.

The better reasoning is to be found in those cases which permit the father's legitimation of his child to operate retroactively so that his assent becomes necessary.[44] So long as the child has been legitimatized before the adoption has taken place, the statutory provision requiring the assent of both living parents to the child's adoption should be controlling. What is important is the establishment of a father-child relationship. When such a relationship has been established by the father's legitimation, the father's interest in that relationship and his rights to his child should not be taken from him without his consent. Moreover, the important question is not whether he has established a "legal" father-child relationship, but rather whether he has established a "positive" father-child relationship. This is the point missed by those cases which reason that since it is expressly provided that the consent of the mother only is sufficient, once her consent is given, that of the father becomes unnecessary.[45] It seems clear that the purpose of such provisions is to deal with those situations where the father is unknown, and to prevent a father who accepts no responsibility and feels no concern for his child from capriciously preventing the child's adoption. To apply such a provision to a case where the child has been legally legitimatized, or where a "positive" though not "legal" father-child relationship has been established, is to extend it to a situation where it was not meant to apply.

THE ROLE OF AGENCIES

Where the rights of the natural parents are involuntarily terminated, almost invariably the child is given to a child welfare agency for subsequent placement. Placement with a child welfare agency is also the usual result where a natural parent voluntarily gives up the child for adoption. In the latter instance, however, the natural parent has available the alternative placement with a private party or a friend, or, as is often the

case, with a third party such as an attorney, who then places
the child with adoptive parents.

These independent adoptions, or, as they are sometimes
called, "private placements," have been widely criticized on the
grounds that they encourage black market adoptions, that they
can be arranged for profit, and that they leave the rights of
both the adoptive and natural parents unprotected. Moreover,
even "a lawyer who is well equipped to handle the *legal* aspects
of adoption may not be qualified to decide many questions
included in placing a child which properly lie within the realm
of *specialized social knowledge*" (emphasis added).[46] It is this
element of "specialized social knowledge" which, though of
great importance, is generally lacking in independent adoptions.

The advantages of agency placement may also be seen in the
services provided by such agencies. These services are directed
toward helping the natural parent with respect to a decision
relinquishing the child, plans for the child (including any preference for its religious upbringing), and insuring confidentiality;
toward providing the adoptive parents with casework services,
help in finding a suitable child and completing the adoption
process, and postadoption counseling; and finally toward
promoting the child's best interests by placing it in an adoptive
home suitable in terms of its developmental history, family
history, and medical and psychological requirements.

THE SELECTION PROCESS

The procedure whereby suitable adoptive parents are found,
or a suitable child found for parents wishing to adopt, is known
simply as the selection process. While courts, prior to the
issuance of the adoptive decree, often conduct their own
independent investigations as to the suitability of the adoptive
parents,[47] this function is for the most part a responsibility of
social service agencies.

There are few legal standards to guide either courts or
agencies in determining adoptive suitability. Generally, any
child may be adopted who is in the state at the time the petition
is filed. A husband and wife may jointly adopt a child, or, if

one of the spouses is already the child's parent, the other may separately adopt him. An unmarried adult may also adopt a child, as may a married adult who has been accorded the right to reside separate and apart from his or her spouse by judicial decree. Further legal restrictions exist as to age, health, religion, and race.

The mere fact that an adoptive couple meets the statutory requirements does not assure their acceptance as adoptive parents. In determining adoptive suitability, child welfare agencies give consideration to a wide variety of social factors. These are reflections of value judgments that may or may not be the consensus of the wider community. Of these, race and religion are perhaps the most important, although others such as ethnic background,[48] age, social position, income,[49] and general life style are also considered but rarely articulated.

Religion as a factor in selection

Many state adoption statutes express a concern for the religion of the child and that of the natural and adoptive parents. This is a reflection of agency adoption practice which is often carried out along sectarian lines.[50] Even nonsectarian agencies, however, attach importance to religious considerations. An example is the former position of the Child Welfare League of America:

A child should ordinarily be placed in a home where the religion of adoptive parents is the same as that of the child, unless the parents have specified that the child should or may be placed with a family of another religion. Every effort (including interagency and interstate referrals) should be made to place the child within his own faith, or that designated by his parents. If, however, such matching means that placement might never be feasible, or involves a substantial delay in placement or placement in a less suitable home, a child's need for a permanent family of his own requires that consideration should then be given to placing the child in a home of a different religion. For children whose religion is not known, and whose parents are not accessible, the most suitable home available should be selected.[51]

While some states require only that the religious affiliations of the parties concerned must be placed on the petition or must be considered in the disposition of the case,[52] others require that the adoptive child be placed with adoptive parents whose religious affiliation is the same as that of the child's. These latter provisions are typically qualified by the words "when practicable"[53] or "when possible."[54]

In *In re Maxwell*,[55] the New York Court of Appeals interpreted the words "when practicable" as discretionary. In that case the issue before the court was whether the New York adoption laws prohibited the adoption of the Maxwell child, since the religion of the prospective adoptive parents differed from that of the natural mother. The relevant statute provided that "in granting orders of adoption . . . the court shall, when practicable . . . give custody only to . . . persons of the same religious faith as that of the child."[56]

Several hours after Mrs. Maxwell's son was born, she signed an affidavit, prepared by the attorney for the Smiths, the prospective adoptive parents, in which she gave her consent to the infant's adoption by them, adding that she did not embrace any religious faith. Adoption proceedings were commenced by the Smiths a few years after Mrs. Maxwell had given her child up for adoption. During those years the child had been living with the Smiths. At the adoption proceedings, Mrs. Maxwell stated that she was a member of the Roman Catholic faith, and that she had not known that the persons to whom the baby had been given were Protestants. She further testified that her affidavit declaring that she did not embrace any religious faith had been signed without knowledge of its contents. On these grounds Mrs. Maxwell demanded return of the child and demanded that, in any event, the child be brought up in the Roman Catholic faith.

The trial court denied Mrs. Maxwell's petition and granted the adoption.[57] On appeal Judge Fuld, writing for the majority, affirmed the lower court's decision. He found the language of the statute, directing the court, "when practicable," to give custody only to persons of the same religious faith as that of the child, to be discretionary. He said:

The statute calls upon the court to give custody to persons of the same religious faith as that of the child when practicable. That term is of broad content, necessarily designed to accord the trial judge a discretion to approve as adoptive parents persons of a different faith from the child's in exceptional situations. Had the legislature intended that in every case the child be adopted by persons of its own religious faith, it obviously would have made its design known by language far different from that which it used. The presence in the statute of the words "when practicable" was to enable the court to relax the requirement in the unusual case such as the one before us.[58]

Judge Desmond dissented, urging that the words "when practicable" were not discretionary, as indicated by the majority, but mandatory. He criticized the lack of effort to find adoptive parents of the same religious faith as the child, declaring that "it is inconceivable that in the city of Buffalo such persons could not be found."[59] However, the dissent seems to miss the main thrust of Judge Fuld's opinion. It was not that other couples could not be found, but that the child had been living with the Smiths for over four years, and that to place him with some other couple, or in an institution, would have had serious consequences as far as his well-being was concerned. Thus, the court stated:

The statute may not be employed as a means of wiping out a relationship between foster parents and child which originated in good faith and has continued for the entire four and a half years of the youngster's life . . . [T]o tear the child from the love and care of these petitioners, the only mother and father he has ever known, and send him instead to an institution until other parents are found, would be inordinately cruel and harsh. No law requires consequences so distressing.[60]

The decision in *In re Maxwell* seemed to place New York with the majority of jurisdictions[61] in interpreting the religious requirements of adoption statutes liberally where the child's welfare is concerned. However, in a recent per curiam opinion in the case of *Starr* v. *DeRocco*,[62] the New York Court of Appeals appears to have reversed itself on this issue and to have aligned itself with those jurisdictions taking a more rigid position on the religious issue.

Starr involved two Roman Catholic children whose father had killed his wife and then committed suicide. At the time of the tragedy one child was three years old and the other less than a year old. The action was brought by Mr. and Mrs. Starr, the brother and sister-in-law of the deceased mother, against the DeRoccos, the brother and sister-in-law of the deceased father, to obtain custody of the children. The Starrs were Protestants living in Massachusetts, while the DeRoccos were Roman Catholics living in Ossining, New York, the scene of the murder and suicide. The lower court awarded custody to the Starrs, stating:

> [T]he court finds that the best interests of the infants would be served by placing them with petitioners Starr. Not only was the court most favorably impressed with them when they appeared before the court, but the court finds that they are of a temperament to best care for the children. They have the experience, that is demonstrated with their present child, they have a home to accommodate the children now, and in placing custody with them, they will be removed from the locale of the tragedy which befell their parents, and thus, in the future, spared possible embarrassment and degradation.
>
> ⁕   ⁕   ⁕
>
> The court is mindful of the difficulties regarding visitation by the DeRocco family with the children occasioned by the removal of the children from the State of New York. However, the court is convinced that the best interests of the children will be served by their removal from the area in which the tragedy befell their parents.[63]

The Appellate Division, in a 3–2 opinion, reversed the decision of the trial court.[64] The New York Court of Appeals, in a per curiam opinion with two judges dissenting, sustained the reversal. The dissenting judges felt that the majority had construed the words "when practicable" as mandatory and in a strong dissent stated:

> [I]f the appellate division majority intended that cause for rejection must be found in the personal character of the DeRoccos to warrant awarding custody to the Starrs, I believe they were mistaken. Such an interpretation of section 32 of article VI would require awarding custody to persons of the same religion as the child in all cases, unless the prospective custodians were total social and moral misfits. Such a view constitutes a blatant disregard for the welfare of the child for purely religious reasons and might well be considered to violate the First Amendment to the Constitution of the United States. . . .[65]

The *Starr* case brought New York into the same camp as Massachusetts, for the Supreme Judicial Court of Massachusetts in *In re Goldman*[66] had construed as mandatory a statute similar to that interpreted in *Maxwell* and *Starr*. In *Goldman*, a Jewish woman sought to adopt twins born illegitimately to a Roman Catholic woman. The twins had been in the custody of the Jewish woman since they were two weeks old. The natural mother consented to the adoption and also agreed to the twins' being brought up in the Jewish faith. The judge of the probate court found that the petitioners were qualified as adoptive parents in all respects, save that they were not of the same religious affiliation as the natural mother of the children. He concluded, however, that since many Catholic couples were available in the area who could furnish the twins a good home, it was "practicable," within the meaning of the Massachusetts provision, to give custody of the children to persons of their own religious faith. The Supreme Judicial Court of Massachusetts affirmed the lower court's decision, applying the test urged by the dissent in *Maxwell*—the availability of other couples of the same religion as the adoptive children. In so doing, the court seemed to interpret the phrase, "when practicable," to mean "whenever it is possible to procure."[67]

The result in *Goldman* seems more extreme than that in *Starr*. In *Starr*, the natural parents were dead and, had they been alive, would presumably have desired that the children be brought up in the Roman Catholic faith. In *Goldman* the natural mother was alive, and even though she, a Roman Catholic, had indicated that raising the twins in the Jewish faith comported with her desires, the highest court in Massachusetts held that the children must be raised as Roman Catholics. In reaching this result, the Massachusetts court seemed to be imposing its own religious preference on the children.

The constitutionality of the result in *Goldman* is, to say the least, questionable (as is the result in *Starr,* though perhaps less clearly). The court in *Goldman* attempted to meet the constitutional objections with this statement: "All religions are treated alike. There is no 'subordination' of one sect to another. No exercise of religion is required, prevented, or hampered."[68] But this is clearly not so. Here the exercise of the Roman Catholic religion is required, even though none of the adult parties to the case desires it, and the exercise of the Jewish religion is hampered.

Religion as a factor in the placement process is intimately connected with the rights of the natural parent. Once those rights are terminated, as they must be for adoption to take place, the desires of the natural parent about the child should be irrelevant. A 1970 amendment to the Massachusetts Act[69] tends to protect the natural mother's desire. If agencies encourage mothers to express a religious preference, this would allow natural parent's religious preference to govern even where it conflicts with the adoptive parent's preference. The effect is that the rights of the natural parent are not terminated but remain in effect, at least to the extent of religious identification or preference. In giving a child up for adoption, its natural parents are in effect stating that they are not themselves capable of promoting its best interests—that another could do so more effectively. Someone else cannot do this, however, if those interests must be sought within narrow strictures imposed as conditions of relinquishment. Rather, since the child's best interests require consideration of the total constellation of social values, there must be complete freedom to weigh all those values.

A problem arises in the case of conditional relinquishment, when a parent desires to give up a child for adoption but will not do so without a promise that certain conditions be met— for example, that it will be placed with parents of a particular religious faith. A private, nonsectarian agency might well conclude that the placement of the child with adoptive parents, even though limited by this condition, would nevertheless be more in the child's interest than remaining with the natural parent if the agency were unwilling to consent to the condition. A similar difficulty exists in the case of secular agencies. Their search for a suitable adoptive couple is necessarily inhibited by their foremost desire: to place the child with a couple of the "proper" religious faith.

Neither of these situations is ideal. Ideally, religious considerations should be relevant only when they further a child's best interests. This is not to say that placement in one religion as opposed to another could be said to further the child's welfare because that religion's tenets are deemed more likely to lead to a child's healthy development toward responsible adulthood. Rather, it is to say that all religions should be considered equally as aids to the healthy development of the child. Religion becomes relevant only when a child has been raised in a particular religion, or has itself a religious preference, and placement with parents who practice a different religion might be confusing or emotionally upsetting to it.

Race as a factor in selection

The other area that has been the subject of controversy in the selection process is that of race. At least two states, Louisiana and Texas, formerly barred interracial adoption altogether.[70] The Texas prohibition on interracial adoption, however, was recently struck down by the Court of Civil Appeals of Texas in the case of *In re Gomez*.[71] While the constitutionality of the Louisiana statute has not been litigated, it is safe to assume that it too is unconstitutional.

In *In re Gomez,* a Negro army sergeant sought to adopt his wife's illegitimate white children, ages ten and sixteen. The couple had been married for nine years, and during that time the husband had supported and acted as father to his wife's children. While fit as an adoptive parent in all other respects, the Negro sergeant was said to be disqualified because of his race. In declaring the Texas statute unconstitutional, the court based its opinion upon the whole line of civil rights cases over the past sixteen years holding racial discrimination in other areas of American life to be a violation of the equal-protection and due-process clauses of the Fourteenth Amendment. Besides the important constitutional aspects of the case, the court pointed out the practical factor that led it to reach its result: "the adoption of the minors would enable them to receive benefits as dependents of a member of the Armed Forces. . . ."[72]

The demise of statutory prohibitions on interracial adoptions does not mean that race is no longer a significant factor in the selection process. Some state statutes, while not barring interracial adoptions, provide that the race of the natural parents, the child, and the adoptive parents be placed on the adoption petition.[73] The effect of this information was at issue in the case of *In re Adoption of a Minor*,[74] decided under the applicable provision of the District of Columbia Code.[75] In that case the petition for adoption was filed by the child's natural mother and its stepfather. Both the child and its mother were white, but its stepfather was a Negro. The district court denied the adoption petition, with the late Judge Holtzoff reasoning that "the boy when he grows up might lose the social status of a white man by reason of the fact that by record his father will be a negro if this adoption is approved."[76]

The Court of Appeals reversed the district court's decision, holding that while a difference in race or religion may have relevance in adoption proceedings, that factor alone cannot be decisive; the child's welfare must be paramount. Judge Bazelon, speaking for the court, reasoned that since the child was happy living in the home of its mother and its stepfather, and since it would continue to live in that home anyway (because its mother had custody of it), denying the adoption would "only serve the harsh and unjust end of depriving the child of a legitimatized status in that home."[77]

Adoption agencies, even in jurisdictions where there are no

statutory restrictions on interracial adoptions, themselves consider race in determining adoptive suitability. Indeed, until very recently the Child Welfare League of America, while arguing that racial background in itself should not be the major criterion in selection, stated their position in these terms:

> [I]t should not be assumed that difficulties will necessarily arise if adoptive parents and children are of different racial origin. At the present time, however, children placed in adoptive families with similar racial characteristics, such as color, can become more easily integrated into the average family group and community.[78]

Recently there has been a discernible trend in some adoption agencies in large metropolitan areas to encourage interracial adoptions. The position of the Child Welfare League of America is now that "families who have the capacity to adopt a child whose racial background is different from their own . . . should be encouraged to consider such child."[79] This trend stems perhaps from the fact that most children available for adoption are of minority or mixed racial origin, while almost all prospective adoptive parents are white. Because until recently children who were members of minority racial groups were not considered acceptable for adoption by white parents, the ratio of suitable adoptive parents to adoptable minority group children was approximately ten to one.[80] By encouraging the adoption of minority group children, these agencies have attempted to meet the demands of couples for adoptable children while at the same time providing homes for children who would otherwise remain in institutions.

RIGHTS AND DUTIES OF ADOPTIVE PARENTS

Once the final decree of adoption is entered, the adoptive parent-child relationship assumes all the characteristics of an ongoing natural parent-child relationship. Specifically, the adoptive parent's duty to control and supervise his adopted child, even to the exclusion of the child's natural family, is preserved in the same way as the identical rights and duties of the natural parent toward his natural child.

Because the adoptive parent-child relationship is artificially established, it may in some instances be terminated for reasons that would not justify the termination of the natural parent-child relationship. Courts, however, are extremely reluctant to set aside an adoption decree or to terminate or annul an adoption without express statutory authority.[81] Even where statutory provisions allow termination or annulment in certain circumstances, such as the child's misconduct, a physical or mental illness unknown at the time of adoption, or when the child's best interests demand termination, courts tend to apply these provisions narrowly.[82] Thus, adoptive parents may not divest themselves of their custodial duties merely because they are dissatisfied with their child, regret their decision about adoption, or think they made a "bad deal."[83] This is true even if the adoptive child's natural parents wish to resume their legal relationship with it and the adoptive parents wish to terminate theirs.[84] Adoption is said to create a "for better, for worse situation."[85]

SUMMARY

Although adoption was originally intended as a means to provide heirs for families whose lineage might otherwise become extinct, modern adoption laws and practices, while protecting biological ties to a limited extent, focus more on a child's need for a family attachment. This ambivalence toward the articulated goal of furthering a child's welfare is evidenced by the major concessions made both to natural parents whose rights in their child are being terminated and to adoptive parents whose rights are being established. Such practices as preserving a natural parent's ties with the child when there is little hope of a permanent reunion, honoring a natural parent's desire to have the child raised in a particular religion, or allowing a natural parent to change his or her mind about placement seem to reflect a strong—perhaps too strong—concern for biological ties. On the other hand, allowing adoptive parents the opportunity to change their mind once an adoption has been decreed gives these parents an inordinate degree of freedom which may be detrimental to a child's welfare.

Nevertheless, because a child's welfare is the official policy in adoption, it is no longer possible to bring a child into one's family and expect it to have a legal status equal to a natural child's without state intervention. State regulation of adoption takes the form of the imposition of a wide range of standards for determining, among other things, who may place a child for adoption, when a child is free for adoption, who may adopt it, how adoption may be accomplished, and what the effect of adoption will be on all the parties involved.

If adoption is meant to serve as a means for providing adequate parental care for children whose natural parents have failed to fulfill the community's expectations of parenthood, it should assume the characteristics of permanence as early as possible. In particular, the state should quickly allow the adoptive relationship to take on all the attributes of a natural one by insuring that the decision to give up a child, once made, is irrevocable; and by insuring that, once rendered (hopefully shortly after placement), the adoption decree is final and the child secure in a permanent family relationship. The process of state intervention that has been discussed in this book should at this point end.

NOTES

1. For a brief discussion of the history of adoption laws in the United States, *see* H. Witmer, E. Herzog, E. Weinstein, & M. Sullivan, Independent Adoptions 19–32 (1963). *See also* F. Infausto, *Perspective on Adoption*, 383 The Annals 1 (1969).

2. Curtis v. Curtis, 71 Mass. (5 Gray) 535, 537 (1856).

3. Ind. Stat. Ann. § 3–120(a)(6) (Supp. 1970); Mich. Stat. Ann. § 27.3178 (543) (1962). Some states require the consent of the parent of the minor parent only when the minor parent is unwed. *E.g.*, Minn. Stat. Ann. § 259.24 (1959). For a discussion of the legal problems raised

by an unwed mother's minority, *see* S. Katz, *Legal Protections for the Unmarried Mother and Her Child,* 10 Children 55 (1962).

4. D.C. Code Ann. § 16–304 (1966).

5. *E.g.,* Ariz. Rev. Stat. Ann. § 8–103B (Supp. 1969); Kan. Gen. Stat. Ann. § 59–2102 (Supp. 1969); Md. Ann. Code art. 16, § 74 (Supp. 1969).

6. Abandonment is "any conduct on the part of the parent, which evinces a settled purpose to forego all parental duties, and to relinquish all parental claims to the child." Winans v. Luppie, 47 N.J. Eq. 302, 304, 20 A. 969, 970 (Ct. Err. & App. 1890). This definition has been endorsed by other jurisdictions: *e.g., In re* Miller, 15 Ill. App.2d 333, 146 N.E.2d 226 (1957); Davies Adoption Case, 353 Pa. 579, 588, 46 A.2d 252, 257 (1946). Pennsylvania has now adopted the *Winans* definition by statute. Pa. Stat. Ann. tit. 1 § 1 (1963).

7. *In re* Anonymous, 80 N.Y.S.2d 839, 845 (Surr. Ct. 1947). Cases utilizing this or similar definitions are collected in Note, *Termination of Parental Rights to Free Child for Adoption,* 32 N. Y. U. L. Rev. 579, 586 n.51 (1957).

8. *E.g., In re* Anonymous, *supra* note 7, at 845; *In re* Hayford, 109 Misc. 479, 481, 179 N.Y.S. 182, 183 (Surr. Ct. 1919).

9. Annot., 35 A.L.R.2d 662, 668 (1954). Since abandonment must be intentional, involuntary separation is generally held insufficient in itself to constitute an abandonment. *E.g., In re* Maxwell, 117 Cal. App.2d 156, 255 P.2d 87 (Dist. Ct. App. 1953) (child taken from parent by order of juvenile court); Welker's Adoption, 50 Pa. D. & C. 573 (Orphans' Ct. 1944) (father imprisoned); Schwaiger v. Headrick, 281 Ala. 392, 203 So. 2d 114 (1967) (parents divorced, father unable to visit or contact child because of friction with mother).

10. *E.g.,* Mo. Rev. Stat. Ann. § 453.040 (Supp. 1969) (one year); Pa. Stat. Ann. tit. 1 § 1.2 (1963) (six months); Tex. Rev. Civ. Stat. Ann. art. 46a § 6 (Supp. 1969) (two years).

11. Cases to this effect are collected in Annot., *supra* note 9, at 678–80. But failure to support alone is not usually held sufficient to constitute abandonment. *See, e.g.,* Johnson v. Strickland, 88 Ga. App. 281, 76 S.E.2d 533 (1953); Smith v. Smith, 67 Idaho 349, 180 P.2d 853 (1947); *In re* Walton, 123 Utah 380, 259 P.2d 881 (1953); *In re* Rice, 179 Wis. 531, 192 N.W. 56 (1923).

12. *In re* Maxwell, 4 N.Y.2d 429, 433, 151 N.E.2d 848, 850, 176 N.Y.S.2d 281, 283–84 (1958).

13. Stalder v. Stone, 412 Ill. 488, 496–97, 107 N.E.2d 696, 700–01 (1952).

14. *Id.* at 496, 107 N.E.2d at 700.

15. Cases are collected in Annot., 47 A.L.R.2d 824, 847–49 (1956), and Annot., 35 A.L.R.2d 662, 688–91 (1954).

16. Cases are collected in Annot., *supra* note 9, 671–72 (1954).

17. *See, e.g., In re* Kline, 24 Del. Ch. 427, 8 A.2d 505 (Orphans' Ct. 1939); Bair Adoption Case, 393 Pa. 296, 141 A.2d 873 (1958); Davies Adoption Case, 353 Pa. 579, 42 A.2d 252 (1946).

18. Some state statutes provide that the consent of a parent who has been divorced and deprived of custody of his child is not required. *E.g.,* Iowa Code § 600.3 (Supp. 1970), which provides that where the parents are not married to each other or where one of them has been deprived of custody by judicial procedure, only the consent of the parent "having the care and providing for the wants of the child" is required. In New Mexico, whether the consent of a parent who has been divorced and deprived of the custody of his child is necessary is a question for the discretion of the court. N.M. Stat. Ann. § 22–2–6(1) (Supp. 1969). However, he must nonetheless be given notice of the adoption proceedings and an opportunity to make known his objections. Miller v. Higgins, 14 Cal. App. 156, 111 P. 403 (Dist. Ct. App. 1910).

In some jurisdictions, whether the consent of a divorced parent is required depends upon the grounds on which the divorce decree was based. Thus, in New York the consent of a parent is unnecessary when he or she has been divorced on the grounds of adultery and deprived of the custody of the child. N.Y. Dom. Rel. Law § 111 (McKinney 1964). Likewise Oklahoma dispenses with the consent of a parent divorced on the grounds of cruelty. Okla. Stat. Ann. tit. 10, § 60.7 (Supp. 1969).

19. Ala. Code tit. 27 § 3 (1958); Alaska Stat. 20.10.020 (1962); Ariz. Rev. Stat. § 8–103(A)(1)(a) (Supp. 1969); Ark. Stat. Ann. § 56–106(b)(III) (1947); Colo. Rev. Stat. Ann. § 4–1–6 (1963); Conn. Gen. Stat. Ann. § 17–62 (1960) (implied); Del. Code Ann. tit. 13 § 908 (1953); D.C. Code Ann. § 16–304(b)(2)(G) (1966) (implied); Ga. Code Ann. § 74–403 (Supp. 1969); Hawaii Rev. Stat. § 578–2 (1968); Ill. Ann. Stat. ch. 4, § 9.1–8 (Smith-Hurd Supp. 1967); Ind. Ann. Stat. 3–120(a)(5) (1969); Iowa Code Ann. § 600.3 (Supp. 1969); Kan. Gen. Stat. Ann.

§ 59.2102 (Supp. 1969); Ky. Rev. Stat. Ann. § 199.500(1)(a) (1969); Me. Rev. Stat. Ann. 19.532 (1964). Md. Ann. Code art. 16 § 74 (1966); Mass. Gen. Laws Ann. ch. 210 § 3 (Supp. 1970); Mich. Stat. Ann. § 25.235 (1957); Minn. Stat. Ann. § 25.9.24(1)(2) (Supp. 1969); Miss. Code Ann. § 1269–09 (Supp. 1963); Mo. Ann. Stat. § 453.040(1) (Supp. 1969); Mont. Rev. Codes Ann. § 61–205 (1962); Neb. Rev. Stat. § 127.040 (1967); Nev. Rev. Stat. § 127.040 (1967); N.H. Rev. Stat. Ann. § 469.30 (1968); N.M. Stat. Ann. § 22–2–6(A)(4) (Supp. 1969); N.Y. Dom. Rel. Law § 111 (McKinney 1964); N.C. Gen. Stat. § 48–9(d) (1966); N.D. Cent. Code § 14–11–10 (Supp. 1969); Ohio Rev. Code Ann. § 3107.06; Okla. Stat. Ann. tit. 10 § 60.6 (1966); Ore. Rev. Stat. § 109.322(c) (1963); Pa. Stat. Ann. tit. 1 § 2 (1963); R.I. Gen. Laws Ann. § 15–7–7 (1970); S.D. Code § 14.0403 (Supp. 1969); Tenn. Code Ann. § 36–108 (Supp. 1969); Vt. Stat. Ann. tit. § 435 (1958); W.Va. Code Ann. § 4755 (1961); Wy. Stat. Ann. § 1–717 (1957).

20. Thus it has been held that, absent a statute to the contrary, there can be no adoption if the jurisdiction requires the consent of the natural parents and one of them is insane, since such a parent is incapable of giving consent. Keal v. Rhydderck, 317 Ill. 231, 237–38, 148 N.E. 53, 56 (1925).

21. 3 Ill.2d 511, 121 N.E.2d 781 (1954).

22. Ill. Ann. Stat. ch. 4 § 9.1–8(e) (Smith-Hurd 1961). This has since been amended, Ill. Ann. Stat. ch. 4 § 9.1–8 (Smith-Hurd Supp. 1970).

23. Nev. Rev. Stat. § 127.040(2) (1967).

24. E.g., Ala. Code tit. 27, § 3 (1958); Ky. Rev. Stat. Ann. § 199.500 (Baldwin 1970); Miss. Code Ann. § 1269–09 (Supp. 1968); Tenn. Code Ann. § 36–108 (Supp. 1969).

25. These statutes would seem to pose constitutional problems. They are perhaps more realistic, however, than those requiring "incurable mental disability" because, as a consequence of the important advances that have been made in psychiatry in recent years (especially in the psychopharmaceutical realm and in the delivery of mental health services), mental illness is generally not a hopeless disability.

26. See Ill. Ann. Stat. ch. 4, § 9.1–8 (Smith-Hurd Supp. 1970); Ohio Rev. Code Ann. § 3107.06 (Baldwin 1969); R.I. Gen. Laws Ann. § 15–7–7 (1970); Wyo. Stat. Ann. § 1–717 (1959).

27. F. Lindman & D. McIntyre, The Mentally Disabled and the Law 206 (1961).

28. *See generally* Comment, *Revocation of Parental Consent to Adoption: Legal Doctrine and Social Policy,* 28 U. Chi. L. Rev. 564 (1961).

29. Skeen v. Marx, 105 So.2d 517 (Fla. Dist. Ct. App. 1958); Ill. Ann. Stat. ch. 4, § 9.1–11 (Smith-Hurd Supp. 1970).

30. *See, e.g., In re* White, 300 Mich. 378, 1 N.W.2d 579 (1942); State *ex rel.* Platzer v. Beardsley, 149 Minn. 435, 183 N.W. 956 (1921); *In re* Adoption of Anderson, 189 Minn. 85, 248 N.W. 657 (1933). This position is grounded on the theory that since parental consent is necessary to an adoption, withdrawal of such consent before the final decree has "vested" any right to the child in the adoptive parents deprives the court of jurisdiction to decree the adoption.

31. *E.g.,* California—Adoption of Pitcher, 103 Cal. App.2d 859, 230 P.2d 449 (Dist. Ct. App. 1951); Connecticut—Bailey v. Mars, 138 Conn. 593, 87 A.2d 388 (1952); Georgia—Hendrix v. Hunter, 99 Ga. App. 784, 110 S.E.2d 35 (1959); Iowa—*In re* Adoption of Cannon, 234 Iowa 828, 53 N.W.2d 877 (1952); Kentucky—Welsh v. Young, 240 S.W.2d 584 (Ky. Ct. App. 1951); Maryland—King v. Shandrowski, 218 Md. 38, 145 A.2d 281 (1958); New Jersey—*In re* S., 57 N.J. Super. 154, 154 A.2d 129 (Essex County Ct. 1959); New York—*In re* Anonymous, 286 App. Div. 161, 143 N.Y.S.2d 90, *motion for leave to appeal denied,* 286 App. Div. 968, 146 N.Y.S.2d 477 (1955). It should be noted that while statutes rarely state whether consent is to be absolutely revocable, irrevocable, or revocable in the discretion of the court, the courts generally profess to find the basis for the rule they adopt in the statutes of their jurisdictions. Thus the District of Columbia and Arizona courts have interpreted statutes providing that the minority of parents shall not be a bar to their consenting to adoption as meaning that consent is revocable only in the discretion of the court. Ariz. Rev. Stat. Ann. § 8–103B (Supp. 1969), *In re* Holman's Adoption, 80 Ariz. 201, 295 P.2d 372 (1956); D.C. Code Ann. § 16.304 (1966), *In re* Adoption of a Minor, 144 F.2d 644 (1944).

32. There is a great deal of difference among the jurisdictions as to when consent becomes absolutely irrevocable. In some, consent becomes irrevocable only after issuance of the final decree: *In re* Harville, 233 La. 2, 96 So.2d 20 (1957); Green v. Paul, 212 La. 338, 21 So.2d 819 (1947). Still other jurisdictions hold consent revocable until the adoption hearing: *e.g.,* Stone Adoption Case, 398 Pa. 190, 145 A.2d 308 (1959). In Michigan, consent is irrevocable after the termination decree. Mich. Stat. Ann. § 170.6 (1968). The North Carolina statute provides that consent becomes irrevocable when the interlocutory decree is issued unless such consent was given to a director of public welfare or a licensed child placement agency, in which case it becomes irrevocable thirty days after it is given;

and in any event consent becomes irrevocable six months after it is given. N.C. Gen. Stat. § 48–11 (1966). Tennessee's very unusual statute provides in essence that consent is irrevocable after the final decree, but absolutely revocable for a period (thirty to ninety days) after it was given if no adoption petition is filed in the interim; if such a petition is filed, consent is revocable in the discretion of the court. Tenn. Code Ann. § 36–117 (Supp. 1969).

33. See authorities cited *supra* note 29. But some states have statutory provisions to the general effect that consent is irrevocable where the child has been given up for adoption to a licensed child placement agency, in accordance with prescribed procedures. E.g., Ohio Rev. Code § 3107.6 (Baldwin 1969); Texas Rev. Civ. Stat. Ann. art. 46a § 6 (1969); Wash. Rev. Code Ann. § 26.32.070 (1961). Such provisions have generally been given effect by the courts. E.g., Kozak v. Lutheran Children's Aid Soc'y, 164 Ohio St. 335, 130 N.E.2d 796 (1955); Catholic Charities v. Harper, 161 Tex. 21, 337 S.W.2d 111 (1960).

34. E.g., In re Adoption of Anderson, 189 Minn. 85, 248 N.W. 657 (1933).

35. Minn. Stat. Ann. § 259.24(6) (1959).

36. Ga. Code Ann. § 74–403 (Supp. 1969).

37. Md. Ann. Code art. 16 § 74 (1966). While the terms of the statute refer only to those cases in which a parent withholds his consent, the Maryland Court of Appeals has ruled that it also applies where consent is given and then revoked. King v. Shandrowski, 218 Md. 38, 145 A.2d 281 (1958).

38. Del. Code Ann. tit. 13 § 909 (1953).

39. Uniform Adoption Act. § 6 adopted in Montana as Mont. Rev. Codes Ann. tit. 61, § 206 (1970) and Oklahoma as Okla. Stat. Ann. tit. 10, § 60.10 (1966).

40. See In re Thompson, 178 Kan. 127, 283 P.2d 493 (1955).

41. See In re Anonymous, 286 App. Div. 161, 143 N.Y.S.2d 90, *motion for leave to appeal denied*, 286 App. Div. 968, 146 N.Y.S.2d 477 (1955).

42. E.g., N.M. Stat. Ann. § 22–2–5(c) (Supp. 1961); N.Y. Dom. Rel. Law § 111(3) (McKinney 1964); Pa. Stat. Ann. tit. 1 § 2(c) (1963); Tex. Rev. Civ. Stat. Ann. art. 46a, § 6 (1969); Wash. Rev. Code §§ 26.32.030(3), .040(5) (1961).

43. *E.g.*, N.Y. Dom. Rel. Law § 111 (McKinney 1964); Ohio Rev. Code Ann. § 3107.06B (Baldwin 1969); Pa. Stat. Ann. tit. 1, § 2 (1963).

44. *E.g.*, *In re* Adoption of Anderson, 189 Minn. 85, 248 N.W. 657 (1933); *In re* Adoption of Doe, 231 N.C. 1, 56 S.E.2d 8 (1949); Sklaroff v. Stevens, 84 R.I. 1, 120 A.2d 694 (1956); Harmon v. D'Adamo, 195 Va. 25, 77 S.W.2d 318 (1953).

Some statutes require the father's consent if he legitimatizes his child. This seems to be the position of the District of Columbia. D.C. Code Ann. § 16–304 (1966) requires the father's consent when "the adoptee has been legitimated according to the laws of any jurisdiction. . . ." A similar provision may be found in Wash. Rev. Code § 26.32.030 (1961). The Arizona statute, however, provides that the father's consent is required if he has acknowledged the child. Ariz. Rev. Stat. Ann. § 8–103A (Supp. 1969). But it would seem that the practical difference between those statutes using the term "legitimation" and those using the term "acknowledgment" is greatly minimized by the fact that the usual cases involving the issue of the necessity of the father's consent are those where there has been both a legitimation of the child by subsequent marriage and acknowledgment of the child by the father. *See, e.g., In re* Adoption of Anderson, 189 Minn. 85, 248 N.W. 657 (1933); Sklaroff v. Stevens, 84 R.I. 1, 120 A.2d 694 (1956).

45. A. v. B., 217 Ark. 844, 848–49, 233 S.W.2d 629, 632 (1950); *see* Adoption of a Minor, 338 Mass. 635, 641–43, 156 N.E.2d 801, 805–06 (1959). For a discussion of the procedural rights afforded fathers of illegitimate children in custody proceedings, *see* Note, *Father of an Illegitimate Child—His Right to be Heard,* 50 Minn. L. Rev. 1071 (1966).

46. Hearings on Juvenile Delinquency Before a Subcommittee of the Senate Committee on the Judiciary, 84th Cong., 1st Sess. 3 (1955) (remarks of Senator Kefauver).

47. There is some variation among the jurisdictions as to whether such an investigation should be mandatory or discretionary. It is mandatory in Illinois, Ill. Ann. Stat. ch. 4 § 9.1–6 (Smith-Hurd Supp. 1967), and New York, N.Y. Dom. Rel. Law §§ 112(5), 113, 115(3), 116(2)–(3) (McKinney 1964) but discretionary in Mississippi, Miss. Code Ann. § 1269–05 (1957), and Nevada, Nev. Rev. Stat. § 127.210 (1967). The District of Columbia makes the investigation mandatory unless the petitioner is a spouse of the natural parent of the adoptee and the natural parent consents to the adoption or joins the adoption petition, in which case the investigation is discretionary. D.C. Code Ann. § 16–308 (1966).

48. For a striking illustration of the effect of ethnic considerations, see

In re St. John, 51 Misc.2d 96, 272 N.Y.S.2d 817 (Family Ct. 1966), *rev'd sub nom.* Fitzsimmons v. Liuni, 26 App. Div.2d 980, 274 N.Y.S.2d 798 (3d Dep't 1966). There a New York state welfare agency sought to deny foster parents the right to adopt their foster child, who had lived with them for four years, on the grounds *inter alia* that the foster parents were dark complected and of Italian descent while the child was a blonde of French and English ancestry. Apparently the denial was based not on statutory grounds but on agency policy. This position was upheld by a lower court, but subsequent public outcry forced the agency to relent before an appeals court had the opportunity to rule on the matter. A fuller description of the case, excerpts from the testimony of parties involved, and judicial opinions can be found in the Appendix, pp. 212–246.

49. Financial security has been considered an important factor in determining the suitability of prospective adoptive parents. As a consequence, many otherwise qualified couples have been denied the opportunity to adopt unless they accept hard-to-place children. Adoption of such hard-to-place children has even been encouraged through state subsidies. California, Illinois, Maryland, Michigan, Minnesota, and New York support adoption in this fashion. For a discussion of how economic considerations foreclose lower-class couples from being selected as suitable adoptive parents, see H. Foster & D. Freed, *Unequal Protection: Poverty and Family Law,* 42 Ind. L. J. 192, 211–13 (1967).

50. For example, Catholic adoption agencies are committed to "the basic principle that any Catholic child being placed for adoption can have his total needs met only in a Catholic adoptive home." Bowers, *The Child's Heritage—From a Catholic Point of View,* in 2 A Study of Adoption Practice 130 (Schapiro ed. 1956). This position is based on the Catholic viewpoint that "religion is something more than a value to the child. It is also an obligation basic to his very nature." *Id.* at 130–31. However, the practice of Catholic adoption agencies varies somewhat where applicants representing a marriage between a Catholic and a non-Catholic are concerned. Some Catholic agencies will consider such applications, particularly "in instances where the mother is Catholic or in families in which the non-Catholic party is willing to take instruction in the fundamental teachings of the Catholic church. On the whole, however, agencies seek to use adoptive couples both of whom are Catholic." National Conference of Catholic Charities, Adoption Practices in Catholic Agencies 50 (1957).

Catholic agencies also place great emphasis on the religious upbringing of the adoptive child and often include in the Adoption Agreement the requirement that the child attend church and Sunday school regularly.

51. Child Welfare League of America, Standards for Adoption Service

25 (1958). In its 1968 Standards, the Child Welfare League modified its position on religion. As now worded, its position reads: "The family selected for a child should be one in which the child will have an opportunity for religious or spiritual and ethical development; but religious background alone should not be the basis for the selection of a family for a child. Child Welfare League of America, Standards for Adoption Service 35 (1968). This would seem to suggest that, while placing the child with parents of the same religious faith should be considered but should not be controlling, the existence of a religious atmosphere as opposed to a nonreligious atmosphere should be controlling. In another provision, the Child Welfare League of America states that while "[o]pportunity for religious or spiritual and ethical development of the child should receive full consideration in the selection of adoptive homes[,] [l]ack of religious affiliation or of a religious faith, however, should not be a bar to consideration of any applicants for adoption." *Id.* at 51. Whether these verbal modifications will have practical significance remains to be seen.

52. *E.g.*, Colo. Rev. Stat. Ann. § 4–1–7(f) (1964) (religious and racial backgrounds of child and petitioner are to be taken into account); Conn. Gen. Stat. Rev. § 45–63 (Supp. 1970) (the preadoption report should indicate the religion of the child and that of his natural and adoptive parents); D.C. Code Ann. §§ 16–305 (1966) (the petition must state the race and religion of the child or his natural parents, and that of the petitioner); Ga. Code Ann. § 74–411 (1964) (suitability of racial and religious affiliations must be investigated); Mich. Stat. Ann. § 27.3178 (545)(o) (1962) (preadoption investigation must consider the racial and religious backgrounds of the child and the petitioner); N.H. Rev. Stat. Ann. § 461.2 (1968) (preadoption investigation is to give due regard to the respective race and religion of the child and the petitioner); Ohio Rev. Code Ann. § 3107.05 (Baldwin 1969) (religious and racial backgrounds of child and petitioner must be investigated prior to the adoption); Wash. Rev. Code § 26.32.090 (1961) (preadoption investigation report must indicate the religion of the child).

53. Fla. Stat. Ann. § 63.011 (1969); Mass. Gen. Laws Ann. ch. 210, § 5B (1958); N.Y. Const. art. VI, § 18; N.Y. Dom. Rel. Law §§ 113, 117 (McKinney 1964); N.Y. Soc. Welfare Law § 373(3) (1966); N.Y.C. Dom. Rel. Ct. Act § 88 (McKinney 1964); R.I. Gen. Laws Ann. § 15–7–13 (1970); Wis. Stat. Ann. § 48.82(3) (1957).

54. Ariz. Rev. Stat. Ann. § 8.236 (1956); Ill. Ann. Stat. ch. 4, § 9–1.15 (Smith-Hurd 1966); Pa. Stat. Ann. tit. 1, § 1(d) (1963).

55. 4 N.Y.2d 429, 151 N.E.2d 848, 176 N.Y.S.2d 281 (1958).

56. N.Y. Soc. Welfare Law § 373(3) (1966).

57. The Smiths agreed, however, to have the child baptized in the Catholic faith and educated in Catholic parochial schools, 4 N.Y.2d at 433, 151 N.E.2d at 850–51, 176 N.Y.S.2d at 284.

58. *Id.* at 434, 151 N.E.2d at 850–51, 176 N.Y.S.2d at 284.

59. *Id.* at 440, 151 N.E.2d at 845, 176 N.Y.S.2d at 289.

60. *Id.* at 434–35, 151 N.E.2d at 851, 176 N.Y.S.2d at 284–85.

61. *E.g.,* Cooper v. Hinrichs, 10 Ill.2d 269, 140 N.E.2d 293 (1957), *reversing* 8 Ill. App.2d 269, 130 N.E.2d 678 (1955); *In re* Adoption of Kure, 197 Minn. 234, 266 N.W. 746 (1936); *In re* Adoption of Duren, 355 Mo. 1222, 200 S.W.2d 343 (1947); Butcher's Estate, 266 Pa. 479, 109 A. 683 (1920).

62. 24 N.Y.2d 1011, 250 N.E.2d 240, 302 N.Y.S.2d 835 (1969).

63. *Id.* at 1013, 240 N.E.2d at 241, N.Y.S.2d at 837.

64. Starr v. DeRocco, 29 App. Div.2d 662, 286 N.Y.S.2d 313 (1968).

65. Starr v. DeRocco, 24 N.Y.2d 1011, 1015, 250 N.E.2d 243, 302 N.Y.S.2d 835, 839 (1969).

66. 331 Mass. 647, 121 N.E.2d 843 (1954), *cert. denied,* 348 U.S. 942 (1955).

67. *Cf.* P. Ramsey, *The Legal Imputation of Religion to an Infant in Adoption Proceedings,* 24 N. Y. U. L. Rev. 649, 657 (1959). This is how the Rhode Island statute is meant to be interpreted. R.I. Gen. Laws Ann. § 15–7–13 (1970) provides: "The word 'when practicable' as used in reference to adoptions shall be interpreted as being without force or effect if there is a proper or suitable person of the same religious faith or persuasion as that of the child available to whom orders of adoption may be granted."

68. *In re* Goldman, 331 Mass. 647, 652, 121 N.E.2d 843, 846 (1954).

69. Mass. Gen. Laws ch. 119, § 33; ch. 210, § 5A (1970).

70. La. Rev. Stat. § 9.422 (1965) ("A single person over the age of twenty-one years, or a married couple jointly, may petition to adopt any

child of his or their race.") Tex. Rev. Civ. Stat. Ann. art. 46a § 8 (1969) ("No white child can be adopted by a negro person nor can a negro child be adopted by a white person.") For a discussion of the Louisiana provision, *see* W. Wadlington, *Adoption of Persons Under Seventeen in Louisiana,* 36 Tul. L. Rev. 201, 205–09 (1962).

71. 424 S.W.2d 656 (Tex. Civ. App. 1967).

72. *In re* Gomez, 242 S.W.2d 656, 659 (Tex. Civ. App. 1967).

73. See statutes cited *supra* note 52.

74. *In re* Adoption of a Minor, 228 F.2d 446 (D.C. Cir. 1956).

75. "The petition or the exhibits annexed thereto shall contain the following information: (4) The race and religion of the prospective adoptee or his natural parent or parents; (5) The race and religion of the petitioner." D.C. Code Ann. § 16–305(4) (1966).

76. *In re* Adoption of a Minor, 228 F.2d 446, 447 (D.C. Cir. 1956).

77. *Id.* at 448.

78. Child Welfare League of America, Standards for Adoption Services 24 (1958).

79. Child Welfare League of America, Standards for Adoption Services 34 (1968). For a discussion of race as a placement factor in agency practice, see S. Crossman, *A Child of a Different Color: Race as a Factor in Adoption and Custody Proceedings,* 17 Buffalo L. Rev. 303 (1967).

80. A recent survey shows that for every one hundred nonwhite children available for adoption, there are only thirty-nine prospective homes, or a ratio of two-and-a-half to one. L. Grow, A New Look at Supply and Demand in Adoption (mimeo, Child Welfare League of America, 1970), cited in U. Gallagher, *Adoption Resources for Black Children,* 18 Children 49 (1971).

81. *See, e.g.,* Allen v. Allen, 214 Ore. 664, 330 P.2d 151 (1958).

82. *See, e.g.,* Buttrey v. West, 212 Ala. 321, 102 So. 456 (1924); Pelt v. Tunks, 153 Colo. 215, 385 P.2d 261 (1963); Mulligaw v. Wingard, 72 Ga. App. 539, 34 S.E.2d 305 (Ct. App. 1945) *trans. from* 198 Ga. 816, 33 S.E.2d 269; Succession of Williams, 224 La. 871, 71 So.2d 229 (1954); *In re* Pierro, 173 Misc. 123, 17 N.Y.S.2d 233 (Surr. Ct. 1940).

83. *See, e.g.,* Parsons v. Parsons, 101 Wis. 76, 77 N.W. 147 (1898); *In re* Adoption of L (Essex County Ct., P. Div.), 56 N.J. Super. 46, 151 A.2d 435 (1959).

84. *See In re* Adoption of L (Essex County Ct., P. Div.), 56 N.J. Super. 46, 151 A.2d 435 (1959).

85. *In re* Adoption of a Minor, 350 Mass. 302, 304, 214 N.E.2d 281, 282 (1966).

A CONCLUDING NOTE: JUDICIAL REFORM

This book has dealt with the subject of public intrusion into the parent-child relationship. The legal basis for this intrusion is *parens patriae*—the power and responsibility of the state to care for those persons presumed to be "incompetent." The purpose is to promote the best interests of the child, defined in this book as encompassing a constellation of social values essential to a child's development into a physically and emotionally healthy and responsible adult. Nevertheless, it should be remembered that intervention is an intrusion into the privacy of the family and hence in itself undesirable. Thus it is important that the ends achieved justify the intervention.

Theoretically, the role of the courts in the process of public intrusion is twofold. First, they must determine when there has been a parental failure or inability to promote even the minimal interests of the child. Usually this relates to adult behavior or environmental conditions defined as "neglect," which may cause or have caused some kind of harm to the child. If conditions constituting neglect have been found to exist, courts are faced with their second task: to dispose of the case in such a way as to promote the child's best interests. This usually involves either state supervision of the parents or a custodial change.

As a practical matter, courts have generally delegated these responsibilities to public welfare agencies. Frequently understaffed by inadequately trained personnel, applying outmoded concepts of child development and often rejecting social values dominant in the community, these agencies operate almost totally independently of the courts in providing protective services for parents and in choosing an appropriate placement—institutional, foster, or adoptive—for the child. Because courts often have no other source of relevant information about the child, the parents, or community resources, they tend to accept agency judgments with little question. As a consequence, these agencies exercise almost unbridled discretion, and their decisions may or may not take into consideration those factors that should be relevant in child placement decisions. Thus, custody decisions, which raise the most important questions to come before a court in this area, and about which "[a] judge agonizes more . . . than about any other type of decision he renders,"[1] are often made in a vacuum without adequate consideration of the competing values which should be balanced.

The basic responsibility facing the court should be to determine what custodial disposition will provide the child with a secure parent-child relationship, thus minimizing the possibility of frequent and perhaps continuous judicial intervention into the life of the child in the future. The fulfillment of this responsibility in a particular case requires inquiries according to more specific criteria. Thus, it should be determined:

1. What disposition will provide the child with an environment that will foster physical and emotional health?

2. What disposition will furnish the child with the economic base necessary for it to become a contributing member of society?

3. What disposition will furnish the child with an environment that will encourage the development of skills and the fulfillment of its intellectual potential?

4. What disposition will provide the child with an environment conducive toward its developing equal respect for all human beings and its maturation into a responsible adult?

Underlying all these considerations should be the basic notion that a child's healthy development is ultimately a question of emotional stability, promoted by a relationship of affection, stimulation, and an unbroken continuity of care. The purpose of posing these questions is to direct the scope of judicial inquiry to particular factors serving community goals. Furthermore, the questions may furnish a checklist for organizing the amorphous data that is produced in child custody matters.

Once the scope of judicial inquiry is narrowed, the next task is an evidentiary one. Judges should draw on the knowledge of various disciplines to add substantive content to the questions posed. Information and perspectives gathered from fields such as psychiatry, psychoanalysis, psychology, social work, sociology, education, and theology may demonstrate the extent to which certain characteristics of the child and the claimants are relevant to the court's objective of securing the child's best interests. The behavioral sciences can also aid in answering more fundamental questions: the effect of parental personalities and behavior on a child, the extent to which environmental factors outside the family, such as schools and churches, affect the child, and the impact on the child of both its maturation and its socialization with peer groups.

But merely outlining questions and asking aid from other disciplines to help answer them does not insure the successful resolution of child custody disputes. As we have mentioned earlier in this book, family law matters, and particularly those relating to children, evoke emotional responses in the decision-maker. It is not that decisionmakers, and particularly judges, should try to suppress these responses. Rather, they should be aware of the influence of their emotions on their decisions and should know when they are interfering with the making of an objective decision.

NOTE

1. B. Botein, Trial Judge 273 (1952).

Appendix

Except where noted, footnotes have been omitted.

JAMES v. McLINDEN

Civil No. 13127 (D. Conn., filed May 23, 1969)

COMPANO, DISTRICT JUDGE.

[Action for injunctive relief based on an alleged deprivation of plaintiff's] constitutional rights as a result of certain actions of the defendants, Judge John McLinden of the Juvenile Court, Mary Bowery, clerk of that court and Commissioner Bernard Shapiro of the State Welfare Department.

✦ ✦ ✦

[T]he Court granted immediate relief to the plaintiff and ordered prompt compliance by the defendants.

✦ ✦ ✦

The plaintiff, Esther James, is a 50-year-old unmarried Negro woman who has resided in New Haven, Connecticut, since 1937. Her sole source of support is a disability allowance of $80 per month subsistence, plus rent, from the State.

On September 27, 1966, Beverly Moore, a heroin addict, gave birth to a baby girl, Sean Renee. Unable to care for the baby, Mrs. Moore turned the child over to her cousin, Rosalind Rogers. In December, 1966, after Mrs. Moore was sentenced to jail, the Rogers woman prevailed upon the plaintiff to take care of the child. Upon Mrs. Moore's release from jail, she visited the plaintiff, gave her a few dollars, and told the plaintiff she could keep Sean and to "take good care of her." The plaintiff has not seen Mrs. Moore since then.

From that date to the present, the plaintiff has raised Sean as her own child. The child regards the plaintiff as her natural mother. Dennis Olson, a social worker employed by the State, testified that the plaintiff has provided Sean with all the care and affection of a "good mother." The plaintiff has fed and clothed Sean from the subsistence money she received; the State has not contributed any additional funds for Sean's support. Medical attention has been fully provided Sean and there is no question she is a healthy, happy child.

On December 26, 1968, the State Welfare Department, through

151

its District Director, filed a "Petition of Alleged Neglect" in the Juvenile Court in New Haven. The petition stated Sean had been abandoned by her parents and "is presently being cared for through an informal arrangement which is neither legal nor healthy." The petition acknowledged that Sean was living with "Mrs. Esther James—Friend."

No official notice of the petition or the hearing scheduled for March 17, 1969, was given to the plaintiff, contrary to the clear mandate of the statute which provided that in such cases a summons, with a copy of the petition, shall be served upon "the parent or parents, guardian, or other persons having control of the child." The statute requires an appearance in court to "show cause why such child should not be dealt with according to the provisions of this part." Conn. Gen. Stat. § 17–61.

However, Olson mentioned during a visit to her home that a hearing was to be held on March 17, 1969 "to take Sean away because of neglect." Believing that she was being accused of mistreating the child, the plaintiff promptly engaged [a legal services attorney] . . . to represent her. [He] attempted to file an appearance in the case, but defendant Bowery refused to accept it on the ground the plaintiff had "no standing."

On March 17, the plaintiff and her attorney attempted to gain entrance to the hearing being conducted in the Juvenile Court Building. Both were denied admittance to the courtroom. All efforts to see Judge McLinden failed.

At the hearing, Miss Bowery was appointed Sean's guardian ad litem. Miss Bowery is not a lawyer and had neither seen the child nor spoken to the plaintiff. At the conclusion of the hearing, Judge McLinden found that Sean was an "uncared for–neglected child" and ordered her into the custody of the Commissioner of Welfare.

[Plaintiff's attorney] thereupon attempted to file an appeal from the court's order, submitting his papers in proper form along with the required $45.00 filing fee. His papers were returned with a letter from Miss Bowery which stated:

We have discussed the matter of your appeal with Judge John F. McLinden and he has advised us that the Juvenile Court cannot accept this appeal.

We are therefore returning your appeal and check No. 6318 in the amount of $45.00.

This action was in direct contravention of a statute which permits appeals by "all persons aggrieved" by any order of the Juvenile Court. Conn. Gen. Stats. §§ 17–61, 17–62, 17–66b, 17–76.

A Superior Court judge refused to entertain plaintiff's writ of mandamus, and all informal appeals to a Justice of the Supreme Court of Connecticut and another judge of the Juvenile Court failed. This action followed.

Upon these facts, it is clear that the plaintiff's rights under the Fourteenth Amendment to due process and equal protection of the laws were denied under color of state law by the proceedings on March 17 in the Juvenile Court, the denial of her right to appeal, and the failure of the Superior Court to grant her relief by way of mandamus.

*   *   *

Under Connecticut law, the plaintiff, as a person "in control" of Sean, was entitled to written notice of the hearing involving Sean's custody. She had a right to appear and be heard, personally and through counsel. To refuse to hear Miss James, who was in the best position to give relevant and weighty testimony on the question of alleged neglect, was a clear violation of the plaintiff's rights under state law. Thereafter, the denial of Miss James' right of appeal infected the proceedings beyond repair within the state legal system. These deprivations reach federal constitutional dimensions and require federal intervention. *Yick Wo v. Hopkins,* 118 U.S. 356 (1886); see also, *Griffin v. Illinois,* 351 U.S. 12 (1956).

Moreover, there is no question that the plaintiff intended to, and did, assume the rights, duties, and privileges of a parent to Sean. She may not have formed such an intention at the moment Sean was placed in her custody or during the first few months she cared for the child. However, within a relatively short time, the plaintiff grew to love Sean as her own and, within the limits of a small income, she fed, clothed, and cared for the child. Having found physical and emotional security with the plaintiff, Sean has responded with the love and affection usually reserved for a mother.

There is no sound reason to deny a person who has voluntarily assumed the obligations of parenthood over a child the same basic rights to due process a natural or legal parent possesses when the State intervenes to disrupt or destroy the family unit. "The policy of our law has always been to encourage family relationships, even those foster in character." *Banks v. United States,* 267 F.2d 535, 539 (2 Cir. 1959).

This is not to say, however, that the State is barred from further action to protect Sean and to insure her welfare. A person in loco parentis must fulfill the obligations of that relationship or else forfeit custody of the child under state law. In any further proceedings, however, the plaintiff must be accorded the same rights as a natural or legal parent. See, *Armstrong v. Manzo,* 380 U.S. 545 (1965); *May v. Anderson,* 345 U.S. 523 (1952).

IN RE CAGER

251 Md. 473, 248 A.2d 384 (1968)

HAMMOND, CHIEF JUDGE.

The Circuit Court for Prince George's County, proceeding under Code (1966 Repl. Vol.), Art. 26 §§ 51 through 71, "Juvenile Causes," and particularly § 52(f) "Neglected child,"[1] found various young illegitimate infants to be living in an unstable moral environment and therefore neglected, solely because each infant lived in a home with the mother and at least one illegitimate sibling, and ordered the infants to be taken from their mothers and placed in foster homes. The appeals are by the guardian *ad litem* of the infants and the three mothers. Planned Parenthood Federation of America, Inc., Planned Parenthood Association of Maryland, Inc., Planned Parenthood of Metropolitan Washington, D.C., Inc. and the Washington Chapter of the Medical Committee for Human Rights filed briefs as amici curiae.

In his opinion Judge Bowen said the three cases:

> are test cases designated to determine whether * * * the State law furnishes a vehicle to assist in the control of the problem of illegitimacy, its mounting costs to the taxpayers, and its mounting costs in human misery and suffering. * * * If the statute * * * is valid * * * we think the State's Attorney's office will proceed with its use in those cases where it applies.

1. Section 52(f) defines a "neglected child" as a child: "(1) who is without proper guardianship; (2) whose parent, guardian or person with whom the child lives, by reason of cruelty, mental incapacity, immorality or depravity, is unfit to care properly for such a child; (3) who is under unlawful or improper care, supervision, custody or restraint, by any person, corporation, agency, association, institution or other organization or who is unlawfully kept out of school; (4) whose parent, guardian or custodian neglects or refuses, when able to do so, to provide necessary medical, surgical, institutional or hospital care for such child; (5) who is in such condition of want or suffering, or is under such improper guardianship or control, or is engaged in such occupation as to injure or endanger the morals or health of himself or others; or (6) who is living in a home which fails to provide a stable moral environment."

* * * As the Court sees it, these cases come before it on * * * the minimum of evidence * * * [O]ther evidence could be brought before the Court of the surroundings in these homes, of the disposition of the parents, of the condition of the children, and a great many other things * * * [T]he charge * * * is supported substantially only by the stipulation of facts.[2] Other evidence can be gleaned perhaps from the birth certificates and from the report which was submitted, but we do not consider that, we consider the case on these facts: * * * these women have conducted themselves in such a way that they have brought into the world more than one illegitimate child, that these children are now living together with their mother under the same roof, or in the same group unit * * *. [T]he question to be decided is whether or not on that set of minimum facts, the Court can find that they are neglected within the meaning of the Maryland law * * *. [A]re these children living in an unstable moral environment.

*   *   *

Most first illegitimate children * * * are the result of a mistake * * *. The second time around we think represents a lack of judgment and demonstrates an unstable moral attitude on the part of the mother * * * that is inconsistent with the minimum moral standard the community requires.

*   *   *

We have no difficulty concluding that the words unstable moral environment relate or were intended to apply to a situation

2. The stipulation was that the appellant Jackson has had three children born out of wedlock, appellant Cager has had four, and appellant Patterson has had three, that all the children are alive and that, with one exception, all of the children born to a given mother are residing with that mother.

In his closing remarks the State's Attorney went beyond the stipulation by giving information as to the ages of the mothers—two were in their teens—of the children, the names of the fathers, which in each instance save one were different, and that their occupations and whereabouts were unknown, and that each mother had had an illegitimate child within the last twelve months.

where a mother has had a series of illegitimate children such as the mothers had in these cases. And that such a series * * * constitutes on the part of the mother neglect of each of the children involved [within the meaning of the statute].

We think that Judge Bowen's conclusion that an illegitimate child can judicially be found to be neglected because of the sole fact that he lives with a mother who has had another illegitimate child who also lives with her is erroneous.

The purposes of § 52(f) of Art. 26 of the Code, as revealed by its legislatively prescribed standards, must be considered in determining as a fact whether a child is neglected. The statute asks whether the person with whom the child lives "by reason of cruelty, mental incapacity, immorality or depravity, is unfit to care properly for such a child." It is concerned with whether the child is under unlawful or improper care, supervision or restraint by any person or entity. Does the child's parent or custodian fail to provide necessary medical care; are the health and morals of the child endangered by his custody, environment or occupation, and finally, does the child live in a home "which fails to provide a stable moral environment." In determining whether a child is neglected because he lives in an unstable moral environment, the court shall consider, *among other things,* whether the person with whom the child lives:

(i) Is unable to provide such environment by reasons of immaturity, or emotional, mental or physical disability;

(ii) Is engaging in promiscuous conduct inside or outside the home;

(iii) Is cohabiting with a person to whom he or she is not married;

(iv) Is pregnant with an illegitimate child; or

(v) Has, within a period of twelve months preceding the filing of the petition alleging the child to be neglected, either been pregnant with or given birth to another child to whose putative father she was not legally married at the time of conception, or has not thereafter married.

The basis for determining neglect must be broader than that on which Judge Bowen rested his determination. Being pregnant with an illegitimate child or having given birth to an illegitimate child within twelve months of the filing of the petition alleging the child to be neglected are two factors to be considered under the statute, "among other things," as indicating neglect but they cannot alone and automatically be found to be indicators of that fact. The "other things" the court is directed to consider in determining whether there is or is not a stable moral environment must include the factors previously enumerated in § 52(f), pertinent to the particular case. Furthermore, that section does not make explicit as a test of neglect the fact that two illegitimate children of a mother live with her and we do not find such a test reasonably or fairly implicit in the statute as a sole determinant.

It is clear that the ultimate consideration in finding neglect which will serve as a basis for removing a child from its mother's custody is the best interest of the child. As we said in discussing the provisions of Art. 26, Subtitle "Juvenile Causes," regarding juvenile delinquents in Ex Parte Cromwell, 232 Md. 305, 308, 192 A.2d 775, 777:

> It is clear that the statute is aimed at the protection and rehabilitation of the child, not its punishment * * *. The power exercised by the State is that of *parens patriae* * * *. The fact that parents may be deprived of the custody of their own children presents no constitutional problems.

The best interest of a child may or may not be served by removing it from the custody of a mother who has had another illegitimate child but the sole test, automatically applied, cannot in fact or law be pregnancy with an illegitimate child or the recent birth of an illegitimate child added to the presence of an existing illegitimate offspring. Cf. Levy v. Louisiana, 391 U.S. 68, 88 S. Ct. 1509, 20 L. Ed. 2d 436. It is equally clear that although a State is permitted to remove a child from a home that has been judicially determined to be so unsuitable as to be contrary to the welfare of the child and to terminate AFDC assistance to a child living in an unsuitable home if it provides other adequate care and assistance for the child, a State may not deny AFDC assistance to dependent children "on the basis of their mother's alleged immorality or to discourage illegitimate births." King v. Smith, 392 U.S. 309, 324, 88 S. Ct. 2128, 2137, 20 L. Ed. 2d 1118, 1129–1130. The cases presently before us would seem to have been instituted not to serve and perpetuate the best interests of the children but rather impermissibly to use the children as pawns in a plan to punish their mothers for their past promiscuity and to discourage them and other females of like weaknesses and inclinations from future productivity.

The brief of the guardian *ad litem* argues that § 52(f) as interpreted by the court below and as applied is invalid under the equal protection clause of the Fourteenth Amendment because it invidiously and purposefully discriminates against the poor who apply for public assistance. The interpretation we give the statute and the limitations of confidentiality we hereinafter find the applicable statutes to impose on state officials will answer these arguments.

The brief of the mothers contends that § 52(f) of Art. 26 is unconstitutionally vague. As we read that section, the standards prescribed by the legislature to determine the presence of neglect are sufficiently precise and definite. Although the judicial determination of neglect is civil in nature, the application of the test of sufficient explicitness needed for a criminal statute shows, we think, that a person of ordinary intelligence could determine from § 52(f) with a fair degree of precision whether a child was or was not neglected, McGowan v. State, 220 Md. 117, 125, 151 A.2d 156; McGowan v. Maryland, 366 U.S. 420, 428, 81 S. Ct. 1101, 6 L. Ed. 2d 393, 400; Richards Furniture Corp. v. Board of County Comm'rs of Anne Arundel County, 233 Md. 249, 196 A.2d 621; Director of Patuxent Institution vs. Daniels, 243 Md. 16, 221 A.2d 397, cert. denied, Avery v. Boslow, 385 U.S. 940, 87 S. Ct. 307, 17 L. Ed. 2d 219 and this is enough to defeat the claim of unconstitutional vagueness.

The mothers also contend that the neglect statute is unconstitutional because it does not apply to Montgomery County which has its own, slightly different, juvenile statute. The contention is answered by McGowan v. Maryland, supra, which upheld the Sunday Blue Laws which varied from County to County in Maryland against attack as unconstitutional for that reason.

It would appear from the record that the State's Attorney of Prince George's County was a prime movant in the apparent campaign or crusade to discourage promiscuity and illegitimacy. His goal may have been laudable but his road toward that goal is attacked by the appellants, justifiably we think, as violative of federal and state requirements of confidentiality in that he used information he gleaned from certain forms the mothers were required to present to him for purposes for which it was not intended to and cannot lawfully be used.

The Welfare laws and regulations required each mother to present in person to the State's Attorney a filled out form 218, "Support of Dependent Child, Notification of Dependency and Request for Report of Action," as a prerequisite to obtaining aid for dependent children. Each applicant enters her name and the names and ages of her children, and information concerning the father. The information revealed by the form is intended only to enable the State's Attorney to obtain information about a non-supporting father so that he may either obtain a warrant for the father's arrest or to institute paternity proceedings. In the cases before us, the forms revealed to the State's Attorney that the names of the children and the fathers did not match, and their use for this purpose led to the investigations which preceded the cases. Title 42 U.S.C.A. § 602(a)(11) requires that law enforcement officials be notified of aid furnished children who have been deserted or abandoned. Section 602(a)(9) requires each State to "provide safeguards which restrict the use or disclosure of information concerning applicants and recipients to purposes directly connected with the administration of aid to families with dependent children." A regulation of the United States Department of Health, Education, and Welfare states that:

> The provisions of the Social Security Act, regarding the confidential character of public assistance information have as their objective the protection of applicants and recipients from exploitation and embarrassment.

By means of Art. 88A, § 5, of the Code and regulations promulgated thereunder, Maryland has complied with the federal requirements. Section 5 requires the State Board of Public Welfare to adopt rules and regulations having "the force and effect of law" governing the use of "records, papers, files and communication of the State and local departments concerning applicants and recipients of assistance." The section further provides that the use of such material "by any other agency or department of government to which they may be furnished shall be *limited to the purposes for which they are furnished* [emphasis added].

The State Department of Public Welfare issued Rule 1000, Confidential Nature of Records, in compliance with the legislature's directive. This rule explains the importance of confidentiality, emphasizing that information in the records may be used only by persons with appropriate authority, and only for purposes *directly* connected with the administration of welfare programs.

The Department states under Part I (2), General Principles and Guides:

The protection of the rights of individuals served by the public welfare department requires that they be safeguarded against identification as a special group and against exploitation for commercial, personal or political reasons.

Departmental regulations do provide for certain situations under which such records may be used. Part IV, Basis for Use of Information Outside the Department, sets forth three circumstances under which information may be disclosed without the consent of the client:

a. Upon proper judicial order when the purpose is directly connected with the administration of the agency's program***.
b. Upon proper legislative order when the purpose is directly connected with the administration of the Department's program.
c. To an officer of the United States, of the state, of the county, or another state, who has a right thereto in his official capacity when the purpose is directly connected with the administration of the Department's program.

We believe this listing to be exclusive in nature.

The use of Form 218 to provide information leading to a neglect proceeding is clearly not sanctioned. The federal and state statutory and administrative provisions all provide that such information is not to be used for purposes extraneous to the AFDC program. The children's eligibility for AFDC is not statutorily designed to be affected by a determination of neglect.

Undoubtedly, a State's Attorney is to be furnished Form 218 for the purpose of proceeding against absent fathers, but the State's Attorney's right is limited to the use of the form for this purpose. Cf. Mace v. Jung (Alaska), 386 P.2d 579; see Terrell v. City of New York (S. Ct. King's County), reported in N.Y.L.J. (Jan. 29, 1968), p. 19, col. 3. Compare State ex rel. Haugland v. Smuthe, 25 Wash. 2d 161, 169 P.2d 706, 165 A.L.R. 1295; Bell v. Bankers Life & Casualty Co., 327 Ill. App. 321, 64 N.E.2d 204.

The mothers urge upon us that to deny them the status of parties to the case—as the lower court did, although he heard them as amici through their counsel—violated their rights under both the State and Federal Constitutions and that had they been made parties defendant, as they should have been, they were entitled to court appointed counsel and the payment of costs and expenses at both the trial and appellate level. Their contentions go too far, in our opinion.

Juvenile Court proceedings were not intended to and, constitutionally, need not be conducted under the usual rules governing court trials or even administrative hearings as long as a standard of fairness is recognized and adhered to. Code (1966 Repl. Vol.), Art. 26 §§ 60, 64; In Matter of Cromwell, 232 Md. 409, 415, 194 A.2d 88. In In re Gault, 387 U.S. 1, 30–31, 87 S. Ct. 1428, 18 L. Ed. 2d 527, the Supreme Court quoted with approval the rule applied to waivers of juvenile jurisdiction in Kent v. United States, 383 U.S. 541, 86 S. Ct. 1045, 16 L. Ed. 2d 84, holding that it applied as well to hearings on delinquency of minors:

> We do not mean ° ° ° to indicate that the hearing to be held must conform with all of the requirements of a criminal trial or even of the usual administrative hearing; but we do hold that the hearing must measure up to the essentials of due process and fair treatment. [387 U.S. at 30, 87 S. Ct. at 1445]

We think the hearings below fully met the required standards of fairness. The infants involved were represented by a guardian *ad litem* who is a practicing attorney who energetically and competently sought to forward their interests. The mothers were given full notice of the actions the State's Attorney took and the ends he sought and were given full opportunity to be heard by the court. We find no basis for holding that the mothers were entitled as a matter of right either to be furnished counsel at public expense or given their expenses in connection with the trial or the appeal. In In re Gault, supra, the Supreme Court, in dealing with judicial determination of delinquency which could lead to removal of the child from his mother's custody and his incarceration for years in a correctional home, said:

> We conclude that the Due Process Clause of the Fourteenth Amendment requires that in respect of proceedings to determine delinquency which may result in commitment to an institution in which the juvenile's freedom is curtailed, the child and his parents must be notified of the *child's* right to be represented by counsel retained by them, or if they are unable to afford counsel, that counsel will be appointed to represent *the child*. [Emphasis added] [387 U.S. at 41, 87 S. Ct. at 1451]

We think that no more is required in respect of proceedings to determine neglect, with the qualifications first that only such proceedings which are or will become contested need there be appointed to represent the child a guardian *ad litem* who is a lawyer or a lawyer to represent a guardian who is not a lawyer and, second, that if the representative of the child and the mother wishes to appeal such a ruling, she should be made a party so that she can appeal to represent the child's interest under the provisions of § 65 of Art. 26 that "any interested party aggrieved by any order or decree of the judge may appeal therefrom to the Court of Appeals." Compare In re Cruse (Ct. App. La.), 203 So. 2d 893; Watson v. Department of Public Welfare, 130 Ind. App. 659, 165 N.E.2d 770.

Prince George's County paid the expenses and costs below, including remuneration to the infants' guardian *ad litem,* but would not pay or agree to pay such expenses and costs on appeal. Section

68 of Art. 26 provides that if the parent or custodian of any child coming before the court "under the provisions of this subtitle [§§ 51 through 71 of Art. 26]" is able to pay the costs of the proceedings against the child and it is proper that he do so, the court may order that he do so, and continues: "except as otherwise provided, *all* costs incurred by the prosecution of *cases under this subtitle* shall be paid by the county commissioners" (all emphasis added). We think that "all costs" includes the costs of an appeal pursuant to § 65 of Art. 26, one of the provisions of "this subtitle." The County Commissioners of Prince George's County shall therefore pay the costs on appeal, other than the costs attributable to the participation of the mothers and the amici, including suitable reasonable remuneration to the guardian *ad litem* for the children. See Chambers v. District Court of Dubuque County (Iowa), 152 N.W.2d 818; Hernandez v. Hardy (Tex. Ct. Civ. App.) 426 S.W.2d 258; In re Karren (Minn.), 159 N.W.2d 402. Cf. Alexander v. Superintendent, 246 Md. 334, 339, 228 A.2d 236.

Orders reversed, costs of the infants and of the State to be paid by the County Commissioners of Prince George's County.

BARNES, Judge (dissenting).

I dissent because, in my opinion, the majority (1) has misinterpreted Code (1957) Article 26, Section 52(f), as amended by Chapter 723 of the Acts of 1963, and (2) has erred in holding that there has been a violation of federal and state requirements of confidentiality in the use of Form 218.

In Article 26, Section 52(f) the General Assembly under the subheading "Juvenile Causes," defines what is a "neglected child." There are *six* separate and alternative criteria, the establishment of *any one of which* will indicate that the child is a "neglected child." These criteria are separately numbered, are marked off by semi-colons and the last criterion is connected with the others by the word "or" and not the word "and." These criteria are as follows: [The Court here quotes Article 26, Section 52(f).]

*   *   *

This sixth criterion [see footnote 1, page 155], which was added to the first five by Chapter 723 of the Acts of 1963, contains five *alternative* criteria which the Court *shall* consider "among other things" to determine whether such stable moral environment exists. These five alternative criteria are whether the parent, guardian or person with whom the child lives:

(i) Is unable to provide such environment by reasons of immaturity, or emotional, mental or physical disability;

(ii) Is engaging in promiscuous conduct inside or outside the home;

(iii) Is cohabiting with a person to whom he or she is not married;

(iv) Is pregnant with an illegitimate child; *or*

(v) Has, within a period of twelve months preceding the filing of the petition alleging the child to be neglected, either been pregnant with or given birth to another child to whose putative father she was not legally married at the time of conception, or has not thereafter married (emphasis supplied).

It can hardly be contended that the six primary criteria are not alternative and that the establishment of any one of them will not justify a finding that the child is a "neglected child." Not only is this clear from the arrangement of the six criteria with separate numbers and separated by semi-colons and by use of the word "or," but a consideration of the subject matter of the various criteria, itself, indicates this. Compare, for example, criterion No. 4 in regard to the failure to supply necessary medical care, when able to do so, with criterion No. 3 in regard to unlawful care or supervision or the unlawful keeping of the child from school. Indeed, if the six primary criteria were not held to be alternative, it would be next to impossible to find that a child was "neglected" as it would be most improbable that all six of the criteria would ever exist simultaneously in a given factual situation.

The same statutory plan is followed in Section 52(e) in its definition of a "delinquent child," which established six alternative criteria. The first criterion in this definition of a delinquent child is a child "(1) who violates any law or ordinance, or who commits any act which, if committed by an adult, would be a crime not punishable by death or life imprisonment; * * *." We indicated in In re

Cromwell, 232 Md. 409, 414, 194 A.2d 88, 90 (1963)—a case involving a determination of delinquency of a child in which the petition alleged only the first criterion already quoted as the *sole* ground for establishing delinquency—that this allegation and the proof supporting it were sufficient to support a finding of delinquency under Section 52(e). This necessarily means that the establishment of *any one* of the six criteria is sufficient for the establishment of delinquency. Inasmuch as Section 52(f) follows exactly the same format, punctuation and use of the word "or," as used in Section 52(e), In re Cromwell supports the position that the six criteria in Section 52(f) are also alternative and that the establishment of one of the six criteria in Section 52(f) is sufficient to establish that a child is "neglected."

As has been observed, the five criteria to establish whether a stable moral environment exists are set forth in the same format, punctuation and in the use of the word "or," as used in Section 52, subsections (e) and (f) in reciting the six criteria in each subsection. It is reasonable to conclude from this legislative usage that the five criteria mentioned under (6) of subsection (f) were also intended by the General Assembly to be alternative criteria so that the allegation and establishment of any one of the five criteria would justify and effectively support a finding that a "stable moral environment" did not exist. This construction must almost necessarily be correct as here again it would be most unlikely that all five criteria would exist simultaneously. If all five must exist simultaneously, it would mean that only a mother who was at the time of the petition "pregnant with an illegitimate child," as provided in criterion (iv), could fail to "provide a stable moral environment," although all of the other four criteria might exist. This appears to me to be a most unreasonable construction resulting in an absurd and unjust consequence which the Court should not assume was the legislative intent. See B. F. Saul Co. v. West End Park North, Inc., 250 Md. 707, 722, 246 A.2d 591, 601 (1968), and prior Maryland cases cited in that opinion.

It is clear to me that the words "among other things" mean that the Court *may* consider facts other than the five criteria which follow, but *shall consider* the five criteria and if any one is applicable in the situation, and the facts support its existence, the Court is then justified in finding that a stable moral environment does not exist. More than one criterion *may* be applicable and established, but only one *must* be applicable and established. This is what the language clearly means to me and it is consistent with the other language in Section 52 as well as with our opinion in In re Cromwell, supra.

When the legislative intent is apparent from the words used, there is no need to look further for the legislative intent. The duty of this Court is to carry out that intention.

* * *

If it is assumed for the argument that the language of Section 52(f)(6) is ambiguous, a consideration of the usual rules of construction in the event of statutory ambiguity leads to the same interpretation already given.

First of all, if the language were ambiguous, the courts should consider the evils or mischief which the Legislature sought to remedy and should construe the language so as to effectuate the general purposes and policies of the legislation. Cooley v. White Cross Health and Beauty Aid Discount Centers, Inc., 229 Md. 343, 350, 183 A.2d 381, 385–86 (1962). Fortunately, Chapter 723 of the Acts of 1963 was an outgrowth of the comprehensive study of the problems of illegitimacy by the excellent Commission to Study Problems of Illegitimacy appointed by Governor Tawes at the request of the General Assembly by its Joint Resolution No. 2 of 1960. This Commission filed its Interim Report with the Legislative Council of Maryland on October 9, 1960, and filed its Final Report with the Legislative Council of Maryland on December 6, 1961. Reference to the Report of the Commission was referred to in the brief of the appellants and in the argument and, in any event, as an official report of a State Commission, this Court may take judicial notice of it. See Dispatch, Inc. v. City of Erie, 364 F.2d 539 (3d Cir., 1966); Department of Public Welfare v. Bohleber, 21 Ill. 2d 587, 173 N.E.2d 457 (1961). See also Ex Parte Cromwell, supra, 232 Md. 305, 309, 19 A.2d 775, 777–78 (1963). This Report contained a number of recommendations for specific legislation, one of these recommendations being, as will be developed more fully later, the addition of subparagraph (6) to Section 52(f). This Report gives the general purpose of the proposed legislation and the policy sought to be effectuated by it. It also gives, in part, the legislative history of the legislation, which the courts may examine to ascertain the legislative intent, if the language is ambiguous. Baltimore Transit Co. v. Metropolitan Transit Authority, 232 Md. 509, 513, 194 A.2d 643, 644–45 (1963). It is a fortunate circumstance in this case that the background of the legislation and a substantial portion of the legislative history are available through this Report, as generally speaking, these are not available in Maryland.

The Report is a comprehensive work of 190 pages (including the Interim Report of October 9, 1960) and contains a bibliography of 135 sources of study, including books, studies, reports, pamphlets, articles and various unbound material. Much of the research was organized and conducted by Adelaide Dinwoodie Nurco, B.S., M.S.W., and the statistical material consists, in part, of some 80 Tables in the various appendixes giving valuable data on the problem of illegitimacy in Maryland.

In its Concluding Statement in Chapter Four of its Report, the Commission stated, in part, the following:

> The Commission is neither so naive, nor so affected by "wishful thinking" to believe that its recommendations individually or in their cumulative effect, will eradicate illegitimacy. However, this Commission does believe that these recommendations, by imposing specific responsibilities upon various agencies of public and private service, and by changing the law upon which society can act, will provide the community with preventative and corrective measures which will have a definite remedial impact upon the problem.
>
> The Commission believes that its recommendations emphasize prevention and treatment, and avoid the imposition of hardships upon innocent children by reason of their parents' conduct. It further believes that its recommendations recognize the duty of the courts as the proper agency of government to determine what is in the best interests of children, to hold parents to their basic responsibilities and to deal with parental neglect as either indicative of a need for help through social services or as an offense to be punished.

Years ago in the interest of children, it became necessary to adopt stern though unpopular laws to enforce school attendance. To retard tuberculosis and venereal disease, the community has passed laws and coordinated all available means of attacking the problems. Today the community stands at a similar point of decision with respect to illegitimacy. Either we must bring into the light of public concern all the ugly facts relating to il-
· legitimacy and attack it through such means, for example, as recommended by the Commission; or accept the alternative of admitting that we are powerless to uphold the Judaeo-Christian concepts of sanctity of marriage, standards of family life and concern for the welfare of children.

The Commission made nineteen recommendations in its Report, Recommendation Two being the addition to Article 26, Section 52(f) with which the case is principally concerned. None of the recommendations is directed toward direct punitive criminal action in regard to the parents of the illegitimate child and, indeed, Recommendation Three specifically recommends against legislation which would punish illicit cohabitation. The thrust of substantially all of the recommendations is toward the welfare of the illegitimate child and the removal of that child from a home which fails to supply a stable moral environment and thus to prevent the rearing of the children in an environment which will likely condition them for the same type of immoral and anti-social conduct as that in which their parents have indulged.

Recommendation Two is as follows:

The Commission recommends that by appropriate legislation approved by the Legislative Council, the definition of "neglected child" as set forth in the State Juvenile Court Act and in Public Local Laws in effect in Baltimore City and certain of the counties, be broadened to provide that a child whether legitimate or illegitimate is neglected if living in a home which fails to provide a stable moral environment; and to further provide that the absence of such stable moral environment is prima facie established if the parent, guardian or person with whom the child lives

(1) Is unable to provide such environment by reasons of immaturity, emotional, mental or physical disability,

(2) Is engaging in promiscuous conduct inside or outside the home,

(3) Is co-habiting with a person to whom he or she is not married,

(4) Is pregnant with an illegitimate child, or

(5) Has, within a period of twelve months preceding the filing of the petition alleging neglect, either been pregnant with or given birth to an illegitimate child in addition to the child whose neglect is complained of.

The "Comment" on Recommendation Two is important and is as follows:

> Existing law provides that a child is neglected if the person having its custody is *unfit by reason of immorality to "care properly" for the child*. The Commission believes, that "immorality" creating an improper environment for a child should be clearly defined in order that public welfare workers and others may know under what specific circumstances they have the duty to file petitions alleging child-neglect.
>
> After reviewing definitions of child-neglect in the statutes of other states, the Commission adopted its five-point criteria. Florida, Minnesota and Wisconsin have reported the successful application of *one or more of these criteria* in handling the problem of illegitimacy and immorality.
>
> It is not the intention of the Commission that neglect petitions be filed under this proposed new section against the woman whose *only child* is an illegitimate child. *Actions hereunder would be for the benefit of any child, legitimate or illegitimate, whose parent or guardian is unable to provide a stable moral environment or whose pattern of behavior constitutes prima facie neglect*. This act would give the court an indirect approach to the parent's unacceptable behavior by relating it to the neglect of other existing children (emphasis supplied).

It seems clear to me that the Commission intended in the preparation of the five sub-criteria, that the establishment of any one of them was sufficient to support a finding of the absence of a stable moral environment.

As introduced into the General Assembly in 1963 as House Bill 6, Recommendation Two of the Commission was substantially followed except the language of sub-criterion (v) was clarified. During the course of the legislation through the General Assembly, however, the words *"the absence of such stable environment is prima facie established if"* were eliminated by amendment and the present language *"In determining whether such stable moral environment exists, the Court shall consider, among other things,"* the parent, guardian or person, etc., was substituted. As I see it, the purpose of this amendment was to *broaden* the power of the court in making the determination of the existence of a stable moral environment, so that *other criteria* than one of the five criteria mentioned *could* justify the court in finding the absence of the stable moral environment. In short, the court *must* consider whether one or more of the specifically mentioned criteria exist but *may* consider in a particular case other relevant facts not specified.

Counsel for the appellants earnestly argued in their brief and before us at the argument, that this change of language indicated a legislative intention that the establishment of one or more of the named criteria would not "prima facie" establish the absence of the stable moral environment. As already indicated, the language indicates to me that the legislative intent was to *broaden* the courts' power in this regard, and was not intended to indicate a *restriction* on the courts' power in reaching the determination. This is made clear to me not only from the language itself, but also by the fact that after the amendment already mentioned was made in the body of the bill, there was no change made in the original title to the bill which concluded "* * * and specifying conditions the existence of which shall prima facie establish the lack of such environment." The amendatory language is consistent with this provision of the title and if it had not been deemed to have been consistent with it, there undoubtedly would have been an amendment of the language of the title to reflect a different intent.

In my opinion, there was evidence in the record in the present case from which the trial court could find and infer that not only subsection (v) of Section 53(f) was involved, but also subsection (ii)—engaging in promiscuous conduct, subsection (i)—inability to provide a stable moral environment because of immaturity or emotional disability, and possibly subsection (iii)—cohabitation with a person to whom the mother is not married. I do not find in the record that the trial court relied *solely and entirely* on subsection (v). On the contrary in colloquy between the trial court and Mr. Bourne, counsel for the amicus curiae mothers, rather indicates the contrary. The colloquy is as follows:

(Mr. Bourne) They are claiming in their argument to this Court that you should take into consideration immaturity and engaging in promiscuous conduct, cohabiting to the person to whom she is not married.

(The Court) But isn't all that simply ramifications and deductions and logical inferences from one fact that is before the Court?

(Mr. Bourne) No, Your Honor. I think that the language of the statute precludes any inference of any of those first four points by the tense of the verb.

(The Court) If so, it is contrary to the natural laws that the Creator put here in the universe.

(Mr. Bourne) Well, the law says "is" unable, is engaging, is cohabiting, is pregnant, those are present tense. Now then on five we go to "has."

I think we have got to go by the tense of the language of the statute.

(The Court) The only facts that they have offered into evidence are the ones they stated to you in the particulars. They stated they intend to prove that these children were living in a house where the mother had illegitimate children. That is all they have proved. What they are arguing from that fact is what is disturbing you.

The arguments and inferences that can be drawn from a fact aren't limited by the particulars. The particulars are limited only to what you are going to prove.

Even if the trial court relied entirely on subsection (v), its findings from the stipulated facts and proper inferences from those facts, were, in my opinion, fully supported and justified. The stipulation of facts in this case was in relevant part as set forth in Note 2 in the majority opinion, and showed that the three appellant mothers had three, four and three illegitimate children, respectively, that all of the illegitimate children were alive and, with one exception, all of the children born to a given mother were living with that mother. Judge Bowen, in making the findings, stated, in part, as follows:

> Now the charge, as we understand it, is supported substantially only by the stipulation of facts. Other evidence can be gleaned perhaps from the birth certificates and from the report which was submitted, but we do not consider that, we consider this case on these facts: *That these women have conducted themselves in such a way that they have brought into the world more than one illegitimate child, that those children are now living together with their mother under the same roof, or in the same group unit.*
>
> *Now the question to be decided is whether or not on that set of minimum facts, the Court can find that they are neglected within the meaning of the Maryland law.*
>
> This brings us to the resolution of the question raised by that law: *are these children living in an unstable moral environment.*
>
> This business of an unstable moral environment encompasses the intangible proposition that exists between human beings who live together as a unit related by ties of blood or marriage. The mere absence of a man from a group is not what we are talking about. Widows and divorcees need not be considered as unstable because no man is involved in their home. What is sought to be elicited in the moral question is the recognition by the community that the relationships between the man in the house and the mother of the children are those which meet the minimum acceptable standards of the community. And the minimum acceptable standards in this community for men and women who wish to live together, to have sexual relations and to bring into the world children in union between themselves is that they be married. And something less than that, we think,

is, under the regulations that society has imposed upon itself, immoral.

*   *   *

The second time around we think represents *a lack of judgment and demonstrates an unstable moral attitude on the part of the mother.* We think for her to continue to conduct herself in such a way as repeatedly to bring illegitimate children into her household, *reflects a weakness in her character, and a demonstrable view of morals on her part, that is inconsistent with the minimum moral standard the community requires. And the reason therefor, that by her deliberate knowing course of conduct in engaging in sexual relations with men, that produce illegitimate children, she has demonstrated in the most forceful and irrefutable way that she either does not care for the views of society on morals, or caring, is unable to conform her conduct to their minimum standards.*

We have no difficulty concluding that the words unstable moral environment relate or were intended to apply to a situation where a mother had had a series of illegitimate children such as these mothers had in these cases. And that such a series of illegitimate children constitutes on the part of the mother neglect of each of the children involved.

Neglect concerns itself not only with the physical aspects of the children's lives, but with their moral and spiritual existence as well. That it is impossible for a mother of less than independent wealth to care for three or four or seven or eleven or twelve illegitimate children on the slender means provided her by the welfare department, we think is axiomatic. *That it is virtually impossible for a mother who continues to have illegitimate children by a series of fathers, that it is impossible for such a woman to provide the moral training and the spiritual counseling that ought to surround the nurture of children of tender years so they will not themselves fall into the difficulties that she has fallen into,* * * *.

In short, gentlemen, *the Court concludes that the unexplained facts presented in this case demonstrate to the Court's satis-*

*faction that these children are neglected within the meaning of
the statute* (emphasis supplied).

There was no attempt upon the part of the mothers, the guardians
ad litem of the children or of any of the other parties to produce any
evidence which would indicate that notwithstanding the prima facie
showing of the absence of a stable moral environment, there were,
in fact, existing conditions which would possibly rebut that prima
facie showing and possibly establish that a stable moral environment
did in fact exist in any of the situations before the Court. The
failure to produce any such evidence and entry into the stipulation
indicates strongly to me that no such evidence was available.

In my opinion, the trial court correctly interpreted the Maryland
statute, and its findings were supported by the record. The record
does not indicate to me that the present cases were "instituted not
to serve and perpetuate the best interests of the children but rather
impermissibly to use the children as pawns in a plan to punish their
mothers for their past promiscuity and to discourage them and other
females of like weaknesses and inclinations from future productivity"
as is indicated in the majority opinion. On the contrary, the record
indicates to me that the removal of the children from a home in
which a stable moral influence does not exist is definitely for the
best interests of those children so that, in the words of the Report
of the Commission on Illegitimacy, the children will not be permitted "to live in homes where promiscuity and non-conforming patterns
of family life become the accepted standards of living for the children to emulate." If as a peripheral benefit of this primary legislative
policy to benefit the illegitimate children, promiscuous parents are
led to abandon their immoral life, the public interest is advanced to
that extent. This, however, is not the primary purpose of the legislation, nor, in my opinion, was it the primary purpose of the institution of the present cases.

The conclusion of the trial court is in accord with the holding in
In re Dake, 180 N.E.2d 646, 648, 649 (Juvenile Ct. of Huron Co.,
Ohio, 1961). In that case, the mother of four illegitimate children,
two of whom were living with her, applied to the Welfare Department of Huron County, Ohio for assistance under the Aid for De-

pendent Children (A.F.D.C.) program. The Welfare Department then sought custody of the two children living with the mother and requested the Ohio Juvenile Court to declare the children neglected in order to deprive the mother of custody permanently. The Juvenile Court of Huron County, Ohio stated the issue before it as follows:

> Briefly stated it is whether a woman who is so devoid of morals and intelligence as to bring forth a series of illegitimate children who must be supported by public funds, is entitled to retain the custody of those children. Is a woman who is incapable of ordering her own life in accordance with the prevailing legal and moral codes, capable of raising children without a father? (180 N.E.2d at 648).

In Ohio, as in Maryland, the primary consideration in determining the custody is: "What is the best interest of the child?" The Court decided that the mother was not entitled to retain custody of the two children living with her, deciding that the best interest of these children would not be advanced by:

> ° ° ° leaving them in their mother's care, without a father, stigmatized as illegitimate, supported mainly by public funds, and in an atmosphere completely lacking in moral decency, rather than by removing them completely and permanently from their natural mother, so that they may have the chance of normal upbringing in a decent home with two loving parents. (180 N.E.2d at 649).

See also In re Turner, 12 Ohio Misc. 171, 231 N.E.2d 502 (Ct. of Com. Pleas, Starr Co., Ohio, 1967).

Nor does the record indicate to me "that the State's Attorney of Prince George's County was a prime movant in the apparent campaign or crusade to discourage promiscuity and illegitimacy," as the majority opinion suggests or that, even though such a goal might have been laudable, his road toward that goal was "violative of federal and state requirements of confidentiality" in the use of information gleaned from "certain forms the mothers were required to present to him for purposes for which it was not intended to and cannot lawfully be used."

The provisions of the various federal and state statutes and regulations are set forth in detail in the majority opinion and need not be further considered here. The end result is that the information on Form 218 of the Welfare Department of Prince George's County may be used for purposes *directly connected* with the administration of the welfare program. There is little question in my mind that the information on Form 218 may be used in the investigation of cases of apparent neglect as such an investigation is directly connected with the welfare program. Indeed, Code (1957) Article 88A, Section 48A, added by the Act of 1963, Chapter 423 in accordance with Recommendation Seven of the Commission on Illegitimacy, as one part of the administration of the welfare program, that child neglect proceedings be instituted when information obtained by the Welfare Department indicates that a child is neglected.

Form 218 was presented to the State's Attorney for Prince George's County as required by the County's Welfare Department. His contact with the mothers seeking aid for dependent children was not that of attorney and client or even of prosecuting attorney and witness. The State's Attorney in this special situation was merely an administrative agent for the Welfare Department and when the fact of apparent neglect of a child appeared, it was the duty of the State's Attorney to file an appropriate petition to ascertain whether or not the child was a neglected child as defined by the statute. This is not only directly connected with the administration of the welfare program by statute, but it is difficult for me to see how the discovery of neglect of a child for whom AFDC assistance is sought would not be directly connected with the administration of the welfare program apart from the statutory provision. It can hardly be contended that it is a purpose of the AFDC program to subsidize those who neglect their children or to provide for the continuance of the neglect of a child! The removal of neglected children from that assistance, the placing of them in proper foster homes or providing for other proper methods of eliminating the neglect must, of necessity, be directly connected with the administration of the welfare program. I see no violation of either federal or state requirements of confidentiality in the use of the information on Form 218 to investigate cases of apparent child neglect.

If, however, it be assumed, arguendo, that there could be such a violation in the use of information on Form 218 for this purpose, in the present case the *means* by which the information was obtained was not before the trial court or before this Court, on appeal, because all of the parties, *by stipulation,* in open Court, agreed that the children were illegitimate. Under these circumstances any supposed breach of confidentiality is not, in my opinion, properly before us for adjudication in the present cases.

I would affirm.

IN RE RAYA

255 Cal. App.2d 260, 63 Cal. Rptr. 252 (1967)

(A Synopsis of the Facts in the Raya Case)

[Mr. and Mrs. Raya separated in 1960. They have not lived together since. Each is presently cohabiting with partners of the opposite sex under a consensual extramarital arrangement; Mrs. Raya and her consort, William Mendoza, have had four children out of wedlock while Mr. Raya and his mistress, a Miss Fernandez, have had three children. As soon as Mr. Raya and Miss Fernandez commenced living together, a divorce was contemplated, but at the time Mr. Raya lacked funds to pay the legal expense. On February 7, 1967, Mr. Raya filed a divorce action, the purpose of which was to affect a change in the relationship of both couples, who have expressed an intent to marry as soon as this may legally be accomplished.

At the time of the separation Mrs. Raya took with her the two children (9 and 7 years of age) born of the marriage, and they remained with her until adjudged to be dependent children within the meaning of Welfare and Institutions Code section 600, subdivision (a). They were first placed with the grandmother who was declared unfit because she was living with another man, and then placed in the Sacramento Receiving Home "pending suitable placement by the Sacramento County Welfare Department." Section 600 provides in part:

> Any person under the age of 21 years who comes within any of the following descriptions is within the jurisdiction of the juvenile court which may adjudge such person to be a dependent child of the court:
> (a) Who is in need of proper and effective parental care or control and has no parent or guardian, or has no parent or guardian willing to exercise or capable of exercising such care or control, or has no parent or guardian actually exercising such care or control.

(Section 600, subdivision (b), also includes a child "whose home is an unfit place for him by reason of neglect, cruelty, or depravity of either of his parents * * *.")

Mr. Raya's divorce complaint alleges Mrs. Raya to be a fit and proper person to have custody of the children.]

PER CURIAM.

During the pendency of the divorce a probation report was ordered. The report, dated April 18, 1967, includes these facts: The Mendoza-Raya family resides in a three-bedroom home in a low rent district. The home is being purchased by the couple. It is described as "neat, clean and quite comfortable * * * and furnished with all necessary facilities." The children lived in the Raya-Mendoza household and accepted Mr. Mendoza as their father and he was a father to them. The Rayas separated when the children were very young and since that time they had little or no contact with their natural father. When they subsequently learned that their natural father was Raya, they became quite disturbed. The report states the children appear well cared for and Raya concedes that Mrs. Raya has been a good mother who gives the children good parental care. The Mendoza-Raya home is one block from the school which the children attend. Their school attendance record is good and they are doing exceptionally well in school. The report's appraisal in this regard is: "These children appear to be happy, healthy, normal youngsters and well cared for * * * bright, friendly." The entire family, of the Catholic faith, attend church each Sunday.

*   *   *

The report's evaluation and recommendation includes: "Your officer is of the opinion that the mother of Timothy and Francis Ray [sic] is a person of good moral character and that she is properly caring for said minors and, too, is seeing that they receive an education as well as spiritual training, and your officer feels that inasmuch as we do have children here of tender age who are in need of maternal love, care, guidance, training, discipline and education, it is to their best interests and welfare that they continue in the custody of their mother. * * * [with] an opportunity to visit with their natural father and to become better acquainted with him."

The *facts* in this report apparently have been accepted by the trial court; but its *conclusions* were not. In fact, a minute order of March 21, 1967 (before the date of the report) reads: "Court finds both parents unfit."

* * *

The trial court found, utilizing the language of section 600, subdivision (a), that the children had "no parent or guardian actually exercising proper and effective care and control and continue[s] to be in need of such care and control," in that each of the natural parents had lived in unmarried cohabitation for more than the five preceding years. This finding cannot be disturbed on appeal if there is substantial evidence to support it. * * * The evidence before the court supplied no substantial support for the finding.

In wardship proceedings the welfare of the child is the paramount concern. * * * Section 600, subdivision (a), of the Welfare and Institutions Code permits an adjudication of wardship when proper and effective parental care or control is lacking. The phrase "proper and effective" offers at best a dim light to discern the point at which a juvenile court is authorized to invade and supplant a parent-child relationship. In one sense the phrase expresses the goal of the child's welfare. In another sense it connotes parental fitness or unfitness. * * * Additional coloration may be gained from the notion of the "neglected child," whose home environment exposes him to physical or moral detriment.

However this may be, the statutory criterion of improper and ineffective parental care denotes a fairly extreme case. A dominant parental right to custody of the child pervades our law. * * * Although expressed more often in divorce and guardianship cases, the dominating right of a parent to custody of his child plays a role in the interpretation of section 600, subdivision (a). Many homes, however blessed by marital vows, fall short of an ideal environment for children. It may be safely assumed that the Juvenile Court Law was not intended to expose such homes to wholesale intervention by public authorities. "It is cardinal with us that the custody, care and nurture of the children reside first in the parents, whose primary function and freedom include preparation for obligations the state can neither supply nor hinder." (Prince v. Commonwealth of Massachusetts, 321 U.S. 158, 166, 64 S. Ct. 438, 442, 88 L. Ed. 645, quoted in Roche v. Roche, supra, 25 G 1.2d at p. 144, 152, P.2d 999.) Thus before section 600, subdivision (a), authorizes the drastic step of judicial intervention, some threshold level of deficiency is demanded. Although a home environment may appear deficient when measured by dominant socioeconomic standards, interposition by the powerful arm of the public authorities may lead to worse alternatives. A juvenile court may possess no magic wand to create a replacement for a home which falls short of ideal. California appellate decisions in wardship cases of the "dependent child" variety demonstrate rather extreme cases of neglect, cruelty or continuing exposure to immorality. * * *

When section 600, subdivision (a), is so viewed, the present facts fall far short of that level of improper and ineffective control which might justify an adjudication of public wardship. Nonconflicting evidence demonstrated that the children were happy, healthy and well adjusted in the home provided by their mother and Mr. Mendoza; that the mother and Mr. Mendoza were satisfying the children's need for familial love, security and physical well-being. The fact that the mother had established a home and was living with a man to whom she was not married supplied the sole evidence which might conceivably support the finding. This piece of evidence was inextricably coupled with a group of accompanying circumstances (1) the relationship was stable, not casual or promiscuous; (2) poverty alone had prevented the Rayas' divorce and the mother's marriage to Mr. Mendoza; (3) as soon as poverty ceased to be a barrier—that is shortly after the Sacramento Legal Aid Society broadened its program to provide legal counsel in such cases—a divorce was instituted, which would legitimize the Rayas' relationships and permit them to establish homes according to prevailing norms. The juvenile court did not face a situation in which the natural parent had surrendered to unmarried cohabitation as her permanent condition, nor need we consider such a case. Given time and freedom from outside interference, the Mendoza-Raya household was in process of transformation into an established family unit. If the wardship order did not block that process, it at least disrupted it and inflicted upon the children the pain and disarray of removal from home and family pending completion of the process. The potential legitimation of relationships cannot be ignored or discounted. * * * Progress toward a cure is a positive factor. The juvenile court's findings took account only of the mother's past and present relationship and ignored the impending legitimation of that relationship. "* * * past indiscretions do not necessarily demonstrate present unfitness * * *."

There was no debate but that poverty had played a major role in producing the home situation which evoked the wardship order. Adequately financed couples can afford divorce. Many take the step nonchalantly, quickly severing their marriages in jurisdictions which invite such business and changing mates with great readiness. The children of quickie marriages and quickie divorces need never find themselves in homes characterized by a permanent liaison such as Mrs. Raya's. For centuries the law has termed such liaisons meretricious or adulterous. Perhaps, in this day of casually created and broken marriages, the label should be applied with less readiness when poverty is a prime factor in producing the relationship. There is a danger here of imposing standards adapted to the well-to-do, who can usually pay for the forms of legitimacy, and ill-adapted for the poor, who frequently cannot. Attempts to apply "across the boards" standards to rich and poor alike may avoid a theoretical discrimination and create a practical one.

Able and vigorous counsel have urged upon us competing moral considerations. On the one hand we are told that there are subcultures in American society whose economic poverty bars them from access to divorce and impels the formation of nonmarital households; that the Aid to Dependent Children provisions of the Welfare and Institutions Code contemplate support of children in their own homes even though, by a 1961 amendment, a "male person assuming the role of spouse" lives in the household; that the 1961 amendment evidences legislative sanction for such nonmarital households among needy citizens; that this sanction should be observed in the application of those sections of the Welfare and Institutions Code forming the Juvenile Court Law. On the other hand, we are told that reversal of the wardship order will evince judicial disrespect for the marriage institution and set the seal of judicial approval on adulterous relationships.

If abstract legal propositions fail to decide concrete cases, abstract moral dogmas accomplish even less. The safest moral guides for the courts are those crystallized in the statutes and case law. In determining whether the evidence supported an adjudication of Mrs. Raya's parental incapacity, the court neither excuses nor condemns. It simply decides that in these particular circumstances the finding of parental incapacity was unjustified by the facts.

* * *

Finally, we deal with an assertion that . . . [stare decisis requires that the judgment of the juvenile court be sustained.] We know of no principle, however—and none has been cited to us—substituting stare decisis for individualized determinations in these cases.

The judgments are reversed with directions to dismiss the wardship petitions.

IN RE NEFF

187 Pa. Super. 79, 142 A.2d 499 (1958)

ERVIN, JUDGE.

On April 10, 1946 the Juvenile Court of Cumberland County adjudged Barbara Ellen Neff, born May 30, 1938, Augusta Ann Neff, born September 9, 1939, Beatrice Diane Neff, born May 19, 1941, and Kenneth R. Neff, Jr., born June 27, 1942, neglected children and committed them to the care and custody of the Child Welfare Service. Act of June 2, 1933, P.L. 1433, § 2, 11 P.S. § 244. The children remained in foster homes for approximately two years and on March 5, 1948 the said court by further order committed them to the care of the Methodist Home for Children, where all but Barbara still remain. When they entered the Methodist Home, they were aged 10, 9, 8 and 6 respectively. When the children entered the Home their father agreed to contribute $55.00 a month to the Home toward their support. He has substantially complied with the agreement. His present salary is $4,100.00 a year. The parents were divorced by a decree entered April 26, 1946. Both parents have since remarried. The father and his second wife now have an additional male child who at the time of the hearing was nearly seven years of age. The father resides in Mechanicsburg, only a few miles from the Home. He and the children attend the Methodist Church in Mechanicsburg nearly every Sunday and sit together. The mother was remarried on March 12, 1949 and now lives in Fair Lawn, New Jersey, in a home valued at $20,000.00, with a mortgage of $12,500.00. Both parents have continued to visit the children at the Home.

On February 11, 1957 the mother presented a petition to the court below to revoke the order of March 5, 1948 and to have custody of the children awarded to her. On June 19, 1957 the court entered an order discharging Barbara Ellen Neff from the care and custody of the Home and placing her in the custody of the mother. Barbara attained the age of 19 on May 30, 1957 and had successfully completed one year in Lycoming College. On August 9, 1957 the court below entered another order refusing the petition of the mother as to the other three children and stated: "This order to be without prejudice to the petitioner to reapply when circumstances so warrant." The mother appealed. It is our duty to review the entire record and to exercise an independent judgment on the merits. * * *

A review of the entire record has convinced a majority of this Court that the best interest and welfare of these three children will be attained at the present time by refusing the prayer of the mother's petition.

We would agree that in the usual case a home environment and family care are more desirable than the finest institution, providing, of course, that the home is adequate and the family care wholesome. But this is not the usual case. As Judge Woodside so well said, 180 Pa. Super., at page 148, 117 A.2d at page 783 in Rinker's Appeal, supra: "It is a serious matter for the long arm of the State to reach into a home and snatch a child from its mother. It is a power which a government dedicated to freedom for the individual should exercise with extreme care, and only where the evidence clearly establishes its necessity. Yet, of course, there are cases where such authority must be exercised for the protection and welfare of children." In this case, however, the mother is seeking to remove the children from the place where they have spent their tender years and the major portion of their minority.

While we did not have the privilege of seeing these children in person, as did the court below, the record convinces us that his observation was accurate. Judge Shughart said: "It is apparent from the appearance of the three who were in Court that they have received the best in physical care. They were well mannered, cheerful and were attractively dressed. It is obvious that all are progressing well in school, the older one having completed her first year in college. In addition, two of them who have shown some talent for music have received special training. Our own observation of their appearance and demeanor furnishes clear and unmistakable proof of the splendid care they have received at the Home from Rev. Victor Hann, the Superintendent, and his staff. These children, their appearance, their excellent records, are the best evidence of the high quality of the care they have received." At the time of the hearing in June of 1957, the children had spent nine years at the Home and two years theretofore in foster homes. At the time of the filing of this opinion the youngest child, Kenneth, Jr., is approximately 16 years of age and Augusta is nearing 19 years of age and probably has completed high school and is ready to enter a hospital for training as a nurse, if she is still of that mind. Beatrice and Kenneth, Jr. should have respectively one year and two years to go to complete high school and will then be ready for college. Dr. Hann testified that all of the children are college material. The girls expressed a desire to go with their mother. This is understandable but their preference must be based on good reasons. Comm. ex rel. Shamenek v. Allen, 179 Pa. Super. 169, 176, 116 A.2d 336. They would undoubtedly enjoy a greater freedom at the home of their mother than they have at the Methodist Home. We are not at all convinced, however, that greater freedom would improve their welfare. Much of the juvenile delinquency present today may be traceable to the enlarged freedom of youth. Some people firmly believe that juvenile delinquency could be reduced by a greater discipline and stricter supervision. Be this as it may, this record convinces us that these children have not been unduly restricted and that they have received a fine religious training which certainly will stand them in good stead in days to come. This is not a case like Com. ex rel. Shamenek v. Allen, supra, where the child, because of the father's treatment of her deceased mother, developed so great an antipathy toward the father that it actually caused her to become ill.

Our conclusion in this case is largely based (as it was in the court below) upon the belief that the mother and her present husband do not fully appreciate the enormity of the expense necessary to keep four children in high school and college at the same time. The mother and her present husband have annual gross earnings of $12,700.00. The husband receives $5,000.00 from his present employment at Curtis-Wright and $3,200.00 retirement pay as an army officer and the mother receives $4,500.00 from her employment. The mother intends to give up her employment to take care of the children if they are awarded to her. This will reduce their gross annual income to $8,200.00 a year. It costs approximately $1,200.00 a year to keep Barbara in college, thus reducing the annual income to $7,000.00 a year. Out of this the two adults must live and then find money to put three more children through high school and college. With costs as they are today, this will be a very difficult thing to do. The failure to do all or any of it will seriously affect the best welfare of the children. If they remain at the Home they will be adequately provided for and their college training will be assured. As was so well said in Com. ex rel. McNamee v. Jackson, 183 Pa. Super. 522, 526, 132 A.2d 396, 398, "by permitting these children to reside * * * [where they are] we are not gambling with their future welfare and happiness, as we would be doing were we to * * * [remove them from their present custody]."

It must be remembered that the court below did not finally foreclose the possibility of releasing all or some of the three remaining children from the present wardship and giving them to the mother. Judge Shughart said, in reference to the order giving Barbara to the mother: "Under the circumstances it might be advisable to see the results of this expense upon the mother and her husband before making a final decision on the other three." At the conclusion of his opinion, he further said: "The petition as to the younger children will, therefore, be dismissed without prejudice to the petitioners to petition again when circumstances warrant." It may very well be that changed circumstances might now dictate the release of Augusta Ann from the present wardship and the award of her custody to the mother if another petition be now presented to the court below.

Our conclusion is that the court below handled a very difficult case in an admirable way and our independent conclusion is that we cannot improve upon it.

Order affirmed.

WRIGHT, J., files a dissenting opinion in which WATKINS, J., joins. WOODSIDE, J., files a dissenting opinion.

WRIGHT, JUDGE (dissenting).
Notwithstanding my high regard for the learned President Judge of the court below, and for my colleagues in the majority, I respectfully submit that it is a clear abuse of judicial discretion to require Kenneth, Beatrice, and Augusta Neff, aged respectively sixteen, seventeen, and eighteen years, who are not delinquent children and are no longer neglected children, to remain in an institution, however worthy, when they desire to be with their natural mother, who has been found presently fit to care for them.

Section 12 of The Juvenile Court Law provides that all orders of the juvenile court shall be subject to amendment or change. Section 16 of said statute (11 P.S. § 258) reads in pertinent part as follows (italics supplied):

If, at any time after the final order of any juvenile court placing or committing any dependent, neglected or delinquent child, *a change of circumstances has taken place which, in the opinion of the parent* or parents or next friend of such child, warrants the revocation or modification of such final order, such child shall, by his or her parent or parents or next friend, have the right to file a petition in such court asking for a revocation or modification of such final order.

Discussing Section 16 of The Juvenile Court Law in Ciammaichella's Appeal, 369 Pa. 278, 85 A.2d 406, 411, the Supreme Court said: "Appellants would limit the 'change of circumstances' as used in this section to a change of circumstances relating to the child and not to the parent. Such construction is not warranted. If the parent or parents of a dependent child become able to and are willing to support the child, surely the Juvenile Court has the right to remand the child to the parental custody."

The majority concedes that this conclusion, as was the conclusion of the court below, is largely based upon financial considerations. However, such considerations are not controlling even in habeas corpus cases, Commonwealth ex rel. Kraus v. Kraus, 185 Pa. Super. 167, 138 A.2d 225, and it is important to note that this is not a habeas corpus proceeding. See Rinker's Appeal, 180 Pa. Super. 143, 117 A.2d 780, 783. As we said in that case: "The family is an institution which preceded governments. Its sanctity was universally recognized before judges or statutes or constitutions or welfare organizations were known to man. The right of a child to a mother and a mother to a child are rights created by natural law. They are rights attributable to the nature of mankind rather than to the enactments of law."

Since few cases involving a contest by an institution for custody of children reach the appellate courts, we call attention to three lower court decisions in which the problem was considered. In Commonwealth ex rel. Field v. Madden, 43 Luz. Leg. Reg. 255, it was stated: "But we are persuaded that a home environment and family care are more desirable than the finest institution, providing the home is adequate and the family wholesome." The uncontradicted evidence in the case at bar is that the mother's home is adequate and the family wholesome. In Commonwealth ex rel. Lyter v. Witmer, 53 Dauph. Co. 377, the court said: "No matter how competent and sympathetic the treatment of a child in an institution may be, it cannot be compared with the loving care received in a normal family life. Only in a totalitarian government do we find the philosophy that 'efficient institutional care' is considered preferable to normal family life." In the case of In re Carol Ann Schuchman, 8 Cumberland L.J. (No. 37) 123, wherein the situation, both procedurally and factually, was markedly similar to that in the case at bar, the Juvenile Court of Franklin County recently directed the discharge of a child of fifteen years from the Scotland School.

I would reverse the order of the court below, and direct that Kenneth, Beatrice, and Augusta Neff be discharged into the custody of their mother.

Judges WOODSIDE and WATKINS join in this dissent.

WOODSIDE, JUDGE (dissenting).
I join in all that Judge WRIGHT has written in his able dissenting opinion. However, I should like to add that I am primarily moved to dissent on the following two grounds: [1] That the Neff children can no longer be classified as neglected; and [2] That it is in the nature of unwarranted punishment to force these young people, now 16, 17 and 18 years of age, to remain in an institution against their will when a parent is willing and able to give them a respectable home.

A neglected child is defined in the Juvenile Court Law of June 2, 1933, P.L. 1433, § 1, 11 P.S. § 243, as follows: "[5] The words 'neglected child' include: [a] A child who is abandoned by his or her parent, * * *; [b] A child who lacks proper parental care by reason of the fault or habits of his or her parent * * *; [c] A child whose parent, * * * neglects or refuses to provide proper or necessary subsistence, education, medical or surgical care, or other care necessary for his or her health, morals or well-being; [d] A child whose parent, * * * neglects or refuses to provide the special care made necessary by his or her mental condition; [e] A child who is found in a disreputable place or associates with vagrant, vicious or immoral persons; [f] A child who engages in an occupation, or in a situation, dangerous to life or limb, or injurious to the health or morals of himself, herself or others."

Because the church home is caring for the Neff children they are not now, in fact, neglected, but neither would they any longer fit into any of the above categories were the Juvenile Court to discharge them from the church home. They are thus no longer neglected either in fact or in law. Although the mother had neglected them at the time that the original order was made, the evidence now before us indicates she is presently willing and able to furnish them a respectable home and to adequately support and look after them. Their mother and her husband live in a $20,000 home and have a combined income of $12,700 per year. There is no suggestion that their home is not a proper place for these children to reside.

As I view it, the order before us is not only contrary to the Juvenile Court Law, supra, but is fair to no person. It is not fair to the mother who seeks to have custody of her children; it is not fair to these young people who seek the experience of living in a home instead of an institution; it is not fair to those who operate and support the institution which is looking after these children whose parent is willing and able to look after them; and it is not fair to the taxpayers of Pennsylvania who are paying for the education of children whose mother lives in an expensive home in New Jersey.

For many years I have known Superintendent and Mrs. Victor B. Hann, who are in charge of the Neff children at The Methodist Home for Children. They are, as the record shows and the court below found, kind, capable, religious people who have performed an outstanding task in rearing these children. Nevertheless, the children's mother is now willing and able to provide a satisfactory home.

It is natural that these children should prefer their mother's home to an institution, however excellent the latter may be. They have emphatically expressed their preference. I think that to deny their request is in the nature of the imposition of punishment upon these unfortunate children, who were brought into juvenile court, not as delinquents, but as neglected children. They do not deserve the stern treatment which they have received at the hands of the law. Their plea to be released from an institution in order to reside in their mother's home is entitled to a more sympathetic ear than the courts have given it.

IN RE JEWISH CHILD CARE ASSOCIATION

5 N.Y.2d 222, 156 N.E.2d 700 (1959)

CONWAY, CHIEF JUDGE.

The purpose of this habeas corpus proceeding is to determine the custody of Laura Neuberger, an infant who is now about five and a half years old. About four and a half years of her short life have been spent in the home of the appellants, Mr. and Mrs. Sanders. Appellants are not related to Laura, nor do they have legal custody. They have her on a temporary foster parent basis pursuant to an arrangement with the respondent Jewish Child Care Association of New York, hereinafter referred to as Child Care.

Child Care is a philanthropic organization chartered by the State of New York to care for children who are in need of custodial care outside of their own homes. It accepts for care children whose parents are temporarily unable to care for them but who are unwilling to place them for adoption. These children are cared for until such time as their own families can properly care for them. While some of these children are placed in a cottage plan institution, the majority are placed in boarding or foster homes. During this boarding period, Child Care's workers assist those in the natural home in preparing for the return of the child's adjustment and preparation for the return to its family. When such a child is placed in a foster home, it is the function of the foster parents to assist in the proper orientation of the child so that it may be prepared and ready for its eventual return to its family. This relationship of foster parent and child is carefully explained to persons who undertake to assist Child Care in its worthy purpose. Such persons are paid an agreed sum of money for the child's room and board, and clothes and medical care are paid for by Child Care. Persons accepting such a child for temporary boarding care do so with the understanding that adoption is not contemplated, that the child will return to its natural parent or parents as soon as feasible, and that one of the primary responsibilities of such boarding parents is to prepare the child psychologically for its contemplated return to its natural home. In order to maintain and strengthen the ties between the child and its parent or parents, the boarding program contemplates periodic visits by the natural parent with the child at the boarding house.

It was in this context that on or about July 30, 1954, the Sanders [*sic*], husband and wife, accepted Laura into their home having applied to Child Care three or four months previously to serve as foster parents. Laura's young mother was unable to care for her after her birth and the child was placed with the Department of Welfare of New York City which in turn commended her welfare and custody to Child Care. When Mr. and Mrs. Sanders first applied to Child Care to participate in its boarding program, that program was explained to them and they were expressly told at that time that Child Care was a boarding agency and not an adoption agency. When they took Laura they knew she had a mother who would visit her, although not for a while in the beginning. The precise chronology of the events that followed during Laura's stay with the Sanders is not clearly revealed by the record. It appears that sometime during the first year that they had Laura, the Sanders acquired a desire to adopt her. They mentioned this to one of Child Care's workers who told them that adoption was out of the question, and explained the necessity for helping Laura to understand who her mother was. Despite this, Mr. and Mrs. Sanders actively sought to effectuate their desire to adopt Laura. In their pursuit of adoption, and contrary to the known policies and rules of Child Care, the Sanders arranged to speak to Laura's mother about adoption. On several occasions they attempted to persuade Laura's maternal grandmother and uncle to interfere and intercede in their behalf and prevail upon Laura's mother to give her up. At one point the Sanders were required by Child Care, as a condition to their keeping Laura, to sign a paper in March of 1957 to the effect that they had Laura on a foster home or boarding home basis only. This occurred after an attorney, representing himself as the Sanders' attorney telephoned Child Care and inquired about the availability of Laura for adoption. Some time prior to Thanksgiving Day in November of 1957, Mr. and Mrs. Sanders asked Child Care if they could take Laura to Florida for that holiday. They were refused permission, one of Child Care's workers explaining to them that by that time Laura might be back with her mother, and that Child Care was working on a plan with the mother toward that end. When thus

advised, Mrs. Sanders became upset and she described her emotional reaction as follows: "I was heartbroken, very worried about
Laurie, about how she would react. In fact, that was my prime
worry, how she would feel being taken away from *her mother and
father*" (emphasis supplied). In their zeal to adopt Laura, the
Sanders persuaded Laura's uncle to discuss his sister's (Laura's
mother) background with the district supervisor of the foster home
department of Child Care. It does not appear what this background
was. At any rate the district supervisor then informed the Sanders
that they would be asked to give up Laura in a few weeks because
they had become too emotionally involved with the child. During
approximately a week that followed, the Sanders intensified their
efforts to persuade Laura's mother to surrender her for adoption.
Mr. Sanders approached Laura's mother both at her place of business
and at her home, but she steadfastly refused to give up her daughter.
He spoke with Laura's grandmother but she refused again to interfere. Finally, Laura's mother telephoned Child Care about these efforts. The district supervisor then informed the Sanders that they
would have to give up Laura and that this course would be kinder
to them in view of their deep emotional involvement with Laura.
When Child Care's representatives came to call for Laura, however,
the Sanders refused to give her up, whereupon Child Care commenced this proceeding. Almost all of the foregoing is based upon
the testimony of Mr. and Mrs. Sanders.

The district supervisor of the foster home department of Child
Care testified, in part, that Child Care has worked with the Sanders
to help them continue to keep Laura while performing their proper
function as boarding parents. However, it became evident that the
child's best interests necessitated her placement in another environment where she would not be torn between her loyalty to her mother
and her boarding parents. According to the testimony of a representative of the Department of Welfare of New York City, that
department was in agreement with Child Care that Laura's best interests required that she be placed elsewhere. A psychiatrist, the
only witness called by appellants, testified in substance that he had
interviewed Laura and the Sanders the afternoon before the trial,
that the Sanders took Laura to satisfy their own parental instincts,
that Laura is well adjusted, that if she were taken from the Sanders

now she might become maladjusted, that the Sanders are the only ones Laura knows as parents, that it would be better to allow Laura's attachment to the Sanders to grow, and that Laura would make a better adjustment to the change to her own mother later on, whenever that should be, if she were left with the Sanders.

Upon this record, the Supreme Court Trial Justice, who had formerly been a Children's Court Justice for 11 years, found that it would be in Laura's best interests if she were taken from the Sanders before, as he phrased it, "further damage is done or a still more difficult situation for her is created." This discretionary finding was expressly affirmed by the Appellate Division. There is no merit to the appellants' claim that the Trial Justice failed or refused to exercise independent discretion as to what is in Laura's best interest, or that he made his determination upon any basis other than her best interests. Consequently, the precise question which this record presents is whether there is such a lack of supporting evidence that we must charge the court below with an abuse of discretion as a matter of law. . . . It should be remembered that "Questions of custody are, generally, for the Supreme Court, in its discretion, and it is rarely that any such determination by it can raise any question of law for us." People ex rel. Portnoy v. Strasser, . . . 104 N.E.2d 895, 896.

In considering what is in Laura's best interests it was not only proper, but necessary, for the Trial Justice to consider the facts in terms of their significance to Laura's eventual return to her own mother. The record pemits no other perspective to be taken, both in view of Laura's mother's steadfast refusal to give her up, and Child Care's declared purpose to return Laura to her own mother when she is able to care for her. Viewing the trial record thus, it supports in a most compelling manner the Trial Justice's determination which has been affirmed by the Appellate Division. It clearly establishes that the appellants have conducted themselves in a fashion inconsistent with their agreement and, indeed, diametrically opposed to their trust. Their own witness testified that Laura had come to look upon appellants as her parents, "the only ones she has known as parents." In short, the content and tone of the record disclose a situation in the Sanders home which has reached such a peak of emotion and possessiveness that it is entirely inconsistent with Laura's future with her own mother, and her need to be prepared for that future. Certainly, the Trial Justice was entitled to find that it would be in Laura's best interests to extricate her now from the emotional entanglement into which she has been plunged by the keen parental desire of the Sanders in which they involved themselves contrary to their own agreement and in violation of their trust. He was entitled to find that to allow Laura to stay longer would make the future transition to her own mother more painful for the child.

That the Sanders have given Laura a good home and have shown her great love does not stamp as an abuse of discretion the Trial Justice's determination to take her from them. Indeed, it is the extreme of love, affection and possessiveness manifested by the Sanders, together with the conduct which their emotional involvement impelled, that supplies the foundation of reasonableness and correctness for his determination. The vital fact is that Mr. and Mrs. Sanders are not, and presumably will never be, Laura's parents by adoption. Their disregard of that fact and their seizure of full parental status in the eyes of the child might well be, or so the Trial Justice was entitled to find, a source of detriment to the child in the circumstances presented. Nor can we sustain an objection that, since the child is not now being returned to her mother, she should be left with the Sanders because the fitness of her next habitation is presently unknown. As the Appellate Division wrote, we may not indulge an assumption, or even harbor a doubt, that Laura will not be properly cared for under the supervision of Child Care which is an authorized agency and which has proven itself most solicitous for the welfare not only of the child and its mother but even of the appellants themselves. From the standpoint of the child's best interests, therefore, we hold that was no abuse of discretion by the Trial Justice.

The nature of this care requires one further basic statement. What is essentially at stake here is the parental custodial right. Although Child Care has the present legal right to custody (Social Welfare Law, [McK. Consol. Laws, c. 55,] § 383, subd. 2) it stands, as against the Sanders, in a representative capacity as the protector of Laura's child relationship which is to become complete in the future. Any future physical legal custody in Laura's mother would be but an empty right, if the emotional substance of that relationship were permitted to be replaced antecedently by the parent-like love and possessiveness of Mr. and Mrs. Sanders. This court has acknowledged that "* * * the right of a parent, under natural law, to establish a home and bring up children is a fundamental one * * *." People ex rel. Portnoy v. Strasser, 104 N.E.2d 895, 896, supra. In support of this tenet we have declared that "Except where a nonparent has obtained legal and permanent custody of a child by adoption, guardianship or otherwise, he who would take or withhold a child from mother or father must sustain the burden of establishing that the parent is unfit and that the child's welfare compels awarding its custody to the nonparent." People ex rel. Kropp v. Shepsky, 113 N.E.2d 801, 804, supra. A proper application of these doctrines requires the conclusion that foster parents may not succeed in a proceeding such as this, where the child temporarily in their care is to return to its natural parent, in accordance with the trust accepted by the foster parents for compensation, in the absence of a clear showing that to return the child to the boarding agency will operate to its grave detriment. The paramount parental right to raise one's own child, which we regard as fundamental, is to be protected not only from direct and immediate incursion, as in the Shepsky and Strasser cases, but also from indirect and less proximate subversion, such as in the case before us.

We are, of course, not unmindful that the result we reach may cause distress to the appellants. However, the more important considerations of the child's best interests, the recognition and preservation of her mother's primary love and custodial interest, and the program of agencies such as Child Care which preserves them, may not be subverted by foster parents who breach their trust.

The order of the Appellate Division should be affirmed, without costs.

DYE, JUDGE (dissenting).
This appeal involves the custody of a minor child. In sustaining petitioner's application for a writ of habeas corpus, a majority of this court is about to say that the best interest of the infant will be served by compelling the approved foster parents, with whom the petitioner had previously placed the child for custodial care, to surrender her back to the Agency, there to be dealt with as they see

fit. This tragic result comes about because of a mistaken notion that the courts are bound to accept an administrative policy of the Agency as controlling their determination rather than to exercise their own traditional power and authority in accordance with the evidence. While administrative practices have a useful place in the handling of ordinary matters of administration, such test is wholly inappropriate in this setting. Here we are not dealing with a routine problem of administration, but rather with the fundamental concept underlying the broad and enlightened social welfare program of the State respecting the care and custody of indigent and neglected children, every aspect of which is to be tested in the light of which will best promote their individual welfare. This idea is neither new nor novel in our society. The State as *parens patriae* has always had a deep concern for its infant wards; from birth to maturity their welfare is paramount, even to that of the natural parent . . . , the determination of which belongs solely to the Supreme Court as successor to the Chancellor . . . , which may not be limited or diminished by the Legislature. . . .

This controversy has not been precipitated by the classic cause arising from abuse and neglect but because these foster parents "have become too emotionally involved," a situation engendered by a feeling of mutual love and affection. In extricating the child from this "emotional entanglement," it seems clear that on this record one of the most fundamental aspects of the child care program, namely the placing of children in a home environment, is being defeated. It is undisputed that the infant Laura was born June 3, 1953. At that time her mother was about 17 years of age and lived with her widowed mother and an unmarried minor brother, a student. The child was thereafter given over to the Department of Welfare of the City of New York who, in turn, gave her to the Agency. When the child was about one year old the Agency placed her with these appellants for boarding care. As might be expected, the foster parents became attached to the child; as the years passed by this attachment grew and was reciprocated by the infant. She flourished under their care and is now almost six years of age. The well-qualified witness, Dr. Pechstein, has described her as a "healthy, normal, well-adjusted child." There came a time when the foster parents proposed adoption, first to the caseworker who disapproved, then to the grandmother, and finally to the mother herself, who temporized and declined to give any definite answer which is regarded as a refusal. The Agency did not like the emotional development as it was their policy to keep the care children in a neutral environment—where there could be no "pull on the child between her loyalty to her foster parents and her mother." To this policy the Agency required the foster parents, as a condition of continued custody, to sign a paper declaring that they understood that Laura could "remain only with the status of a foster child." However, this failed of its intended purpose. The foster parents continued to hope for an adoption while the Agency considered this was impossible under the circumstances, demanded the return of the child and, when refused, commenced this proceeding. At the hearing the Agency freely conceded that the foster parents were well qualified in every respect, had taken good care of the child and were providing her an excellent "home environment" but, even so, that their love and affection for the child had created a situation which would make it difficult for Laura to return to her mother if and when, at some unknown time in the future, if ever, the mother would be in a position to care for her. The mother did not appear at the hearing and so far as it appears she is in no position to care for the child at this time or in the near future—or for that matter is there anything in the record to indicate a maternal interest in the child. Concededly, the Agency intends to replace the child in a neutral environment not presently designated. The Agency, as we have said, asserts that the foster parents were quite unfair in yielding their love to the compulsive attraction of the infant's helplessness at the same time conceding that the child is in a good home environment. There is impartial, disinterested and informed testimony that the child's best interest will be promoted by not disturbing the placement at this time. In the words of Dr. Pechstein, "This child is at a critical period. * * * This is by far the worst time to consider changing the placement * * * if this child is moved now * * * She will be uprooted from * * * the only ones she has known as parents * * * from her home in Levittown, where she has made friends and is about to start in kindergarten with children that she knows. She will be taken out of an environment which has made her the healthy, normal, well-adjusted child that she is. That is going to open up the possibility of all kinds of maladjustments. * * * I can't see where they [the Agency] get this notion of placing a child in a neutral environment, without love and without hate, possibly, without this, without that. It is as though you are taking the child and placing it in a bare environment with nothing but food. * * * Where a child has been by necessity placed in such an environment, where they are just handed the bare necessities of life * * * food, shelter, clothing; * * * these children have not grown. * * * In my experience [on placement] we have sought homes where they can get this type of love, where there is care and attention and concern which might duplicate that of a parent * * *. A child learns to react to others by reacting to the emotions * * * of liking and disliking, of love and hate. This is normal. * * * If you take a child and deprive him of that, you are depriving the child of the essentials of life. * * * Here these people are taking the child; the agency is taking the child away from these people, and they treat this child as their own, offering the child the best that the child could get. I really don't understand why the agency feels this way. * * * I think these people would make better parents since they have raised the child this far and they have made an attachment to the child and the child has made an attachment to them. * * * I think the child will make a better adjustment to the change to the mother later on, whether it is a year or five years from now, if she is left exactly where she is."

When this uncontradicted testimony is analyzed in the light of surrounding circumstances, it seems convincingly clear that the child's best welfare is to be served by continuing the placement with these appellants. In so ruling, we are not unmindful of the mother. Under the applicable statutory scheme of child care and placement, the natural parents have first consideration, but even this right must be tested in light of what is best for the child. Here there is no evidence justifying return of custody to the natural mother. She does not ask it and she is in no position to assume the care and education at this time or in a reasonably foreseeable future time. All that remains then is to apply the test of what is best for the welfare of the child and, when applied in this instance, it points convincingly to the desirability of leaving the child with the foster parents. The Agency does not disagree with the best interest test, but, nonetheless, feels that their policy of neutrality should be accorded precedence. This, as we see it, is not for the child's best interest but rather for the best interest of the Agency, a specious result in any event for, even if custody remained with the appellant, the Agency may continue supervision and visitation. The courts of New York have repeatedly taken their stand on the side of the child . . . The Supreme Court has the power and the duty to promote and protect the best interest of the State's infant wards. The failure of the Supreme Court to exercise its inherent powers in this habeas corpus proceeding in accordance with the evidence was tantamount to an abuse of discretion.

The order should be reversed.

FROESSEL, JUDGE (dissenting).

I concur with Judge Dye for reversal. We are not here concerned with the respective rights of the Sanders [*sic*], the Child Care Agency, or the mother, for it is undisputed that the Sanders have no rights as against either of the latter. The mother may have her child, Laura, whenever she wishes, subject to the provisions of section 383 of the Social Welfare Law. Our only concern is Laura's best interests in the meantime. The problem presented rightly troubled the learned Justice at Special Term, and the Appellate Division was sharply divided.

Laura was born on June 3, 1953. Her mother delivered her to the Department of Welfare of New York City, who thereupon turned her over to the Agency. On July 30, 1954 the Agency gave the child to the Sanders for boarding care, at which time she was not quite 14 months old. Seymour Sanders at the time of the hearing was 30 years old, his wife 28, and they are childless.

Laura's mother visited her but once a year for the first two years. Small wonder then that the Sanders thought she had little interest in Laura, and therefore, inquired about adopting her, despite the fact that they had been told by the Agency that Laura could not be adopted. Its order having been disobeyed, the Agency sought to place the child in another home. The Sanders were told they "were too attached to the child"; they "loved her too much." For that entirely normal human reaction of the average person to the love of a child, Laura is to be transferred to strangers in the sixth year of her life.

The Agency took the position, at the hearing, that it could not function properly if a "foster family was in position to question our judgment, even if our judgment, if you weigh it, might turn out to be wrong." Perhaps they are right (Social Welfare Law, § 383), but certainly the courts have the power, as Judge Dye has pointed out, to determine what is in the best interests of the child, our paramount concern.

In 1954 Laura was boarded on a temporary basis. More than four years later, we do not have the slightest indication as to when, if ever, the mother will want her child. If Laura is to be bandied about meanwhile from family to family until she is transferred to her mother, each such change will be extremely difficult for the child, as testified to without contradiction by the psychiatrist at the hearing. Why multiply the shocks? And if the mother never chooses to take Laura, and that does not appear to be unlikely from the record before us, the child could not find a better home than she now enjoys.

I am of the opinion that the Agency, however well motivated, has committed grave error here, contrary to the best interests of the child; that the courts below were in no small measure erroneously influenced by the so-called rights of the Agency, rather than by the welfare of the child, and that there is no substantial evidence to support their determinations. Accordingly, I would reverse the orders below, and dismiss the petition.

* ☼ *

Order affirmed.

IN RE ALEXANDER

Circuit Court of Hillsborough County (Florida)
No. 155465–C (March 24, 1967)

PATTON, JUDGE.

This cause came on for final hearing before this Court on February 8th, 1967 and again on a continuation of said hearing on March 15, 1967. At each of said hearings both of the Petitioners were present with counsel, and the Department of Public Welfare was represented by one or more representatives and by its counsel. At each of said hearings testimony was presented by the Petitioners and by said Department of Public Welfare, which is hereinafter referred to in this judgment as Department for sake of brevity.

* * *

This proceeding was commenced by the filing of a Petition by the Petitioners, on September 23rd, 1966, whereby they sought a judgment of this Court permitting them to adopt a white male child known as Baby Boy. . . . At the time of the filing of said Petition, the Petitioners were represented by other counsel who subsequently voluntarily withdrew pursuant to Order.

The Petition alleges that Baby Boy [was born in 1964] . . . , and shortly after his birth was permanently committed to the Department for subsequent adoption by Order of the Juvenile and Domestic Relations Court of Hillsborough County, Florida, pursuant to Florida Law. Immediately after such commitment the child was placed in the foster care of the Petitioners by the Department, and at that time Petitioners entered into a printed form of Placement Agreement prepared and used by the Department. Among other things this Agreement, a copy of which is filed in evidence in this cause provides: "No action for adoption or guardianship may be taken."

The Petition further recites that the child remained in the foster care of the Petitioners continuously from the said date of placement until the filing thereof. On or about October 12th, 1966 custody of the child was surrendered to the Department under the conditions hereinafter set forth. The child was placed by the Department in another foster home in Hillsborough County at that time and has remained there continuously to the present time. That on or about October 12th, 1966 the evidence shows a meeting was held at which there were present the Petitioners and their original counsel and the attorney for the Department. The attorney for the Department advised the Petitioners and their then attorney that it was his opinion that the Petitioners would not be permitted to adopt the child because of the permanent commitment to the Department and the provisions of the Placement Agreement. Petitioners' original counsel apparently agreed with the Department's contention and advised the Petitioners that it was his opinion that they should surrender custody of the child to the Department, which they state they reluctantly did in reliance upon such advice. As quickly as it was possible for them to do so, Petitioners, with consent of their original counsel, sought further legal advice from their present counsel who advised them that they were of the opinion that Petitioners were not barred from pursuing their effort to adopt the child. It was at this time that the Petitioner's original counsel withdrew.

After the Petition was filed, the Department filed a Motion to dismiss same upon the grounds of lack of jurisdiction over the subject matter and over the parties. On a hearing on this Motion, it was the argument of the Department that same should be sustained because of the permanent commitment to the Department and because of the aforesaid Placement Agreement. This Motion was denied and the matter ordered to be heard on the merits.

Shortly after obtaining their present counsel, the Petitioners filed a Motion to regain custody of the child pending final hearing. This Court considered said Petition at a hearing held December 21st, 1966, pursuant to notice, and denied the Motion, without prejudice to the Petitioners, on the ground that it would not be in the best interests of the child to move him again until a final determination was made. At the same time the Court ordered the Department not to move the child from Hillsborough County until such determination.

At the final hearing, the Court heard the evidence offered on behalf of the Petitioners and the Department which, in brief, established the following:

On behalf of the Petitioners it was shown that, in addition to the facts set forth in the Petition, that they presently live in a home owned by a son of Nepa Alexander by a former marriage, which home is located in a middle class residential district in Tampa, and is sufficient to adequately meet the needs of the child; that the Petitioners also are purchasing a home in Tampa which they are presently renting; that Nepa Alexander is a housewife and is not employed, and that her husband, Steve Alexander, is presently employed in a full daytime job and is also working additional part-time at night. His income, while not unusually large, is sufficient to provide for the needs of the child and the Petitioners; other witnesses testified as to the good character of the Petitioners and of their love and care of the child during the time he was in their custody, the child was subject to an allergy which required much additional care and attention by the Petitioners, although the Department provided the necessary medical attention and medicines; testimony of the Petitioners and others was to the effect that Nepa Alexander devoted herself unselfishly to the child during this ordeal; that the child has now, according to medical reports, overcome this allergy; it has also been shown that the Petitioners are active in religious work and that Steve Alexander gives time to working with boys of the church.

On behalf of the Department the evidence shows: that the Petitioners had signed Placement Agreements with respect to other children to whom they furnished foster care for the Department; that the Petitioners were compensated for all such employment, including the care of Baby Boy . . . ; that both of the Petitioners are older than the Department believes is to be the best interests of the child for purpose of adoption; that Nepa Alexander has four sons by a previous marriage, none of whom have been adopted by Steve Alexander, and that none of these sons completed a high school education; that the Petitioners are indebted and that within the past ten years Steve Alexander failed in a business venture; that Nepa Alexander has contributed to financial difficulties by her mismanagement of bank accounts, etc.; that shortly before the filing of the Petition herein, the Department had been in contact with persons it believed would be interested in adopting the child, and that these persons were younger, better off financially, and more desirable, in the opinion of the Department, as adoptive parents. These persons, however, are no longer available as prospective adopting parents.

The Department, however, was frank and fair enough to concede that if this had been an adoption proceeding involving a natural parent or a licensed child-placing agency not opposing the adoption, that the Department probably would not have opposed such adoption because of any of the aforesaid matters.

The real objection of the Department to this adoption is that the Petition was filed and the proceedings brought without the consent of, and over the continuous opposition of the Department. Counsel for the Department, while not actually denying the jurisdiction of this Court, in effect contends that the proceeding should have been dismissed as soon as the Department filed its objections because of the permanent commitment by the Juvenile Court and because of the Placement Agreement. Again, in fairness to the Department, it should be made to appear that in the past they admit they have consented to adoptions by persons providing foster care for the child adopted pursuant to a Placement Agreement. The Department says these have been unusual situations.

After hearing the evidence and considering the arguments of respective counsel, this Court finds:

1. That it has jurisdiction of the subject matter of these proceedings and of the Petitioners, the Department and the child sought to be adopted.

2. That under the present adoption laws of the State of Florida, the fact that the child sought to be adopted was previously permanently committed to the custody of the Department by Order of said Juvenile Court, does not require the consent of the Department as a prerequisite to the entry of a judgment of the Court permitting Petitioners to adopt said child. This Court is of the opinion that this is a fact to be considered and it has been seriously considered by this Court. It is the opinion of this Court that the Department is in no stronger position than a natural parent who is resisting an adoption, and in fact should not be in an equivalent position because it is assumed that it is the aim and purpose of the Department to seek the adoption of such children. It is the further opinion of this Court that if the consent of the Department is to be a pre-

requisite to such an adoption, the Legislature should amend the existing adoption laws to provide this.

3. For the same reasons set forth in the preceding paragraph, it is the opinion of this Court that the provisions of the Placement Agreement signed by the Petitioners do not oust this Court of jurisdiction of this proceeding nor preclude the Court from permitting the Petitioners to adopt the child. Again, the Court is of the opinion that the provisions of the Agreement are entitled to serious consideration, and such consideration has been given.

4. That the contentions of the Department with regard to the effect of the permanent commitment and of the Placement Agreement have been set forth in this Judgment with some detail so that there be no doubt that such contentions have been seriously argued by the Department and carefully considered by the Court.

5. That the evidence of the Department as to the availability, as of the time of the filing of the Petition herein, of other persons as prospective adoptive parents should not now be a factor in the determination made by this Court. In any adoption proceeding there can always be the possibility of the existence of other persons who might prove to be better parents. Age and financial condition of other persons must be compared against the evidence of the love, care and attention given this child by the Petitioners over a period of about two years.

6. That the Petitioners, despite their age, are, in the opinion of this Court based upon the evidence in this cause, well suited to become the adopting parents of the child, and the child is suitable to be adopted by the Petitioners and that the best interests of the child will be served by permitting such adoption.

7. That the paramount issue before this Court is the best interests of the child sought to be adopted. From the evidence produced before this Court, it appears without question that the Petitioners were devoted to this child during the entire time they had custody of him; that they afforded him as much care and attention as could have been expected of natural parents and

that this care and attention was obviously given, not for the financial return which the Petitioners expected to receive from the Department, but on account of their love for the child; that from the evidence produced before this Court, it appears that it would be contrary to the best interests of this child to deny the Petitioners the right to legally adopt him.

WHEREUPON, IT IS ORDERED, ADJUDGED AND DECREED:

1. That the prayer of said Petition is hereby granted and the Petitioners, Steve Alexander and Nepa Alexander, husband and wife, are hereby permitted and authorized to adopt the said minor child, Baby Boy . . . , and are hereby decreed to have adopted said child.

2. That the name of Steve Michael Alexander is hereby given to said child, and he shall hereafter be known by the name of Steve Michael Alexander.

3. That the said child is hereby decreed to be the child and heir of the Petitioners, Steve Alexander and Nepa Alexander, husband and wife, and is further decreed to be entitled to all the rights and privileges, and subject to all the obligations, of a child born to the Petitioners in lawful wedlock.

4. That the Bureau of Vital Statistics of the State of Florida, is hereby authorized and directed to issue a Birth Certificate for said minor child by his new and legal name, to-wit: Steve Michael Alexander.

5. That upon the entry of this Final Decree of Adoption the Department of Public Welfare of the State of Florida shall immediately deliver the custody of said minor child to the Petitioners.

✻　✻　✻

IN RE ALEXANDER

206 So.2d 452 (Fla. 1968)
(District Court of Appeal of Florida)

ALLEN, JUDGE.

The appellants appeal a final decree of adoption from the Circuit Court of Hillsborough County. The petitioner-appellees brought a petition for the adoption of one Baby Boy . . . after having cared for him as foster parents since November 25, 1964, the date of his birth. Baby Boy . . . had been permanently committed to the care of appellant for subsequent adoption by order of the Juvenile and Domestic Relations Court of Hillsborough County, Florida, pursuant to Florida law.

The petitioner-appellees, as foster parents, signed an agreement with the respondent-appellant. This agreement contained a clause stating that, "no action for adoption or guardianship may be taken."

The petitioners cared for Baby Boy . . . continuously until October 12, 1966, when custody was surrendered to the respondent under conditions set forth in the final decree of the trial court. The respondent did not give its consent to the adoption of Baby Boy . . . by the petitioners.

The respondent has presented several points on appeal. We feel that the appeal centers around two main questions.

1. Does the agreement signed by petitioners, which contained the clause, "No action for adoption or guardianship may be taken," bar them from seeking the adoption of a child?

2. Does the lack of consent by the respondent to the adoption preclude the trial court from granting the petition for adoption?

To both of these questions we must answer in the negative. In the final decree granting the petition for adoption, the court below has stated: [The court here quotes the lower court's seven findings.]

* * *

The record shows that the court below carefully considered the contentions raised by respondent-appellant and took the best interests of the child, Baby Boy . . . as the paramount issue before it.

The trial court, after careful consideration, granted the petition for adoption allowing the petitioners to adopt the said minor child.

Finding no error in the record, we affirm the ruling of the lower court granting the petition for adoption of Baby Boy . . . by the petitioner-appellees.

We find the additional arguments and issues propounded by respondent-appellant to be without merit.

Affirmed.

LILES, C. J., and SHANNON, J., concur.

IN RE ST. JOHN

51 Misc.2d 96, 272 N.Y.S.2d 817 (Family Ct. 1966),
rev'd sub nom.
Fitzsimmons v. Liuni, 26 App. Div.2d 980,
274 N.Y.S.2d 798 (3d Dep't 1966)

(A Synopsis of the Facts of the Liuni Case)

[Elizabeth was born on July 4, 1962 in New York. Her mother was legally married at the time and indicated to the Ulster County Welfare Department that the father of the child was not her legal husband. Five days after the child's birth, she was placed in the home of Mr. and Mrs. Michael Liuni, a couple in their mid-forties who had three children of their own and who were frequently used by the Ulster County Welfare Department as foster parents. At the time Elizabeth was placed with the Liunis, the Department did not indicate the duration of the placement. The boarding arrangement was accomplished without the Liunis' signing a formal agreement.

During the end of the first year of Elizabeth's stay in the Liuni home, Mr. and Mrs. Liuni inquired of their caseworker if the child were available for adoption. The caseworker told them that it was not the policy of the Department to place children locally for adoption. Moreover, the Liunis were advised that the adoption of Elizabeth was not possible because of legal entanglements.

On March 18, 1964, Elizabeth's mother legally surrendered the child to the Commissioner of Welfare of Ulster County. On December 4, 1964 when Elizabeth's father was located, he also signed the necessary forms for a legal surrender.

In November 1965 while Mrs. Liuni was caring for her own three children and two foster children (besides Elizabeth), she was hospitalized for about four weeks because of a mental depression which accompanied her menopause. Mrs. Liuni had received shock therapy during her hospitalization as part of the treatment for involutional melancholia. During Mrs. Liuni's confinement her mother took care of all the children in the home. On April 29, 1966 Mrs. Liuni had a physical examination and was found to be fit. The family physician said that she exhibited no signs of mental depression.

On February 17, 1966, when Elizabeth was about three and a half years old, she was evaluated by a child guidance clinic to determine whether she was ready for a pre-adoptive placement. Instead of placing the child immediately upon her legal availability, the Department had wanted to wait because Elizabeth had been born with an obvious birth mark or blemish on the left side of her face extending from the left temple downward. Physicians agreed at Elizabeth's birth that the blemish was susceptible to surgical treatment but that time should be allowed to determine whether the birth mark might become less noticeable or fade as Elizabeth's face matured. In 1966 the Department decided that the birth defect, although still visible, had receded to a point where Elizabeth would be acceptable for adoption.

The child guidance clinic's evaluation read, in pertinent part, as follows:

> Elizabeth is a beautiful, blue eyed blond who looks and acts more like a five year old. She is bright, probably superior, child who relates appropriately to adults, although in a somewhat exaggerated fashion.

> From the history of the boarding mother's emotional difficulties, we suggest that plans for permanent placement be initiated promptly, giving appropriate consideration to the boarding mother's vulnerability. It would be well to emphasize to the boarding father the hazard to his wife's mental welfare if this ambiguous relationship is continued indefinitely. Certainly, he should be helped to see that extended requirements of rearing another child, not yet school age, is likely to impose too great [a] stress on his wife during the menopausal period of life, which is difficult for most women and may prove somewhat overwhelming to her.

> This in no way suggests that we are unmindful of the problems which may arise both for child and mother as separation is proposed and effected.

Acting on this report, the Commissioner of Welfare advised the Liunis on March 18, 1966 that an adoptive home had been provided for Elizabeth and that the Department would like to start to introduce her to her adoptive parents with the co-operation of the Liunis. At the request of Mr. Liuni a meeting was arranged with the Department officials at which time he advised the Department that he and his wife wanted to adopt Elizabeth. They were advised that their request for adoption could not be approved for the following reasons:

1. They were too old (Mr. and Mrs. Liuni were both 48 years old and it was not departmental policy to approve of adoptive parents who were beyond normal child bearing years).

2. Mrs. Liuni was not physically able to care for a young child in light of her four week hospitalization and the emotional difficulties associated with the menopausal period of her life.

3. The child who is blond, blue-eyed and of fair complexion, did not match the Liunis' ethnic background.

4. As foster parents, the Liunis had no legal claim to a child committed to their care on a boarding arrangement.

The Department of Welfare then demanded that the Liunis deliver the child to them. This demand was refused. The Commissioner of Welfare then obtained a writ of habeas corpus returnable before the Supreme Court, Ulster County on April 25, 1966.

The following testimony was given when the case subsequently went to trial.

IN RE ST. JOHN

Excerpts from the Testimony of Witnesses
[Family Court, Kingston, New York, June 1–3, 1966—
Docket No. R 4 66]

Hon. Hugh R. Elwyn, Judge, Family Court, County of Ulster, Kingston, New York

Mr. Griggs, Counsel for Petitioner, Joseph Fitzsimmons, Commissioner of Public Welfare

Mr. Avis, Counsel for respondents, Mr. and Mrs. Michael Liuni

Mrs. M., Social Worker for Ulster County Welfare Department

Mr. Michael Liuni, Respondent

Excerpt No. 1. (Record, Pp. 164–85)
Direct and Cross Examination of Mrs. M., Social Worker

Q: Mrs. M. [Social Worker] would you state your full name and legal address for the record please?

A: Mrs. M., L. Lane, R., New York.

Q: And it is Mrs, M., is it not?

A: It is.

Q: And Mrs. M., do you have children of your own?

A: I have three.

Q: Would you indicate to the Court if you have any official relationship with the Ulster County Welfare Department?

A. I am employed by the department as a Case Worker, I was formerly in the field of unwed mothers and pre-adoptive babies, but presently as adoptive home finder.

Q: How long have you been with the department, Mrs. M.?

A: For a year and a half.

Q: Now, would you indicate what your educational background is, Mrs. M., insofar as it relates to the work that you are doing in the department?

A: I received my AB degree from Vassar College in 1947; I did graduate work at the University of Missouri and Columbia University; I had married and had three children.

215

Q: I believe you indicated that you and your husband and your children reside in R.?

A: Yes, we do.

Q: Now Mrs. M., have you had experience as to what the basis is for the adoptive parents selection program for the Welfare Department?

A: Both from specific and in service training and also from general reading.

Q: And would you indicate to the Court what the basis for the adoptive selection program is in the Ulster County Welfare Department?

A: Generally speaking, we look for couples who are mature, stable, have a great deal of love, plenty of it to share and are able to take a child into their family; we also look for a specific couple that would be able to fill the needs of a specific child and help to develop to its fullest potential.

Q: Now Mrs. M., I believe you were present and heard the testimony of Mrs. G as to the standards of adoption with the department?

A: I did.

Q: Mrs. M., have you had any experience in removing a child from a foster home for placement in an adoptive home?

A: This was my job prior to the present position.

Q: And what sort of experience did you find it to be? in removal?

A: It depends entirely upon the cooperation between the foster parent and the worker in preparing the child for the change.

Q: Do you do anything to seek the cooperation of the foster parents or the boarding parents?

A: Indeed we do, plus the entire time that the child is in foster care, if he is old enough to understand, he is given to know that we are looking for permanent parents for him, but these are not his parents but that they love him and are going to care for him until a permanent home is found, and they do help us to move the child.

Q: Now Mrs. M., is it in the departmental policy that prior to the time a child is going to be placed for adoption that a child be taken to the psychiatric evaluation section of the child guidance, of the Albany Child Guidance Center?

A: It is.

Q: And did that time come with respect to Elizabeth when she was taken for psychiatric evaluation?

A: It did.

Q: And were you the worker who took the child to Albany?

A: I transported the foster mother and the child to Albany.

Q: And did you receive a report from the Center in Albany relative to their evaluation of Elizabeth?

A: The day following the visit which had been made on the 17th of February, a report was written to our department, as it always is.

Q: And did this report favor a removal or did it favor the child staying in the foster home?

MR. AVIS: Objection on the grounds it is against the evidence rules, question of the report being present.

THE COURT: Sustained.

MR. GRIGGS: I might respectfully point out to Your Honor that these reports are submitted to the County Welfare Department in a matter of routine and each and every one of these are actually sent in due course of business as reports which are made part of the file of each infant child which is being placed for adoption. On that basis I believe that it would fall within the best evidence rule and I am asking her to refer to the records as they hold.

MR. AVIS: Routine records are usually applied to business records, doesn't apply to questions of this type.

THE COURT: The objection was made and the basis of the objection was that the document itself was the best evidence of the contents and I sustained the objection on that ground. Her version of content is not the best evidence. Now, I haven't heard any other offer of the report, have you made any offer of report?

MR. GRIGGS: I withdraw the question Your Honor it is fact.

THE COURT: All right.

MR. GRIGGS:

Q: Mrs. M., I show you three papers stapled together and I ask if you can identify them?

A: This would appear to be a copy of the child's record of Elizabeth ———— in which the majority of the dictation is under my signature.

Q: And were you responsible for the preparation of this report?

A: Yes, as a matter of routine investigations are written up as soon
     as possible after they are made.

Q: May I have this logged for identification as Petitioners Ex-
     hibit?

"PETITIONERS EXHIBIT 1 FOR IDENTIFICATION"

MR. GRIGGS: Now, Mrs. M., I show you Petitioners Exhibit 1 for
     identification and I ask you whether this exhibit contains any
     entry concerning your trip to Albany with the Infant and the
     Boarding Home mother?

A: Yes, it does.

Q: And what is the date of that visit, Mrs. M.?

A: 2/17/66.

Q: Did you make any entries on that report concerning your visit
     to Albany?

A: Yes, I did.

Q: And are there any entries sustained thereon concerning any
     reports you received from Child Guidance Center?

A: Yes.

Q: And what are those remarks?

A: Shall I read them or simply—

Q: What is the substance of them?

A: The substance of them is that following the examination of the
     foster child and the foster mother the attending psychiatrist
     called the worker into the office and regular routine matters,
     [sic] to see if there were any questions and to give a verbal
     report.

Q: Were you the worker?

A: I was, which would supplement the written report.

Q: And did you receive any verbal report?

A: I did.

Q: What was that report?

A: The report suggested strongly the removal be made as soon as
     possible in the long term interest of the child, and that while
     the removal would be stormy that it would certainly be in the
     long range interest that it be done, that we receive the coopera-
     tion of the Guidance Center in doing it.

Q: Now, this exhibit pertains to other dates and remarks and what else prepared by yourself?

A: The area ones were, the contact was best during 1965, were primarily mine, following that there were those of the new worker [*sic*].

Q: When was your most recent contact with Beth?

A: Professionally speaking, 2/17/66, I have seen her since.

Q: You have seen her since Feb. 17th?

A: Non professionally.

Q: Non professionally?

A: Yes.

Q: But your last professional contact on behalf of the department was on 2/17/66?

A: That is true.

Q: Now, were these statements prepared by you in the usual course of your employment with the Welfare Dept.?

A: I make it a practice to write up interviews as soon as possible because obviously . . . one's memory fails if you don't do it immediately.

Q: And these in turn become a part of the file on a particular child?

A: They do.

Q: Your Honor, I offer Petitioners Exhibit 1 for identification as Petitioners Exhibit 1 in Evidence.

THE COURT: Show it to your . . . [adversary].

A: Your Honor, may I make a remark?

THE COURT: Not at this time, No.

MR. AVIS: I object to the introduction of this report as not . . . bringing . . . Mr. and Mrs. Liuni . . . , that there was no notice or knowledge submitted to Mrs. Liuni that she was undergoing examination, and [the] report I presume [com]prises some psychiatric [information] and that such relationship that existed is a privilege[d] . . . communication.

MR. GRIGGS: Mr. Avis, these do not involve Mrs. Liuni, this involves Elizabeth.

MR. AVIS: That is solely on the basis of the child?

MR. GRIGGS: Of the child only, this is not, nothing there, there is nothing in there concerning any, no psychiatric evaluation of Mrs. Liuni.

MR. AVIS: It is in the nature of a self serving declaration, I still object to it as not binding on the Respondent or this infant.

THE COURT: It is however in my judgment Mr. Avis admissible as a memorandum made in the regular course of business, and I will on that basis allow it, and the objection is overruled, the exhibit is received.

MR. AVIS: Exception.

EXHIBIT MARKED "PETITIONERS EXHIBIT 1 IN EVIDENCE."

MR. GRIGGS: I have no further questions of the Petitioner, Your Honor.

MR. AVIS CROSS EXAMINING WITNESS:

Q: Mrs. M., how often did you visit the Liuni home while the child was there?

A: I would hesitate precisely [to] say Mr. Avis without consulting [the] records, but I think I visited at least a half a dozen times, on several occasions taking the child out for a ride and on a visit or so to the office.

Q: Now, in your opinion was the child being well taken care of in the Liuni home?

A: The child was receiving good foster care.

Q: Now, could you tell us why this child, why the department permitted the child to remain for a period of four years at this particular home?

A: As it has already been stated there were legal complications. There was a complication of finding the right family. May I say that as a matter of policy we try to place the child outside the area where the natural mother lives, sometimes this causes delay because a couple may not apply, this is [sic] a rural family unit may not apply from the right section. We are bound by religion, and we are bound by natural national background.

Q: Now, would it have been possible to have the child in several foster homes during this four year period?

A: It would not have been advisable.

Q: Now, the department permitted this child to remain for four years in the Liuni home is that correct?

A: This is correct.

Q: And what objection would the department have to consent to the adoption of this child by the Liunis?

A: Basically speaking, as it already has been brought out, they would not meet the specific requirements of our standards.

Q: That is—

A: As adoptive parents.

Q: That is the age requirement?

A: That is one of them.

Q: There is no other factor that is existing except the age?

A: Yes, there are.

Q: What are those factors?

A: There is a factor of nationality background, this child is [of] . . . French and Irish and German extraction; they are Italian on both sides; there is a coloring; there is the physical makeup of the natural parents and of the adoptive parents, foster parents in this case; there is geography.

Q: This little child is an American Girl, is she not?

A: Just as we all are.

Q: And so are the Liunis?

A: Nationality background is the thing that we look for.

Q: Why should nationality background be a factor?

A: Because human beings have a desire to belong, to be one of a group, to take pride in their national heritage, all of us are—

Q: Have we not seen cases where white people would adopt dark children?

A: In the County of Ulster I have not seen it Mr. Avis, it might exist it undoubtedly does.

Q: That would be a serious objection by your department, is that correct?

MR. GRIGGS: Objection Your Honor, this witness has not been qualified as the department head or one who gives or issues directions to the department and on that basis I think it is an improper question.

THE COURT: Objection is overruled, I think she has indicated . . . that she has had enough acquaintship [sic] with the policy of the department that she can make a statement with regard to it and I will weigh the effect to be given to it when I read the entire record.

A: May I answer that, Your Honor?

THE COURT: Yes, you may, the objection is overruled.

A: A child is not living with a wife and family it lives in the community, the County of Ulster does not . . . to my knowledge [have] a community that would accept this type of placement.

MR. AVIS:

Q: Now, isn't it a fact that other couples are married with different nationalities?

A: Certainly, this child is also a mixture.

Q: And what objection would there be if the nationality of the parents were different, they are all human are they not?

A: This is one of many considerations, it is not the guiding one, it cannot be separated from the others.

Q: Those are some of the general rules, the particular rules the agency has set up, is that correct?

A: They are standards by which we go, one has to have some standard.

Q: Now, there are other children entrusted to Mrs. Liuni, is that correct?

A: There were.

Q: And the department never found any fault with the bringing up of these children that were entrusted to the Liuni care?

A: Both children in infancies, they were well cared for, Mrs. Liuni is an excellent foster mother.

Q: Now, do you realize the repercussions that would occur if the child is taken from the Liuni home?

A: I've performed such removal before and found them handleable.

Q: You found them—

A: Able to be handled.

Q: Without noticing the effect of such actions.

A: If the preparation has been sufficient, the effects are negligible.

Q: Now, four years, would you call that a temporary residence with foster parents?

A: I have placed other children that have been in foster homes that length of time.

Q: Now, the question is would you consider this a temporary arrangement, four years, with a child in one household?

A: It was not a permanent plan for this child.

Q: Not what?

A: It was not a permanent plan for this child.

Q: But the fact remains therefore four years is that correct?

A: This is true.

Q: No further questions.

MR. GRIGGS EXAMINING WITNESS

Q: Mrs. M., an application, a formal application has been filed with the Court by Mr. and Mrs. Liuni concerning the adoption of Elizabeth ———— and if you were asked to make a written recommendation to the Court would you recommend an adoption?

MR. AVIS: I object to the question as to form, it calls for a conclusion.

THE COURT: Certainly it does, but this is her job to make judgments, at least she is in a position to testify as to what her judgment would be if she were asked in this particular case, objection is overruled.

MR. AVIS: Exception.

A. If I were asked to make the judgment I presume I would be given the opportunity to do a home study, to the depth and degree that we usually do, and I would feel that I would have done that before I would give an answer. You can't make a snap judgment. We have done a home study as a foster home, which is very different than the one we do as an Adoptive Home.

MR. GRIGGS:

Q: But, would the studies that you have from the observations of the home and from the records that you have kept and maintained in this particular matter, would you feel that you would make a favorable recommendation?

A: It is extremely difficult to say without having done a complete home study, but on the basis of my present knowledge of the child, of the family, of the medical records and of the psychiatric evaluation, I think I should be very hesitant.

Q: Now Mrs. M., did you not, were you not the caseworker who removed one foster child previously from the Liuni home?

A: Yes, I was.

Q: Was there any difficulty?

A: None whatsoever, the Liunis cooperated pretty well.

Q: Is that child placed for adoption?

A: Yes, it was. They have had him since birth.

Q: How long ago was that?

A: I am not good at dates, Mr. Griggs, but I would say last year, oh, possibly in the Spring.

Q: Thank you, Mrs. M.

A: The late Spring.

MR. AVIS EXAMINING WITNESS

Q: Mrs. M., speaking of this last child that was removed, how old was that child when he was placed in the foster care of Mrs. Liuni?

A: I believe it was a newborn infant, I would have to look up the records.

Q: You don't know is that correct?

A: It may have been, it was an infant, I could not tell you the exact day because I don't know, I did not make the placement.

Q: And how old was the child at the time you took it from the Liuni home?

A: Again guessing, I would say about 8 months, 7 or 8 months.

Q: It was just an infant?

A: Yes Sir.

Q: And how long was it at the Liuni home?

A: Again guessing, I do not remember the dates, I would say probably about 7½ months.

Q: That was the temporary period, was it not?

A: Yes Sir it was.

Q: And they cooperated in that direction, did they not?

A: Yes they did, they understood that that was a temporary, just as they had with the other placements.

Q: Now, do you recall the conversations that were had in the Liuni home by you and Mrs. Liuni regarding the adoption of the child?

A: Are you referring to the little boy?

Q: To Elizabeth.

A: I don't recall ever having discussed adoption.

Q: Mr. and Mrs. Liuni discussed this request for adoption of the child with you?

A: Not with me.

Q: Now, you say you have done graduate work?

A: Yes.

Q: In what field was that?

A: In Social Sciences.

Q: Dealing with adoption of children?

A: I beg your pardon?

Q: Did it deal with the subject of adoption?

A: Not during my college years, no.

Q: No further questions.

MR. GRIGGS: No further questions Your Honor. May it please the Court, at this time the Petitioner rests its case.

Excerpt No. 2 (Record, Pp. 229–35)
Direct Examination of Michael Liuni

✻   ✻   ✻

Q: Now, regarding your children, you say you have a son how old?

A: Fourteen, Michael.

Q: What is the color of his hair?

A: He has blondish hair, dark brown with bluish eyes.

Q: And what color is the hair of Elizabeth?

A: She has blonde hair and blue eyes.

Q: Now, during the period of time in which you had practically six children in the house; is that correct?

A: That's right.

Q: Was the wife capable of undertaking the housework and the details to take, to rear three infant children?

A: These were—these—this was hard with the three foster children, but this was only temporary, practically five, six weeks. We didn't know this when we took the third child. They did not tell us they were going to take the little boy away. He was there a short while. He was ten months old at the time. We were heartbroken because we had gotten to love him, but we knew this was the way the system worked. We did not fight it. We cooperated.

Q: Now, with what caseworker did you come in contact with?

A: I had most of my contacts with Mrs. Strong who set us up in the foster home, brought the child to us originally, and Mrs. Gray brought the next two kids, and I only met her once in my home, and Mrs. McCord has been—has contacted my wife, and Mrs. Ambrose—Miss Ambrose—I only saw once in my home and I have met them in the Welfare Office.

Q: Did you have opportunity of speaking to Mrs. Strong regarding the adoption of Elizabeth?

A: Yes, I did have conversation with Mrs. Strong, and Mrs. Gray at the one time I saw her in my home, and also Miss Ambrose about the possibility or the probability of our keeping Beth throughout the four years. After the first year, we wanted this child. We had grown to love her, and she became part of our family and each time I brought up the suggestion I was told it was a complicated case and the longer you keep a child the better change [chance] you have of keeping her. Nobody ever made any promises but the implication was there. The older she got the better change [chance] because we or they could not find her father. Now, the natural father and the legal father is all mixed up and I don't even want to bother straightening it up.

Q: Now, where did your conversations take place, as a rule?

A: In our home.

Q: When they visited your home?

A: That's right, mostly with my wife, but as I say, I did have conversations with Mrs. Strong and Mrs. Gray on this point.

Q: Did they at any time in the period that you had these children, have any complaints of the manner in which the children were being kept, fed, maintained?

A: No, we are always complimented on our bringing up of these children, and in fact, the first boy I had, Paul, Paul Kent, was premature, and he was actually skin and bones, five pound baby, and I think he was 24 days old, and then when he left he had a double chin and he was working on his triple chin. There is a point I would like to say, and that is, the way I understand these things, they gave Beth the surname of Stevens and they gave Paul the surname of Kent. The other two, they used letters, and when I questioned this, they said that usually the ones who got names and the ones who get letters are different categories, the ones that are names are not up for adoption and the ones who had the letters are adoptable. So Beth was given the name of Stevens and the way I understood it, she was not up for adoption.

Q: I want to ask you this question: Why do you and Mrs. Liuni desire to adopt Elizabeth?

A: She has become part of our family, she is loved by my sons and my daughter, they have been sent home from school all during this time of this proceeding. It all started because they have nervous stomachs and they are getting sick over it. They know they might lose their sister. We love this child as much or more than our own, and I don't see any valid reason for taking her away from us.

Q: How many years have you had her in your home?

A: We had her since she was four days old, five days old and she will be four years old next month.

Q: She has been there a period of about four years?

A: Right.

Q: Now, is the child treated like your natural children?

A: I would like to quote from the book furnished us by the Welfare Department, and refute something that Mrs. Gray said yesterday, that she has made a statement that the kids are put in our home for room and board, p-e-r-i-o-d. There is nothing else added to that statement. This is a rule book we are supposed to go by, paragraph 58, "No license or certificates shall be issued unless it is understood and agreed that children receive the board, mingle freely and are equal in the—other children in the household and in the community and shall be accepted as members of the household and share its pleasures and responsibilities." That certainly goes a little more than room and board, and that is the way we have interpreted it and that is the way we have lived our lives with this child and all the children we have.

Q: The child attends church with you and other members of the family?

A: That's right, she does, she is baptized and my sons were present when she was baptized. She—we did not bring an adult there because we did not want to know the true nationality of the child at this time and if I may quote from the other paragraph of the book of rules, 350, "No more than two children under the age of two years shall be boarded in any home. No children under the age of two years shall be boarded in any home" This is repetitious, "if the foster parents have two children under that age. However, if they have one child under two the home may be used for one boarding child under two years of age." I just want to bring that up because they did practically force three children on us even though their regulations say two, and the fact that we originally settled for one.

Q: What is this book that you have in your hands?

A: It is, it says, "The Problem of Social Welfare, Boarding Home Register."

Q: And who gave you this?

A: Mrs. Gray when they brought the first child and her writing is in here noting the date that we brought each child.

Q: Are there any other records regarding the children other than this book you just read from?

A: No, except who brought them.

Q: I am going to ask that this document be marked for identification.

IN RE ST. JOHN

51 Misc.2d 96, 272 N.Y.S.2d 817 (Family Ct. 1966)

ELWYN, JUDGE.

[H]abeas corpus proceeding by the Commissioner of Public Welfare of Ulster County to regain custody of Elizabeth St. John, a four year old female child from the respondents, Mr. and Mrs. Michael Liuni. . . . The Commissioner has legal custody of the child. . . . The respondents are not related to Elizabeth, nor do they have legal custody. They have her on a temporary foster parent basis pursuant to an arrangement with the Commissioner of Welfare whereby the Department of Welfare assumes full responsibility for the support and maintenance of the child, including medical expenses, and the foster parents receive compensation for their services in providing board and care.

Pursuant to such a general arrangement, . . . the Department on July 9, 1962 placed Elizabeth in the Liunis' care when she was only five days old. With the exception of the first five days of her brief life she has known no other home and no other parents. It is conceded by the Commissioner that the Liunis have provided Elizabeth with a good foster home and that their services as boarding parents have been wholly satisfactory.

* * *

Upon the trial of the issue the respondents contended that the best interest of the child required that she be permitted to remain in the care of the Liunis because (1) the child considers herself a member of this family; (2) that Mrs. Liuni was fully capable of taking care of the child and assuming her role as foster mother and that her prognosis was good; and most importantly, (3) to remove Elizabeth from the Liuni home at this stage of her young life would be disastrous to the child's welfare. Moreover, it is pointed out that Elizabeth has never seen or met the adoptive parents proposed by the Welfare Department and that the only parents she knows are Mr. and Mrs. Liuni her present foster parents.

In addition to stressing the fine qualities and capabilities as parents of Mr. & Mrs. Liuni, which the Welfare Department virtually concedes, the respondents rely principally upon factor number three—i.e. the disastrous effects which may be expected to befall Elizabeth if she is removed from her foster parents' home, to demonstrate that her welfare and interest will be best served by permitting her to remain.

In preparation for the trial of this issue the Liunis, without the consent of the Commissioner, permitted Elizabeth to be seen and evaluated by Dr. Donald Schultz, a psychiatrist who testified on their behalf at the trial. Counsel for the Commissioner has moved to strike out all of Dr. Schultz's testimony regarding his appraisal of the emotional stability of the Liuni family and the neurotic symptoms Elizabeth would be likely to develop were she to be taken from the Liunis upon the ground that the basis for his testimony was illegally obtained inasmuch as he had not first secured the Commissioner's permission to make his examination of Elizabeth. The contention is without merit and the motion to strike Dr. Schultz's testimony is denied. The development in the federal courts and in many state courts of a rule of exclusion to illegally obtained evidence has its application to criminal matters. It has no application to this proceeding to determine the best interest of a child. Apart from evidence obtained as a result of an unreasonable search and seizure, Mapp v. Ohio, 367 U.S. 643, 81 S. Ct. 1684, 6 L.Ed.2d 1081, has not changed the traditional common law rule followed in New York which sanctions the admissibility of illegally obtained evidence [citations omitted].

At the threshold of any consideration of the issues presented by this contest between a Commissioner of Welfare and boarding parents for the custody of a child committed to the latter's care stands a question as to the power of the courts to review an administrative determination concerning the child's welfare. It is, of course, firmly established by many authorities that in proceedings for the custody of a child, the child's welfare is the supreme consideration [citations omitted]. On this the Courts and the agencies would agree—the real point at issue being whether an authorized agency has by virtue of the provisions of Section 383 of the Social Welfare Law any "superior right" to the custody of a child which the Courts are bound to respect at the cost of diminishing their traditional role as *parens patriae* to do what is best for the welfare of the child. A resolution of this issue is necessary before we reach the question—what is best for the welfare of the child in this case?

For his authority to remove Elizabeth from the Liuni home and to place her with other foster parents for adoption the Commissioner relies upon Subdivision 2 of Section 383 of the Social Welfare Law which vests in him the custody of the child during his minority and provides that "any such authorized agency may in its discretion remove such child from the home where placed or boarded."

The Commissioner does not claim that his discretion is unfettered and uncontrolled, but contends that the Liunis have no legal right with respect to the child's custody and have no standing to contest his determination that it would be in the child's best interest to place her with other foster parents for adoption, merely because of their demonstrated love and affection for the child and her affection for them and the devoted care which they have given her while she was in their home. Moreover, he argues "[i]n a proceeding such as this, custody could be determined on consideration only of the superior right of the authorized agency [citations omitted]." "Any other result," it has been said, "would give a boarding parent the right to substitute her discretion and judgment for that of the public welfare officials and authorized agencies as to what is best for the welfare of the child, and destroy their supervision and control generally." (In Matter of Convent of Sisters of Mercy v. Barbieri, supra, 113–114, 105 N.Y.S.2d 4.)

This latter argument—that decisions depriving the Commissioner of legal custody of the children committed to his care might result in a breakdown of the placement system was effectively answered by Mr. Justice Hart in Matter of Mary I—— v. Convent of Sisters of Mercy in Brooklyn, 200 Misc. 115, 121, 104 N.Y.S.2d 939, 944, 945, a case in which the boarding parents succeeded in retaining the child over the claim of the Commissioner as follows: "The placement system in these particular proceedings must yield to the welfare of the individual child. This Court refuses to sacrifice this infant's interests because of a claim that the interests of children, not before the Court, will be affected by a possible impairment of a placement system, nor is the fact that the result reached may be operative as a precedent in future cases of any great moment. Each case will require an approach with respect to the facts therein presented and weighed accordingly. In other cases there may well be lacking the fact here presented of permitting an infant of the age of 6 months to remain in a boarding home for 4 years with the resultant attachment of the child for the boarding parents."

As for predicating a decision with respect to this child's custody "on consideration only of the superior right of the authorized agency" it may be observed that this is directly contrary to the oft repeated concept that in a custody proceeding the court does not act to determine rights between the parties whether parents or non-parents, but solely for the protection of infants, qua infants (Finlay v. Finlay, 240 N.Y. 429, 434, 148 N.E. 624, 626, 40 A.L.R. 937), a fact noted by the dissenters in the Appellate Division in Matter of Jewish Child Care Association. . . .

Moreover, it is impossible to reconcile the foregoing statement with respect to the "superior right of the authorized agency" for which People ex rel. Our Lady of Victory Infant Home v. Venniro, supra, 126 Misc. 139, 212 N.Y.S. 745 appears to be the source and upon the basis of which the actual decision in favor of the agency was made with earlier statements made by the court in the same case rejecting the argument that the courts were powerless to interfere with the exercise of the agency's right to remove the child from the home of boarding parents and asserting the equitable jurisdiction of the Supreme Court, formerly exercised in Chancery to act as parens patriae for the welfare of infants.

The case of People ex rel. Converse v. Derrick, 146 Misc. 73, 261 N.Y.S. 447, although not directly in point since it involved a custody dispute between a Public Welfare Commissioner and a natural parent who sought to revoke an instrument of surrender, nevertheless contains some apt observations on the need for the power of the courts to review the decisions of welfare agencies. The court says (pp. 77–78, 261 N.Y.S. p. 452): "The State of New York stands in relation of *parens patriae* to minor children in the state, and representing the state, it is the function of the Supreme Court to determine the custody of such minors, and such determination is to be based solely on the welfare of the minors. This power of the state and function of the Supreme Court evidently transcends legislative action and contract between individuals (citing cases). This office of the Supreme Court descends from king to chancery and from chancery to the Supreme Court of this State. Born in a time when the question of custody could be changed on the misbehavior of parents or of guardians chosen by parents, this power must still be available even in these days of social service organizations and welfare officers so that errors of heart or errors of judgment on the part of officials, as well as misbehavior by parents and by guardians, can be remedied by the court."

The argument that the court is powerless to act for the benefit of the child in view of the discretion conferred upon an authorized agency by § 383 of the Social Welfare Law was also rejected by the court In People ex rel. Catholic Charities of Buffalo v. Hagstotz (unofficially reported), Sup., 117 N.Y.S.2d 818, 823, wherein the court said "° ° ° To me it is a startling proposition that the legislature could, or if it could that it did, intend to take away from the Supreme Court the power which it has always had to determine the custody of children and to grant that power to a welfare agency and to assert that under any and all circumstances, once a child has been boarded out by an agency, that the Supreme Court is powerless to determine what is best for the interest and welfare of the child."

Considering these views to be sound, I should unhesitatingly opt in favor of the supremacy of the inherent equitable power of the Supreme Court over the administrative determination of welfare agencies as respects the welfare of infants, were it not for the fact that substantially the same views were vainly asserted by the dissenting judges in both the Appellate Division and the Court of Appeals and that their views did not prevail nor serve to prevent a child care association from regaining the custody of a child placed with boarding parents in the one case in the Appellate Courts of this state dealing directly with the competing power of the Courts and the agencies (Matter of Jewish Child Care Association . . .).

How much validity is left then in the assertion of the dissenting justices of the Appellate Division In Matter of Jewish Child Care Assn. . . . with respect to the responsibility of the courts for the welfare of infant children? It is still true, as they say, that "In the proceeding at bar it is not respondent's judgment as to what is for the best interests of the child, but that of the court which is determinative (?) The custody of an infant may not be controlled by the estab-

lished practice of any organization no matter how noble its motive
may be. Like any other qualified witness, respondent was entitled to
present proof before the court, but the responsibility for determining
what course would aid the child's welfare was solely and independently the duty of the court in the exercise of its vast powers to deal
with the custody of infant children."

Apparently Judge Dye, one of the dissenting judges in the Court
of Appeals thought that the effect of the majority holding in the
Jewish Child Care Assn. case was virtually to set at naught the power
of the courts for in his dissent he writes: "In sustaining petitioner's
application for a writ of habeas corpus, a majority of this court is
about to say that the best interest of the infant will be served by
compelling the approved foster parents, with whom the petitioner
has previously placed the child for custodial care, to surrender her
back to the Agency, there to be dealt with as they see fit. This tragic
result comes about because of a mistaken notion that the courts are
bound to accept an administrative policy of the Agency as controlling
their determination rather than to exercise their own traditional
power and authority in accordance with the evidence." (In Matter of
Jewish Child Care Assn. . . .)

Although the Child Care Association prevailed over the efforts of
the boarding parents to retain custody of the child, I do not believe
that the majority opinion of the Court of Appeals in Matter of Jewish
Child Care Assn. . . . compels any such conclusion as Judge Dye suggests as being the "mistaken notion" supporting the decision. A careful reading of the majority opinion written by Chief Judge Conway
shows that the result reached was not predicated upon the superior
right of the agency as the Appellate Division said might be done, but
rather upon an express finding that "There is no merit to the appellants' claim that the Trial Justice failed or refused to exercise independent discretion as to what is in Laura's best interests, or that he
made his determination upon any basis other than her best interests.
Consequently, the precise question which this record presents is
whether there is such a lack of supporting evidence that we must
charge the court below with an abuse of discretion as a matter of
law [citations omitted]. It should be remembered that "Questions of
custody are, generally, for the Supreme Court, in its discretion, and

it is rarely that any such determination by it can raise any question of law for us [citations omitted]."

"* * * From the standpoint of the child's best interests, therefore, we hold that there was no abuse of discretion by the Trial Justice." 5 N.Y.2d pp. 227–228, 229, 183 N.Y.S.2d p. 69, 156 N.E.2d p. 702.

The precise holding of the majority opinion of the Court of Appeals in Matter of Jewish Child Care Assn. . . . although affirming the order of the Appellate Division awarding custody of the child to the agency, does not, in my judgment, imply approval of their reasoning or rejection of the power of the Supreme Court over the administrative determination of welfare agencies with respect to the welfare of infants committed to their care. The observations of Judge Dye (dissenting) with respect to the power of the Supreme Court are therefore still apposite to a determination of this case.

While administrative practices have a useful place in the handling of ordinary matters of administration, such test is wholly inappropriate in this setting. Here we are not dealing with a routine problem of administration, but rather with the fundamental concept underlying the broad and enlightened social welfare program of the State respecting the care and custody of indigent and neglected children, every aspect of which is to be tested in the light of which will best promote their individual welfare. This idea is neither new nor novel in our society. The State as *parens patriae* has always had a deep concern for its infant wards; from birth to maturity their welfare is paramount, even to that of the natural parent (Matter of Bock (Breitung), 280 N.Y. 349, 21 N.E.2d 186), the determination of which belongs solely to the Supreme Court as successor to the Chancellor [citations omitted].

Substantially the same issues as are presented by this case were before the court in N. Y. Foundling Hospital v. Strozak (N.Y. Law Journal, Dec. 23, 1965, p. 11, col. 6) decided by the Supreme Court of Nassau County which likewise involved a custody dispute between foster parents who sought to retain custody of a child who had been placed in their care for nearly five years and the Foundling Hospital which sought to remove the child for placement with its grandparents. Mr. Justice Brennan in denying the writ and continuing the child in the custody of the boarding parents states what I conceive to be a correct position for the courts to take in cases of this kind. The Justice says: "This court is well aware of the broad discretion granted to authorized agencies, as defined in Section 371 of the Social Welfare Law and as set forth in Section 383 (1) of that law with respect to the care and custody of children entrusted to them. It is also recognized that this discretion is not absolute, but is subject to the ultimate equity powers of the Supreme Court as successor to the Court of Chancery [citations omitted]. The court is also convinced that the opinion of the agency is entitled to great weight, but that the court, in the final analysis, must make its own independent judgment, from all the facts as to what is in the best interests of the child (Matter of Jewish Child Care Assn. . . .)."

This court will therefore form its own independent judgment concerning this child's custody, based not on any superior right of the Commissioner of Public Welfare, but solely on what I conceive to be for the welfare and best interest of the child. In making this judgment the Family Court has the same jurisdiction and may exercise the same powers as possessed by the Supreme Court (N.Y. Const. Art. 6, § 13, subd. c; Family Court Act § 651).

The Liunis' efforts to retain custody of Elizabeth are undoubtedly sincerely motivated by their great love and affection for this blond, blue eyed pretty little girl of four. The depth of their affection and the sincerity of their motives were epitomized by Mr. Liuni when he said: "The way my wife and I felt was that God sent us a foster child to replace the one he took from us." Moreover, it is conceded by the Commissioner that the Liunis have provided the child with a good home and have been excellent foster parents.

If only the immediate and short term interests of this child were at stake, it would be an easy matter for the Court to conclude, as is so strenuously urged by the respondents and the Adoptive Parents Committee, Inc., that her present welfare might best be served by leaving her in the security of the only home she has ever known to be reared by the only persons she knows as her parents. Such a determination would, of course, absolve the Court and all concerned from the responsibility for creating what Dr. Donald Schultz, the psychiatrist who examined the Liuni family and testified on their behalf, saw as such an emotional shock in the life of this young child as would cause her to "suffer for a good period of her life, perhaps all of her life, with neurotic symtomatology; indeed," he said, "she has already developed them."

On the other hand, Dr. Bartholomew J. Dutto, the medical advisor to the County Welfare Department while conceding that "there would be a temporary trauma at the separation" stated that "given young parents and an adequate home and the attention that would be lavished on her I think that memory at that age is very short, I think that the child would adjust." Dr. Dutto's view is also shared by Dr. Lenore M. Sportsman, the Director of the Albany Child Guidance Center to whom the child was referred for pre-adoptive evaluation. Dr. Sportsman, a psychiatrist of eminent qualifications and vast experience in the making of pre-adoptive studies of children to determine their suitability for adoption testified: "* * * I would expect that of course she would have some reaction from being changed from one environment to another, because she has formed love, affectionate relations with people, but having formed good, warm relations, it is my belief, my professional experience, that persons who have had good affectionate relationships make others quite readily. Therefore, I would not expect that there would be lasting harm to the child * * *." Upon questioning by the Court, as to the severity of the emotional shock to be anticipated by the removal of the child from the foster parents' home Dr. Sportsman replied, "In my experience, Your Honor, I cannot say that would—with the stable personality which I observed in the little girl months ago—five—that I would expect this would be an excessive traumatic experience." Dr. Sportsman did, however, emphasize that the severity of the emotional reaction upon the child depended largely upon the way in which the transition was handled and strongly recommended that if the child were to be placed elsewhere for adoption that the change should not be brought about abruptly but gradually and with the full cooperation of the foster parents and the social workers of the adoption agency. In sum, both Dr. Dutto and Dr. Sportsman felt that the need for finding more suitable adoptive parents for Elizabeth far outweighed the risks of any temporary emotional disturbance the child might suffer as a result of her removal from the Liuni household.

With the experts differing so widely in their opinions as to the severity of the emotional conflicts expected to be generated by the proposed placement of the child with other foster parents the Court must evaluate these conflicting opinions as best it can. Frankly, I am inclined to view Dr. Schultz's fears for the neurotic symptomatology which he predicts would befall Elizabeth were she to be removed from the Liuni household as somewhat exaggerated. In any event, I find these fears insufficient reason to frighten the Court into making a judgment which while preserving intact the mother image Mrs. Liuni represents and freeing the child from "this worry about the mother leaving," would at the same time create for Elizabeth and her future security more problems than the psychiatrists have dreamed of. Important as they are, the emotional needs of this child for love and security are not the only, nor are they indeed, the paramount consideration in determining this child's best interests.

In my judgment any consideration of this child's welfare which fails to take into account her future *status* in the family and the community as well as the control and custody of her person is not only short-sighted, but is lacking in an understanding of the importance of status as a source of legal rights (see Matter of Ziegler, 82 Misc. 346, 143 N.Y.S. 562) and an appreciation of the realities of the social structure. In a case involving issues similar to that presented here and which resulted in the award of custody to the foster parents over the claims of the agency the Court said, "[t]he question of adoption or its frustration is not controlling on these habeas corpus proceedings." (Matter of Mary I—— v. Convent of Sisters of Mercy in Brooklyn, supra, 200 Misc. 115, 123, 104 N.Y.S.2d 939, 947). I disagree.

Other courts when confronted with essentially the same issue have considered the feasibility of legal adoption to be a relevant factor in a complete appraisal of the child's welfare. For instance, in People ex rel. Our Lady of Victory Infant Home v. Venniro, supra, 126 Misc. 135, 139, 212 N.Y.S. 741, 746 the Court in sustaining the right of the agency to the custody of the child justified its holding by observing that, "[i]t may be said, too, as an additional reason, that since the child cannot be adopted without the consent of the relator, it cannot acquire the complete rights of a child, nor enjoy the benefits of a complete parental relationship." Also in N. Y. Foundling Hospital v. Strozak, supra, the case on which the respondents and the Adoptive Parent's Committee, Inc. chiefly rely to justify an award of custody to the boarding parents, the Court expressly recognized the importance of adoption in formulating a permanent plan for the placement of the child. In the latter case the boarding parents had made formal application for adoption when the child was a year and a half old and during the subsequent years the case worker for the Foundling Hospital had cooperated with the boarding parents with a view toward having the child adopted by them. The record showed a cooperative attitude on the part of both the foster parents and the agency to achieve an adoption. This circumstance undoubtedly influenced the Court in permitting the foster parents to retain custody of the child, but in making this decision the Court recognized that it had left some loose ends in so far as the child's future was concerned for it concluded with the following apology and pious hope: "The Court is also aware of the fact that a permanent plan of placement is far superior to a temporary one, and that perhaps this decision does not finalize the relationship. It is earnestly hoped that means may be found by which the boy may become the adopted son of the Strozaks." N.Y.L.J. Dec. 23, 1965, p. 11, col. 6, supra.

While the issue in this proceeding is essentially one of custody the matter of status which for this child can only be achieved through legal adoption is so inextricably interwoven with any consideration of her welfare that it simply cannot be ignored. A moment's reflection upon the status of this child and the responsibilities of the Liunis of an award of custody to them will show why this is so.

In Judge Dye's dissenting opinion in Matter of Jewish Child Care Assn. . . . he says that giving precedence to the Agency's policy of neutrality is a specious result in any event for, even if custody remained with the appellant, the Agency may continue supervision and visitation. Such a statement can only be the result of a confusion between "legal custody" and "physical custody." The Commissioner of Welfare has the legal custody of this child now (Social Welfare Law, § 383, Subd. 2). The Liunis have physical custody now; by resisting the Commissioner's right to remove the child from their home they are in effect asking this Court to take the legal custody of the child from the Commissioner and give it to them. If that isn't their purpose then there is no point to this proceeding. If the legal custody of this child, as opposed to physical custody, is awarded to the Liunis, then it must follow that the Commissioner no longer would have legal custody. The legal custody of this child with the attendant right to influence and even control its destiny can't be in both the Commissioner and the Liunis at the same time.

But what of the responsibility for the child's support which up until now has been assumed by the Department of Public Welfare? If the Commissioner were deprived of the legal custody of the child, ought not the Department of Welfare also be absolved of responsibility for future support and that responsibility shifted to the Liunis who up until now not only have had no responsibility for the support of the child but have been paid for their services. "Ay, there's the rub," for without the Liunis assuming their full responsibilities as parents through the medium of legal adoption, they have no enforceable responsibility for the support of this child, and if despite their good intentions they should ever fail to meet their responsibilities as parents the County Welfare Department would have no alternative but to assume responsibility for the support of the child. Merely providing instruction and care for the general welfare of this child without also an assumption of the responsibility for the support of the child is insufficient to place the Liunis in *loco parentis* (Miller v. Davis, 49 Misc.2d 764, 268 N.Y.S.2d 490). To award legal custody of this child to foster parents without their simultaneous assumption of the full responsibilities of parents and the legal guaranty of the rights and benefits that only adoption can provide, is not to assure this child's future security and welfare, but to cast her to the wolves.

By contrast through legal adoption the foster parents and the foster child sustain toward each other the legal relation of parent and child and have all the rights and are subject to all the duties of that relationship including the rights of inheritance from and through each other, and the foster child has all the rights of fraternal relationship with natural children, including the right of inheritance from each other (Domestic Relations Law § 117).

It, therefore, becomes essential, in my judgment, to any thorough and complete consideration of this child's welfare to ascertain whether the child's adoption by these foster parents is legally feasible. Unlike the Strozaks, the Liunis never made a formal application for the adoption of this child prior to the Institution of this suit. In fairness to the Liunis, it must be mentioned however, that they made known to their caseworker their desire to adopt Elizabeth, but their interest in adopting the child never came to the attention of the case supervisor of the Child Welfare Division or to the Commissioner. Subsequent to the commencement of this suit a petition for adoption was filed, but the application cannot be processed because it is not accompanied by an agreement and consent executed by the Commissioner, nor by any of the other supporting documents required by law or the Rules of the Family Court. The Commissioner, although approving of the Liunis as boarding parents has, for the reasons previously mentioned, found them unsuitable as adoptive parents for Elizabeth and has testified that he would not consent to this child's adoption by them.

The respondents and the Adoptive Parent's Committee, Inc. contend that the Commissioner of Welfare cannot arbitrarily withhold his consent to an adoption of this child by the Liunis and that in withholding his consent for the reasons he has given he is acting arbitrarily and capriciously. Moreover, they contend that the Family Court has the power to approve an agency adoption without the Commissioner's consent if the Court finds that he is arbitrarily withholding his consent.

If the Commissioner is arbitrary or capricious in withholding his consent to the Liunis' application for adoption of this child, or is guilty of an abuse of discretion the Liunis may have a remedy through a Proceeding against Body or Officer under Article 78 of the CPLR, but if so, such remedy must be sought in the Supreme Court (CPLR 7804(b)). By Section 113 of the Domestic Relations Law it is provided that "[a]n authorized agency may consent to the adoption of a minor in its lawful custody. The agreement of adoption shall be executed by such authorized agency." Section 114 of the Domestic Relations Law provides that "If satisfied that the moral and temporal interests of the foster child will be promoted thereby the judge or surrogate shall make an order approving the adoption * * *." The power to approve the proposed adoption necessarily carries with it the power to disapprove. However, the Court's power to approve or disapprove of an adoption to which an authorized agency has given its consent is not tantamount to nor so broad as to include the power to make the selection of the foster parents for the agency or to compel the agency to consent to an adoption by foster parents of which it disapproves.

Even though the Family Court may in this custody proceeding

exercise all the powers of the Supreme Court (N.Y. Const. Art. 6, 13, subd. c; Family Court Act § 651), it must be remembered that even the Supreme Court with all its inherent equity powers cannot grant an adoption (Erlanger v. Erlanger, 102 Misc. 236, 237, 168 N.Y.S. 928), jurisdiction of which as of September 1, 1967 is exclusive with the Family Court. An option was unknown to the common law and exists in this country only by virtue of statute [citations omitted]. In this state an adoption can be consummated only under the conditions prescribed by statutory authority [citations omitted]. And like all statutory proceedings there must be strict observance of the statute (Matter of Santacose, 271 App. Div. 11, 16, 61 N.Y.S.2d 1, 5).

In Matter of Santacose, supra, the Commissioner of Welfare having custody of a child surrendered for adoption attempted to take a neutral attitude as between two sets of proposed foster parents who sought to adopt the child, saying that he would be satisfied with whatever determination the Court made. The Appellate Division, however, upon reviewing an order of adoption made without the Commissioner's consent condemned such a hands-off attitude by the Commissioner saying that the responsibility for making a selection of adoptive parents was placed by statute on the Commissioner and that he couldn't shift the responsibility for making the initial choice of adoptive parents to the County Judge. Moreover, the Court held p. 18, 61 N.Y.S.2d p. 6 "that the two statutes" (referring to Section 384 of the Social Welfare Law providing for the surrender for adoption of a child to authorized agency and Section 113 of the Domestic Relations Law providing for the agency's consent to an adoption) "contemplate and intend that, in such a situation as the present one, the only basis for an adoption is the *execution* by the Commissioner of Public Welfare of a *written consent* which takes the place of, and is so intended, the written consent of the natural parents required in the case of a voluntary adoption." The statutory requirement of obtaining the Commissioner's consent not having been obtained, it was held that the adoption lacked jurisdictional basis and consequently the order of adoption was reversed and vacated.

It, therefore, appears that unless the Commissioner of Welfare gives his consent to the adoption of this child by the respondents, which he has said he will not give, an adoption may not be consummated and any order or adoption made by this Court without his consent would be without jurisdictional basis. Although they cite no authority for their contention the Adoptive Parents Committee Inc. urge that the power to approve an agency adoption without the agency's consent may be found in the language of Section 141 of the Family Court Act. Broad as is the "wide discretion" and heavy as are the "grave responsibilities" given to Family Court Judges by Section 141 of the Family Court Act, I do not think that these Findings of the Legislature are intended to confer any unrestrained grant of power to disregard the plain language of other statutory enactments. Discretion is not the equivalent of unbridled power.

The Adoptive Parents Committee have, however, suggested an ingenious way to escape the dilemma. It is this. Let the Court in this proceeding find that the welfare and best interest of the child require that its custody be awarded to the foster parents and make an award accordingly. Section 111 of the Domestic Relations Law prescribing whose consent shall be required for adoption provides in subdivision 4: "Of any person or authorized agency having lawful custody of the foster child." The foster parents now having *lawful custody* of the child pursuant to the order of this Court in these proceedings, only their consent to their own adoption of the child would be necessary. The authorized agency's consent would no longer be required since it has been deprived of lawful custody.

Some acceptance of this specious reasoning may be found in the opinion of the Supreme Court Justice in Matter of Mary I—— v. Convent of Sisters of Mercy in Brooklyn, supra, 200 Misc. 115, 123, 104 N.Y.S. 2d 939, 947, which he frankly acknowledges to be in the nature of obiter where he says: "Moreover, it may well be that if the result reached in this case is sustained" (i.e. an award of custody to foster parents) "that a Surrogate may find that lawful custody as is here determined, is in Mr. and Mrs. I—— and not in the authorized agency and that the consent of respondents as indicated in section 111 of the Domestic Relations Law is unnecessary."

The flaw in this line of reasoning is, of course, that it assumes that the best interest and welfare of the child, which alone can support an award of custody of any child may in a contest between boarding parents and an authorized agency having lawful custody of the child be determined without reference to any permanent plan for the placement of the child or stabilization of its status through legal adoption. This premise I reject for the reasons heretofore stated.

Stripped of all irrelevancies and emotionalism the resolution of this contest between the agency and the boarding parents for the right to determine this child's future resolves itself into a balancing of the relative importance to this child and her future of her immediate, short term need for a home with familiar surroundings, a mother's love and a child's sense of security against her long term needs for lasting acceptance into a family with greater life expectancy and which more nearly coincides with her ethnic and cultural background and her need for a permanent social and legal status in the family and the community. The temptation to be swayed by the immediate emotional needs of this child for familiar home surroundings and the love and affection of the only persons she has ever known as parents is strong indeed. It is, however, a siren song, which if followed, will I believe, lead this child only to heartbreak, emotional insecurity and a questionable social and legal status.

I am keenly aware that to remove this child from the only home she has ever known and from the physical custody and control of the persons she regards as her mother and father will cause some emotional shock to this child, the extent of which may not be accurately measured as evidenced by the wide divergency of opinion of two qualified and competent psychiatrists. Nevertheless, in my judgment the need to find a permanent placement for the child through the medium of legal adoption, but which may not be achieved in the context of her present placement so far outweighs the emotional pull of the appealing but delusive temporary expedient of leaving the child with the boarding parents, that the risk, incalculable as it is, has to be taken. In making this judgment, I am also not unmindful of the plight of the foster parents who have become so emotionally involved with the fate of this child whom they have come to love as their very own. However, they must realize that unlike natural children who have no choice in the selection of their parents, children who are wards of the State have the right to have their adoptive parents carefully chosen for them and that it would not be in their best interest to allow prospective adoptive parents arbitrarily to select the child they wished to adopt.

Finally, it is urged that nothing is known about the adoptive parents the agency has selected for Elizabeth, so that the Court has no basis for comparing the proposed adoptive parents with the Liunis. This is true. The answer to this, however, is the same as that made by the Court of Appeals in Matter of Jewish Child Care Assn. . . . to a similar objection. The Court said: "Nor can we sustain an objection that, since the child is not now being returned to her mother, she should be left with the Sanders because the fitness of her next habitation is presently unknown. As the Appellate Division wrote, we may not indulge an assumption, or even harbor a doubt, that Laura will not be properly cared for under the supervision of Child Care which is an authorized agency and which has proven itself most solicitous for the welfare not only of the child and its mother but even of the appellants themselves."

In my judgment this child's welfare and interests will be best served by her return to the physical custody of the Commissioner of Public Welfare for placement for adoption. However, in effecting such a placement heed should be paid to the admonition of Dr. Sportsman, Director of the Albany Child Guidance Center, that the transition from foster home to adoptive home be made gradually and be preceded by adequate preparation of the child by all concerned so as to smooth the way for her adaptation to her new environment.

The writ is therefore sustained and the legal custody of the child is awarded to the Commissioner of Public Welfare.

FITZSIMMONS v. LIUNI

26 App. Div.2d 980, 274 N.Y.S.2d 798 (3d Dep't 1966)

PER CURIAM.

Appeal from a judgment of the Family Court of Ulster County which sustained a writ of habeas corpus directed to respondents-appellants Liuni and awarded custody of Elizabeth St. John, an infant, to petitioner-respondent Commissioner of Public Welfare in a proceeding commenced in the Supreme Court, Ulster County, and by order of said court referred to said Family Court for hearing and determination. It is conceded that the Judge of the Family Court, by whom the proceeding was heard and determined, is a first cousin of the wife of the respondent Commissioner. Consequently, he was disqualified from acting, being "related by ° ° ° affinity to [a] party to the controversy within the sixth degree," and the proceedings before him were and are void. (Judiciary Law, § 14; *People ex rel. Union Bag & Paper Corp. v. Gilbert*, 143 Misc. 287, affd. 236 App. Div. 873.) The proceedings had in the Supreme Court prior to the reference were, of course, valid and under all the circumstances of this particular case, the matter should be remitted to that court. Consideration should there be given to the propriety of designating a guardian ad litem to represent the infant concerned and to the advisability of proceeding with the hearing and determination of the case in that court; but in each respect we prefer to leave the Special Term's discretion untrammeled. Judgment reversed, on the law, without costs, and thereupon vacated and set aside and proceeding remitted to the Supreme Court for further proceedings not inconsistent herewith. Stay continued. Order signed. Gibson, P. J., Herlihy, Reynolds, Staley, Jr., and Brink, JJ., concur.

Index

247